PRAISE FOR *SEARCH MARKETING*

Cutler's expertise in search marketing shines through every page of this thoughtful and practical guide to search marketing. This is a book that will help marketers at all levels think strategically about how to apply search to profitably grow their businesses, get the most out of their search marketing spend and enrich their customer interactions. Cutler's writing brings the same energy, enthusiasm, and passion to this subject as she does to the classroom and readers will surely be the beneficiaries.

Jonathan Copulsky, co-author of *The Technology Fallacy* and *The Transformation Myth* and author of *Brand Resilience*

In *Search Marketing*, marketing expert Kelly Cutler unveils a groundbreaking guide that will transform the way you navigate the digital landscape. Whether you're a seasoned marketer or just dipping your toes into the world of search marketing, this book is your go-to resource for mastering the art of SEO and SEM.

Jim Lecinski, Associate Professor of Marketing at the Kellogg School of Management and former Vice President Sales and Services, Google, Inc.

In essence, this book is a distillation of everything one would need to plunge headfirst into the world of SEO and SEM. It doesn't merely instruct; it guides you through the process with an ease that makes learning not only straightforward but also empowering. For marketers who have longed for an accessible, all-in-one package to truly comprehend and master the dynamics of SEO and SEM, your pursuit ends here. With this book, you'll find yourself not just understanding but confidently leading your business's digital marketing efforts. In the world of digital marketing, this book is not just an accessory – it's a necessity.

Sabine Gutsche, Head of Marketing, Deutsche Leibrenten Grundbesitz AG

Kelly Cutler's *Search Marketing* is the new must-read guide for all marketers. Search marketing remains the strongest results-driver of all digital marketing strategies. Kelly distills the complexity of SEO and SEM as only a successful veteran entrepreneur of the dot com boom, turned highly respected digital marketing professor at one of the country's top universities could. This book truly cements her guru status.
Karrie Sullivan, Founder, Culminate Strategy Group

From beginning steps to full integration, Kelly unmasks the mystery of the digital marketing sphere. Using her detailed map of SEO and SEM, she gives you a blueprint to develop your strategy seamlessly. Kelly, being an entrepreneur and a professor, is the insider you have been looking for.
Steve Tullar, Managing Director, JonesTrading

Kelly Cutler's innovative Three-Pronged approach offers a fresh perspective on SEO. Her book serves as a valuable guide, providing essential foundations for a comprehensive and effective SEO strategy suitable for experts and newcomers alike. It's a must-read for anyone looking to understand the art and science of digital marketing.
Herman Bulls, Marketing Professional, 2015 MBA Duke's Fuqua School of Business

Cutler injects her engaging and effective teaching style by starting each chapter with clear objectives and key results you can expect to achieve by implementing these best practices in your organization today. You'll leave each chapter empowered with confidence and knowledge to incrementally improve your Search Marketing strategy and drive key business results.
Mara Sackfield, Global Product Manager, Stryker

Whether you have been around since the early days or are brand new to search marketing, Kelly offers fresh perspectives, tactical tools, and real-world examples to help you better optimize SEO and SEM strategies and stay one step ahead of the latest trends.
Jennifer McGinn, Senior Director Marketing, Informatica

Kelly Cutler has been my go-to expert for all things SEO for 15 years and she's finally sharing her knowledge with the world in this book. A must-read for both SEO newbies and experts looking to fine-tune their craft.
Ajay Goel, CEO of Gmass

Kelly Cutler has masterfully crafted a comprehensive guide that demystifies the multifaceted world of Search Engine Optimization (SEO) and Search Engine Marketing (SEM). Her expertise shines through as she breaks down the intricate strategies and techniques that drive online success in this space. This book is a must-read for entrepreneurs, marketers, and business owners looking to maximize their online visibility and drive results.

Tanya Norwood, Chief Officer, Marketing and Membership, ASCP

Search Marketing

A Strategic Approach to SEO and SEM

Kelly Cutler

KoganPage

First published in Great Britain and the United States in 2024 by Kogan Page Limited

2nd Floor, 45 Gee Street
London
EC1V 3RS
United Kingdom

8 W 38th Street, Suite 902
New York, NY 10018
USA

4737/23 Ansari Road
Daryaganj
New Delhi 110002
India

www.koganpage.com

Kogan Page books are printed on paper from sustainable forests.

ISBNs

Hardback   978 1 3986 1282 2
Paperback   978 1 3986 1280 8
Ebook   978 1 3986 1281 5

British Library Cataloguing-in-Publication Data

A CIP record for this book is available from the British Library.

Library of Congress Control Number
2023948918

Typeset by Integra Software Services, Pondicherry
Print production managed by Jellyfish
Printed and bound by CPI Group (UK) Ltd, Croydon, CR0 4YY

To my family: Vic, Sydney and Jesse

Your unconditional support, love, and use of random acronyms has been essential throughout this process. Also, thank you to my furry companion, Rudy. Your snoring and antics provide amusement, laughter, and delight, even on the toughest days. Thanks to my most important role models: my parents and grandparents.

CONTENTS

PART THREE

SEM

ACKNOWLEDGMENTS

I would like to thank the contributors who helped make this book a success. Thank you to ExpandTheRoom, part of Infinum, Be Found Online, AMA Chicago, and the talented team from Qualitest. Your knowledge and expertise are awe-inspiring. Thank you to Kogan Page and huge gratitude to Paisley, the best work study student anyone could ask for.

Additionally, there are so many friends and colleagues I would like to thank for their support and guidance. Thank you to my students at Northwestern University, who inspire me each and every day, and to all the teachers, advisers, clients, and coworkers I have had over the years. You know who you are. My expertise and passion for search marketing started back in the late 1990s and somehow continues in the ever-evolving, AI-inspired, digital marketing world of today. I hope this book can encourage the next generation of search marketers to stay curious, ask questions, and continue learning.

PART ONE

The Fundamentals of Search Marketing

1

An Overview of Search

Introduction

Marketing has been around for thousands of years, dating back to ancient Greek, Roman, and Chinese times when merchants would use techniques such as hand-painted signs and public performances to promote their goods. The Golden Age of advertising is often considered the 1950s and 1960s, or the "Mad Men" era, when businesses began using television, radio, and print media to reach consumers. This gave rise to what is now known as the digital era and the introduction of internet and digital technology beginning in the 1990s and 2000s. Businesses began using more technical methods of reaching consumers, including email, SEO, and social media platforms like Facebook. Today, marketers have become increasingly sophisticated in their digital marketing, focusing on personalization and automation. As technology continues to advance, marketers must stay on the cutting edge, embracing new systems and processes as well as finding fresh ways to communicate with customers.

My personal journey into the world of digital marketing goes all the way back to 1997. With a shiny undergraduate diploma, this Michigan girl moved to the Windy City to try and get a job in the booming new economy. Although I studied English and film in college, the dotcom craze took hold of me, and I accepted a job at an up-and-coming company called Apartments.com. The concept was that renters looking for an apartment in Chicago would sign up online to meet with a rental agent. The agent would identify the apartments meeting their criteria—say a one-bedroom in Lincoln Park that allows dogs—and would take the renter to view each apartment. This concept, while novel at the time, quickly took off and the company grew, as Classified Ventures (CV), and went on to include Cars.com and NewHomeNetwork. I clearly remember the celebration party when we were able to secure the domain cars.com from its original owner—what a great decision that turned out to be!

The job at CV led to several other "internet companies", as they were called then, when I landed at America Online (AOL) in 2000. At that time, AOL was the way most consumers accessed the internet. Similar to newspapers, there were sections within AOL—like Business, Auto, Real Estate, and Entertainment. My job was to sell advertising within those sections. We had the technology to geographically target ads as well. In the early years of digital marketing, our products were advanced. AOL had also begun its merger with traditional media conglomerate Time Warner and it was an exciting time to be in the industry.

Working with my advertisers led to a common question being asked: "How do I get my company to show up on the page where people type in different words and find companies that match their search?" At the time, Yahoo was a popular content provider, but there really was no concept of search engines, as we know them today. Again, this was the early 2000s, so I had no idea how that specific technology worked. But I decided to figure it out. From there, I started my first digital agency, focused on search engine optimization (SEO), which would eventually include paid search (SEM), web analytics, social media marketing, and more.

Soon after I left AOL to pursue my own business, Yahoo and Google emerged as important ways to search and find information. Businesses were realizing that their websites needed to rank on those results pages in order for potential customers to find their products and services. As search engines became more sophisticated, businesses began advertising with sponsored links, primarily on Yahoo, Overture originally, but eventually on Google as well. In 2000 Google introduced AdWords, a self-service platform for businesses to build and oversee campaigns on Google. Over time, AdWords evolved to include features like audience targeting, day parting, ad extensions, and quality score. Now called Google Ads, Google has also introduced a variety of other SEM tools, including Google Analytics, Search Console, and Tag Manager.

Following advertising, SEO began to emerge as a technique to get to the top of search engine results pages (SERPs) by using keywords and linking strategies. As search engines became more advanced, SEO became an important marketing technique. Websites continue to evolve and so does SEO and how it is used for marketing purposes. Content, keywords, and linking are still fundamental components of SEO, but there is much more competition now, and, as a result, SEO has become more complex. The process includes both art and science and a special attention to detail. Common misconceptions about SEO can still plague businesses and marketers, including what's known as black-hat SEO, or use of unethical and aggressive techniques to try and improve rankings on SERPs. This can include keyword stuffing, hidden text, cloaking (showing different content to search engines and users), or anything else that is considered deceptive. Black-hat SEO can in some cases produce short-term results but can also lead to irreparable damage. Black-hat SEO must be avoided at all costs, and the best way to avoid it is to be armed with the knowledge and information about what is called white-hat SEO, or, the right way to go about search engine optimization.

Both SEO and SEM have grown to become essential and fundamental components of a digital marketing strategy. Businesses that follow best practices and keep up with the latest trends, algorithms, and consumer insights can use search marketing to improve visibility, attract qualified website traffic, and ultimately drive conversions and revenue. Websites that are built with SEO in mind will garner more traffic, leads, and sales while also delivering a better user experience. Similarly, landing pages and content are keys to successful ad campaigns. Spending marketing dollars on both SEO and SEM can pay off in dividends when done effectively.

This book is meant to serve as a guide for marketers who describe themselves as "knowing enough to be dangerous." It will help them learn the ins and outs of search marketing at a more detailed level so they can ask the right questions of their internal teams, agencies, and partners. In my many years of teaching this topic in university and professional settings, marketers crave more detailed knowledge about search marketing so they can effectively market their businesses, collaborate with teams, structure their digital marketing strategy, understand technology and website/app development better, and generally arm themselves with knowledge.

My sincere hope is that this book will offer an in-depth, but not intimidating, look behind the curtain at search marketing, including both SEO and SEM. This book is intended for mid- to senior-level marketing strategists and digital marketers, including chief marketing officers (CMOs), chief brand officers, senior marketing strategists, VPs of marketing, senior product marketers, search marketing managers, marketing managers, e-commerce managers, marketing consultants, and marketers enrolled in programs to further their professional development. The writing is meant to be technical and detailed enough to really learn and understand search marketing, but without the unnecessary pressure of jargon, buzzwords, and acronyms that are all too common in the business of digital marketing.

What is Search Marketing?

Quite simply, search marketing refers to both the organic and paid capabilities for businesses to promote themselves through search engine listings on Google, Bing, and others. Search marketing is a powerful tool for businesses to reach potential customers through search engines and to capitalize on searches that best align with their business. SEO involves optimizing the website and its content to rank higher in organic search results for relevant keywords. This involves creating high-quality, relevant content, building authoritative backlinks, and optimizing the website's technical and on-page elements. By improving the website's ranking in organic search results, businesses can attract more targeted traffic to the website and increase brand and product visibility.

SEM, on the other hand, involves placing paid ads on search engine results pages. These ads appear above or below the organic search results and are marked as "sponsored." With SEM, businesses bid on specific keywords and pay for clicks or actions. This can be an effective way to quickly generate traffic and increase conversions, particularly for businesses with a new website or limited organic prominence. SEM can also be used for brand awareness, as a competitive tactic, and for local visibility.

Search marketing is particularly effective for businesses targeting customers who are actively searching for products or services that they offer. By optimizing the website and content for relevant keywords and leveraging paid search advertising, marketers can reach these customers at different phases throughout the buying cycle.

To succeed with search marketing, it's important to have a deep understanding of your target audience, their search behavior, and the competitive landscape in your industry. By investing in search marketing and staying up to date with the latest SEO and SEM best practices, marketers can improve visibility in search results, attract more qualified leads, and ultimately drive more revenue.

With both SEO and SEM, specific action items related to the use of keywords will build visibility. We will take a closer look at the use and importance of keywords later in this book. An important concept to remember is that the combination of both SEO and SEM can be exponentially powerful, versus using only one tactic or the other. While both are key components of a digital marketing plan, they are often overseen by separate groups because SEO is more technical in nature and SEM is considered a paid media tactic. However, SEO and SEM each have advantages and disadvantages. While SEM delivers immediate listings on search engines and allows control over the placement and ranking, there are forces such as search volume, cost, and quality score which are harder to control. Relatedly, SEO cannot ensure positioning or ranking but can be much more cost-effective than SEM. SEO is considered a longer-term, lower-cost method, while SEM can deliver fast impact while also incurring higher costs. In essence, SEO and SEM are two sides of the same coin.

It is important to note that volume of searches and competition are key indicators of how Google ranks both paid and organic listings on results pages. Not surprisingly, the metric "clicks," as measured by click-through rate (CTR), are typically the highest and top-positioned organic listings. Top organic rankings get the most clicks and are thereby the most valuable. However, these are also the most competitive, thus the hardest to achieve.

Digital marketing strategy cannot rely on SEO alone. Although marketers covet the high CTR and conversions of top organic listings, these can be elusive and thus are best balanced with paid ad campaigns. However, although SEM offers greater control for marketers, consumers are often aware of the difference between ads and organic listings. This means that the highest organic listings usually obtain more clicks and conversions than sponsored ones. Also noteworthy, as search engines continue to evolve, is the way search listings appear on the page continues to change. Ads, or sponsored listings, seem to be taking up more above-the-fold real estate than ever before, to accommodate multimodal listings (including images, videos, and more) and other new features like chatbot and AI-generated content. We will explore the ever-changing world of search engines in Chapter 12.

For the reasons we have explored, this author's position is that a solid SEO strategy combined with effective SEM campaigns creates a strong foundation for a digital marketing plan. Further, search marketing campaigns, both organic and paid, should include a wide and evolving keyword strategy focused across brand keywords that include all variations of business, product, and category names, combined with non-branded keywords that include categories, products, descriptors, and more. Search marketing is fluid and should always be a focal point deserving clear and specific goals, objectives, budgets, resources, and reporting. This approach will ensure that the SEO strategy does not become stagnant but continues to evolve.

Search in the Context of Digital

Digital marketing is the practice of promoting a brand, product, or service through digital channels such as search engines, social media, email, and other digital platforms. It involves various tactics and strategies that businesses can use to reach and engage with their target audience, build brand awareness, and drive sales and revenue. SEO and SEM are two important components of digital marketing. In my opinion, SEO is the most important element of digital marketing because, without it, businesses can miss out on top visibility for the most targeted and qualified audience—those searching for the specific company, products, and keywords.

While SEO and SEM are fundamental to a digital marketing strategy, there are many other types of digital marketing that can be combined to create broad visibility across online channels and platforms. Additional types of digital marketing include:

1 **Social media marketing:** Social media marketing involves using social media platforms like Facebook, Twitter, LinkedIn, Snapchat, TikTok, and Instagram to promote a brand or product, build a following, and engage with customers. This can increase brand awareness and drive qualified website traffic.

2 **Content marketing:** Content marketing involves creating high-quality content such as blog posts, videos, and infographics to attract and engage with a target audience. This can increase brand authority and build trust with potential customers and is also an essential element of the SEO strategy.

3 **Email marketing:** Email marketing involves sending targeted emails to a list of subscribers to promote products or services, provide value, and build relationships with customers. This can generate leads, drive sales, and improve customer retention.

4 **Influencer marketing:** Influencer marketing involves partnering with influential people on social media to promote a product or service to their

followers. This can increase brand awareness and credibility, and generate visibility, leads, and sales.

5 **Affiliate marketing:** Affiliate marketing involves partnering with other websites or influencers to promote a product or service in exchange for a commission. This can generate leads and sales and increase brand prominence.

To use these types of digital marketing effectively, businesses should first identify their target audience, goals, and budget. They should then develop a comprehensive digital marketing strategy that includes a mix of these tactics, tailored to their specific needs and objectives. Effective digital marketing requires ongoing testing, tracking, and optimization to ensure that campaigns are generating the desired results.

How to Use This Book

This book is intended for those interested in a deeper dive into search marketing, both SEO and SEM, and is therefore meant to be read beginning to end. However, it can also be a useful tool for those marketers and business leaders interested in one or the other, either SEO or SEM. That is why the book is divided into parts. In my classes and through surveys, I have found that SEO is by far the most intriguing area of digital marketing and that which students have the greatest desire to learn more about. Interestingly, SEM is rarely if ever listed as the component of digital marketing that students want to learn more about. However, I often find that students actually know less about paid search than they think. For those reasons, my hope is that this book sheds light on both areas of marketing while also bringing them closer together, as they should be in any well-run marketing team within an organization.

As I know that we all have busy schedules and growing to-do lists, I have tried to include helpful tools and tips throughout this book. Also, at the end of the book, there is a glossary of key terms. Hopefully all of these assets can serve as tools for those looking for something in particular or looking for additional information.

Below is a list of tools and tips included in this book and how they can be beneficial.

What to Expect

At the beginning of each chapter is a list of what to expect. This is a summary of topics within the chapter.

Objectives and Key Results

A goal management framework popular in technology organizations, the objectives and key results (OKR) framework helps implement and execute strategic initiatives. In this book, every chapter will include objectives, which are specific and measurable goals, and key results, which are the measurable outcomes demonstrating progress toward achieving the objective. OKRs are typically used in a collaborative and iterative process. They help to prioritize, align, and measure important outcomes.

Step by Step

In some cases, a particular tool or process can be used to drive a specific goal or outcome. In those cases, I have included a step by step for how to go about using that tool or process. These can be important ways for marketers and their teams to accomplish specific tasks or techniques within SEO and SEM.

Lookouts and Sidebars

As with all types of marketing, there are voluminous ways to do things and countless tools to use in the process. Lookouts are text boxes that provide helpful tools and insights for marketers looking to expand their understanding of a particular topic or technique.

Case Studies

Throughout the book there are several case studies highlighting work within the areas of search marketing. Case studies are real-world examples of how the knowledge and skills described within this book have been utilized for companies and organizations focused on SEO and SEM. These cases can be used to exemplify and illuminate concepts and strategies within the text.

Chapter Summary

At the end of each chapter there is a summary of what was contained within. This recaps the most important points within that chapter and makes it easier for readers to digest and retain those key points.

Reflection Questions

Also at the end of each chapter are a set of questions to help the reader reflect upon how their team or organization has approached the topics from that chapter. These questions are meant to be open-ended and thought-provoking. They can be conversation starters for the next marketing meeting or talking points for the next presentation. Ideally, they will provide fodder for an ongoing conversation about SEO and SEM within the organization and into the future.

Additional Resources

There are countless sources for information on the topics of search marketing, SEO, and SEM. These sources include online publications, books, videos, podcasts, and more. Below is a subjective and curated list of resources that may be helpful in addition to or in combination with this book:

1　Moz: Moz is a leading SEO software provider and also offers a wealth of free resources on its website, including guides, articles, and videos covering a wide range of SEO topics.

2　Search Engine Journal: Search Engine Journal is a popular online publication that provides news, insights, and resources on search engine marketing and optimization.

3　Search Engine Land: Search Engine Land is another popular online publication that covers the latest news, trends, and best practices in SEO and SEM.

4　Semrush: Semrush is an all-in-one digital marketing platform that offers a variety of SEO and SEM tools, as well as valuable resources on its blog and academy.

5　Ahrefs: Another popular SEO tool provider is Ahrefs, offering a range of free resources on its blog, including guides, case studies, and tutorials.

6   HubSpot: HubSpot is a leading inbound marketing and sales platform that offers a variety of resources on SEO and SEM, including guides, webinars, and templates.

7   SEO 101: Hosted by Ross Dunn and John Carcutt, this podcast covers a wide range of SEO topics, from basic to advanced techniques.

8   The Search Engine Journal Show: Hosted by Brent Csutoras, this podcast features interviews with leading SEO experts and covers the latest trends and best practices in SEO and SEM.

9   Search Talk Live: Hosted by Robert O'Haver and Matt Weber, this podcast covers all aspects of SEO and SEM, from keyword research to link-building and beyond.

10 Experts on the Wire: Hosted by Dan Shure, this podcast features interviews with leading SEO professionals and covers a wide range of SEO topics, from technical to creative aspects.

11 The Paid Search Podcast: Hosted by Chris Schaeffer and Jason Rothman, this podcast focuses specifically on Google Ads and provides valuable tips and insights for optimizing your ad campaigns.

12 SEO Bits: Hosted by Rebecca Gill, this podcast covers a wide range of SEO topics, from on-page optimization to local SEO and beyond.

PART TWO

SEO

2

Search Engines and Web Traffic

WHAT TO EXPECT

- The Definition of SEO
- The Customer Decision Journey
- The Three-pronged Approach to SEO
- Timeline for SEO
- Hiring for SEO
- Case Study: Hill Labs
- Reflection Questions

OBJECTIVES AND KEY RESULTS

- Define search engine optimization (SEO) in the context of general marketing and digital marketing.
  - SEO, when done effectively, drives high-quality website traffic through organic listings on search engines.
- Recall the customer decision journey and the place for SEO within it.
  - SEO, in conjunction with content marketing, can build awareness, increase consideration, drive purchasing, and influence post-purchase behavior such as referrals and loyalty.

- Interpret the three-pronged approach to SEO and understand each of the elements: on-page SEO, off-page SEO, and content.
  - The three-pronged approach will deliver all the meaningful elements of an aggressive and goal-oriented SEO campaign, resulting in increased conversion metrics and overall business growth.
- Explore a representative timeline for SEO strategy and implementation.
  - Set realistic timing expectations for key stakeholder groups involved in SEO and marketing efforts within the organization.
- Uncover the best practices and key skills to look for when hiring SEO professionals.
  - Hire SEO professionals who represent key skill sets for successful collaboration, contribution, and promotion of SEO efforts.

The Definition of SEO

SEO is defined as the continual process of improving the quality and quantity of website traffic to a website or web page from a search engine. It is commonly used as a technique to increase visibility on search engines for specific queries or keyword searches by internet users and potential new customers. Digital marketing consists of many different platforms, strategies, and tactics aimed at driving qualified website traffic which converts into customers and sales. In the early days of digital, if you were doing SEO, you could accomplish a lot. Now digital has become complicated with distracted users and cluttered platforms. It is much harder to stand out. A modern digital marketing plan may include email, SEO, paid search, social media, influencer marketing, display, and retargeting, across platforms like Facebook, Google, Microsoft, Amazon, Snapchat, and TikTok, just to name a few. In that increasingly chaotic and crowded landscape it is more competitive and costly to achieve results.

This is where SEO provides an opportunity. Most users of search engines today have an understanding of the difference between a paid and a natural or organic listing. Therefore, we typically see higher click-through rates, conversions, leads, and sales from traffic coming from organic search. It is usually the highest-performing traffic source outside of direct traffic. This means that SEO is worth the effort. In addition, SEO provides continuity across the customer decision journey, considered a key aspect of any marketing tactic. Customers experience brands at different moments within that journey. A strategic SEO campaign can meet those customers where they are, when searching out of curiosity, consideration, need, or want.

There are many important factors to consider and to build upon for a successful SEO strategy. In this chapter we will examine a three-pronged framework that assembles and organizes these factors into the following areas: on-page SEO, off-page SEO, and SEO content. We will look closely at each of the three areas while also learning about the appropriate expectations for timing of SEO. Finally, we will review the best practices and most important considerations when hiring for SEO roles and functions.

The Customer Decision Journey

An important concern with an SEO strategy is the customer decision journey, or CDJ. Successful marketers use the CDJ as the roadmap for all of their marketing efforts and SEO is no exception.

As illustrated in Figure 2.1, the CDJ is a continuous loop and marketers must determine their customer's path and how their strategies, platforms, and materials can help customers move decisively along that path.

The Three-pronged Approach to SEO

When used effectively, SEO can contribute across these different stages of the CDJ. First, on-page SEO helps businesses develop websites and increase awareness and consideration by improving the usability of the website. Next, off-page SEO is a critical authority-building opportunity for marketers to increase earned media and deliver increased value outside of their owned properties, increasing consideration and purchase intent. Chapter 3 provides an in-depth look into the framework for the digital marketing trifecta—paid, earned, and owned media. Finally, content must be used in different strategic ways across each stage of the CDJ. Every piece of content developed by a brand holds the intrinsic chance to include keywords, key messages, consistent tone, and voice, which are all fundamental to search engine optimization.

FIGURE 2.1 The Customer Decision Journey

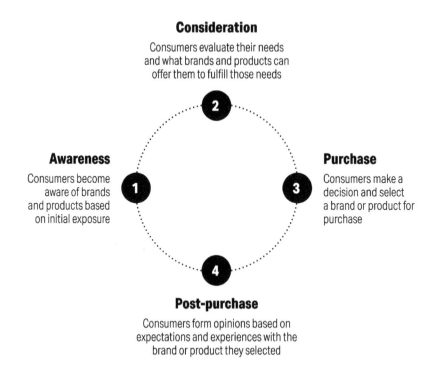

Consideration

Consumers evaluate their needs
and what brands and products can
offer them to fulfill those needs

Awareness

Consumers become
aware of brands
and products based
on initial exposure

Purchase

Consumers make a
decision and select
a brand or product for
purchase

Post-purchase

Consumers form opinions based on
expectations and experiences with the
brand or product they selected

There are many pertinent factors included in a robust SEO strategy. Let's explore the three-pronged approach that I have developed to help arrange SEO into meaningful sections that can be executed simultaneously or one by one. In many cases, multiple coworkers and teams will be involved in these sections. For example, it is not uncommon for one SEO company or agency to oversee all off-page SEO while an internal team is responsible for the on-page SEO and yet another group is tasked with the content creation. These three sections rely on unique skill sets that may be best fulfilled by individuals or teams with a unique and specific expertise within each.

The three-pronged approach provides organization into three distinctive categories, which are on-page SEO, off-page SEO, and content. On-page and off-page SEO elements require some technical capabilities, while content is a critical component that increases page relevance while also serving as a foundational element to an overall marketing plan. While most SEO professionals work within these general concepts, the three-pronged approach is a framework developed by the author. In Figure 2.2 we can see the basic

FIGURE 2.2 The Three-pronged Approach to SEO

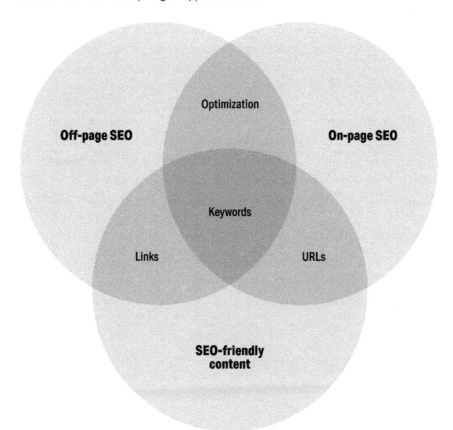

layout of the three-pronged approach to SEO and recognize where there are overlaps.

Each of the three prongs share certain elements like links. However, their most important shared element is keywords. Website designers and developers must think like their customers to place the proper keywords at the center of the SEO strategy. Keywords should be thought of as the very center of search engine optimization and should be a collaboration opportunity across departments and teams. Sales, marketing, technology, and executives should all take part in keyword research and brainstorming. Developing a strategic and cohesive set of keywords delivers consistent messaging across an organization while also benefiting SEO in each of the three sections.

It can be confusing to learn about the differences between on-page and off-page SEO. The easiest way to differentiate is to consider that on-page

SEO is everything we control within our owned properties. On-page SEO sends signals to search engines that we have followed best practices for everything within our control, while also providing an optimal user experience (UX) for our customers. Off-page, on the other hand, includes everything happening outside of our owned properties that helps us earn more authority and value over time. Off-page SEO provides a way to earn that authority and value by participating in dialogue that happens outside of our control.

In Table 2.1 we have a list of elements included in the two sections. It is important to remember the division of each section to avoid duplication of efforts. While there must be collaboration across sections, they also should be considered separate to ensure an exhaustive and thorough approach to each.

Now, let's explore each of the three prongs of SEO in more detail.

TABLE 2.1 On-page vs. Off-page SEO

On-Page SEO	Off-Page SEO
Site structure	Backlinks
Keywords	Directory submission
Title tags	Local SEO
Meta descriptions	Social media
Alt tags	Public relations
Images	Brand mentions
Page Speed	Sponsorships
Schema markup	Guest posting
Header tags	Social bookmarking
Internal linking	Blog commenting
Anchor text	Press releases
Sitemaps	Influencer marketing
Canonical tags	
Structured data	
Featured snippets	
Domain authority	
URL structure	

1. On-page SEO

Every search involves a user typing keywords, key phrases, or queries into a search engine. From there, search engines like Google rely on algorithms with crawlers identifying the best pages to match the user's search (more on this in Chapter 4). Proper attention to on-page SEO aspects will ensure that website pages can easily be read by users and search engine crawlers.

As we will discover in Chapter 4, the use of solid on-page SEO best practices will help with two very important components of search ranking systems: crawling and indexing. Because search engine databases contain massive amounts of data and billions of web pages, without the signals sent by on-page SEO it is difficult for search engines to learn and understand what individual web pages are about and determine the relevancy of pages for search queries. Consider these on-page SEO signals as shortcuts for search bots and spiders to find what they need in a consistent format across different websites, web properties, and web pages.

On-page, sometimes called on-site, SEO elements assist the search engine bots and spiders by directing them to the correct keywords, content, and pages. When on-page SEO is ignored, there is a risk that the site will not be properly indexed in a search engine database. This can lead to a site being buried on Google, or possibly not ranked at all.

Understanding if and how a site is indexed is one of the first steps to on-page SEO. The Step by Step below offers a quick and easy way to check if a site is being indexed by search engines. Google also offers a more in-depth URL Inspection Tool, which provides useful information about the indexing of specific pages as well as the ability to test whether a URL is indexable. There is additional information in Google Search Console's help section.

Common uses for the URL Inspection Tool are:

- View status of a URL in the Google index (indexed or not indexed).
- Learn why a URL is or is not indexed.
- Inspect a live URL to determine if it is indexable.
- Request the indexing of a specific URL to be crawled by Google.
- View a rendered version of a page to see how Googlebot views the page.
- Troubleshoot why a page may be missing from the index.

Website structure is one of the most important and manageable ways to optimize a site for search engines. Website structure is an overarching SEO category that includes many components like utilizing correct naming and tagging conventions. Properly naming and tagging website elements like images, videos, pages, and URLs will lead to better on-page SEO, and thus higher rankings and increased organic search traffic.

Search engine bots and spiders currently cannot see or read visual or audio elements including images and videos. Thus, written descriptions are considered an SEO best practice. Using alternative, or alt, text for visual or audio elements is a quick and easy way to increase accessibility of your site while also following an SEO best practice. The Step by Step shows how to add or edit alt text. That alt text creates an efficient way for spiders and bots to understand what a visual element is because the alt text describes it.

FIGURE 2.3 Meta Description

RunToTheFinish
https://www.runtothefinish.com › running-high-arches ⋮

7 Best Running Shoes for High Arches (+Exercises)

2 May 2023 — The **Hoka Clifton is a great** option for runners with high arches.
Thanks to a large midsole and a lightweight breathable upper it feels ...

NOTE Screenshot of Google search, 2023, keyphrase: best womens running shoes for high arches.
Google and the Google logo are trademarks of Google LLC.

Similarly, meta descriptions are used to summarize a web page for ease of use by search engines. These descriptions are equally as important because they can be the first or second thing a user sees on a search engine result listing—it is usually displayed right after the headline. See the example in Figure 2.3 of how a meta description appears within a Google search result.

On-page elements include some factors which can be automated with software, artificial intelligence, and machine learning. For instance, naming conventions for URLs should follow SEO best practices. Software or AI can be used to implement the proper naming conventions across a site with thousands of URLs. The Lookout box includes several tools that can assist with the process of on-page SEO. Also, please note that many website builders like WordPress, Wix, and SquareSpace offer on-page SEO tools, as do plugins and extensions for browsers like Firefox, Edge, and Chrome.

LOOKOUT

On-page SEO tools

1 **Screaming Frog:** Finds broken links, ensures redirects, analyzes tags, discovers duplicate content, and generates sitemaps.

2 **Yoast SEO:** A WordPress SEO plugin: add titles, meta descriptions, and structured data to posts and pages.

3 **SEOcrawl:** Offers rank checking, crawl monitoring, a cannibalization tool, visibility tracking, and task management.

4 **MetaTags.io**: Previews how tags, URLs, and meta descriptions will look in search results.

5   **ShortPixel:** Compresses and optimizes images.

6   **Generator:** Creates structured data.

7   **Schema Markup Validator:** Validates embedded schema.org based structured data.

Here is a compiled list of several important on-page SEO elements to consider as part of an overall strategy. This is not meant to be a fully exhaustive list, rather it provides ways to understand and implement many of the best practices for on-page SEO:

- Use on-page **SEO tools** offered by search engine companies to understand the current state of on-page SEO. Conduct a technical SEO audit. We will explore technical SEO more in Chapter 3, including the steps to performing an audit:
  - o   Google Search Console
  - o   Bing Webmaster Tools
- Organize **site hierarchy** and **accessibility:** when websites are effectively structured, following best practices, they will be indexed and crawled more regularly:
  - o   Ensure **navigation** is simple but well organized and naturally flowing.
  - o   Use **breadcrumb** listings so users can easily navigate back to a previous section or page.
  - o   Use **text**, rather than images, for navigation.
  - o   Create an **XML sitemap** to ensure that search engines discover new and updated pages.
  - o   Consider using an **image sitemap** to increase crawling of images within the site.
  - o   Use **standard image formats** like .JPEG, .GIF, and .PNG.
  - o   Create **custom 404 error pages** so that if a page or link is broken, users can easily navigate.
  - o   Optimize URLs and avoid deep nesting of subdirectories as those will lead to long URLs with unnecessary characters.
- SEO-friendly **URL structure** should be simple for both readers and search engines:
  - o   Use one to two keywords within a URL, don't "keyword stuff."

- o   Remove extra, unnecessary words or symbols.
- o   Use lower case.
- o   Use HTTPS (secure) if feasible.
- o   Remove dynamic parameters—URLs should be static when possible.
- Customize page and site **titles, headings and tags,** using keywords where appropriate:
  - o   site title
  - o   SEO title
  - o   blog post titles
  - o   headings (H1s, H2s)
  - o   categories, subcategories
  - o   create SEO-friendly, keyword-rich tags, categories, and links
- Create **crawlable links:** internal or external pages, navigation, email, map, location, files, and phone numbers.
- Optimize visual content using **alt text.**
- Write expressive **meta descriptions** for site and pages.
- Study **tagging** opportunities like canonical and "nofollow" tags.
- **Structured data:** help search engines understand content by providing structured information about website pages. Structured data also enables special search result features and enhancements like graphical search results. The Lookout box lists some helpful tools for developing and managing structured data for SEO. We will study structured data in Chapter 3.

LOOKOUT

Tools for Structured Data for SEO

1   Google Data Highlighter

2   Google Structured Data Markup Helper

3   JSON-LD Schema Generator by Merkle

4   Yandex Structured Data Markup

5   Structured Data Testing Tool

6   Google Rich Results Tester

FIGURE 2.4 Featured Snippets

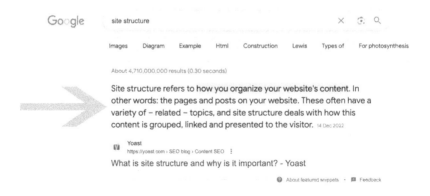

NOTE Screenshot of Google search, 2023, keyphrase: site structure. Google and the Google logo are trademarks of Google LLC.

- **Featured snippets** sometimes appear in search results as special boxes showing the description of the content first rather than after a link to a page. These special boxes might be found on their own or within another section of the search results page. Featured snippets can be blocked but not added and their content does not come from structured data. Google determines whether a page would make a good feature for a user's request. Featured snippets appear in position zero, or above all other organic results, and can provide users with quick answers to their questions. There are different types of featured snippets, such as definitions, lists, and tables. Figure 2.4 shows an example of a featured snippet about site structure for SEO.

- **Schema markup** helps search engines understand the information on the website by adding code to a page to communicate its main ideas. Schema markup—which is an agreed-upon vocabulary by search engines including Google, Yandex, and Bing—can provide a better user experience with **rich results** (formerly called rich snippets), information that is set apart from the rest of the listing that helps users decide where to click. Examples of content in rich snippets can include items from the list below:

  o review
  o rating

- price
- image
- podcast
- FAQ
- book
- Q&A
- video
- event
- local business
- how-to
- product
- video
- recipe

Search results pages are becoming rich and engaging experiences (see the screenshot example in Figure 2.5 when doing a search for a specific guitar from Fender). The results page can include images, news, questions with answers, ads, shopping, and more. These rich results are part of the new and continuously improving user experience on search engines and are not "for sale," they must be earned.

Along with the list of on-page SEO tactics, there are also many important things to avoid. Content should be original, fresh, and unique, and websites should avoid creating duplicate content or use canonicalization, 301 redirects, or "noindex" to direct crawlers and to address duplicate content issues. Also steer clear of any disruptive techniques like interstitials, pop-up dialogues, iframes, heavy images, or disruptive advertising. These can all affect page load time and should be limited or not used at all. Google's Advanced SEO Guidelines offer additional detailed information on these topics.

Remember that along with on-page elements like naming, tagging, and descriptors, Google also includes mobile-friendliness, site speed, use of secure sockets layer (SSL), and internal linking as additional on-page SEO factors. Quality guidelines are provided by search engines like Google and Bing and are constantly changing and being revised. It is considered a best practice for SEO professionals to become familiar with these and revisit them frequently for new and revised information and guidelines.

FIGURE 2.5 Example of Rich Results on Search Engine Results Page

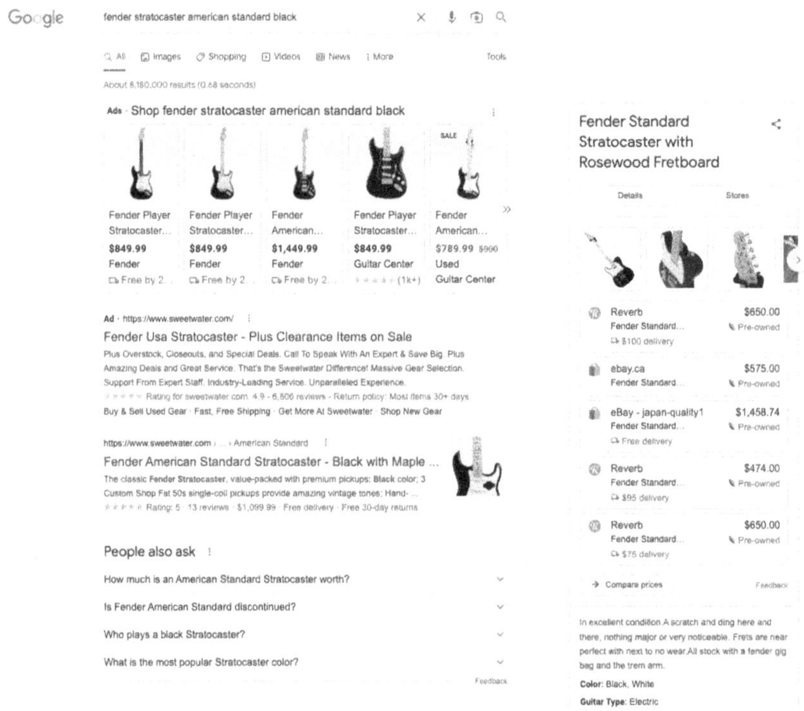

NOTE Screenshot of Google search, 2023, keyphrase: fender stratocaster american standard black. Google and the Google logo are trademarks of Google LLC.

2. Off-Page SEO

Off-page SEO denotes all the things that must be done outside of the website to increase authority with search engines. The biggest off-page SEO factor is the number and quality of backlinks (also called inbound or one-way links) to your website. *PageRank (PR)* is an algorithm used by Google Search to rank web pages in their search engine results. It is named after both the term "web page" and co-founder Larry Page. PageRank is a way of numerically measuring the importance of website pages. According to Google, PageRank works by counting the number and quality of links to a page to determine a rough estimate of the website's importance. Other ranking factors include page speed, page longevity on the web, and user behavior, including metrics like time on site and bounce rate. Tools like DNSChecker.com can be used to check PageRank.

FIGURE 2.6 How Backlinks for SEO Work

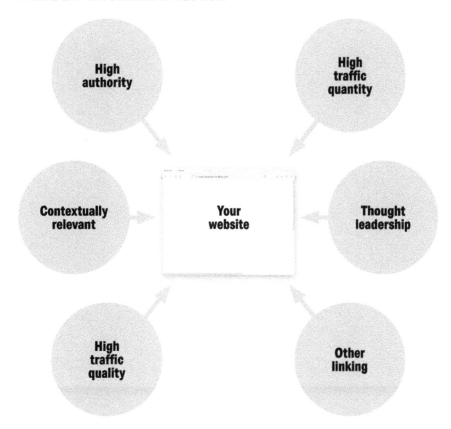

Keeping in mind that high authority or quality is more important than volume, SEO involves researching ways to increase site content authority by utilizing backlinking, social bookmarking, directory submission, and content distribution strategies.

Figure 2.6 demonstrates the concept of using backlinks from other websites to build authority for your website.

Although Google continuously evolves their algorithm, backlinks have always been, and continue to be, of great SEO importance. Google uses links to determine reputation and their search result ranking is partly based on those links. Figure 2.7 shows the relationship between backlinks and Google search positions and their direct relationship.

ALGORITHM UPDATES

Google is famous for algorithm updates with cute names like Penguin and Hummingbird, and some with less cute names like Link Spam Update. These

FIGURE 2.7 Total External Backlinks

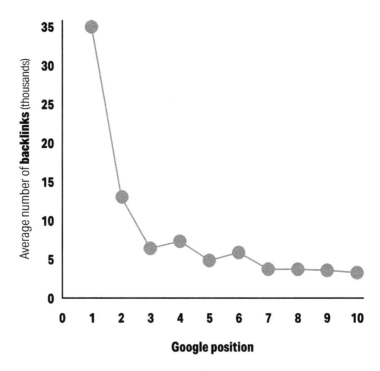

updates can cause changes to the way search engines display organic search results and can instantaneously cause widespread negative impact on an SEO strategy. While these updates are unavoidable, marketers and SEO engineers can prepare as much as possible to avoid getting caught by an update. Most SEO professionals keep track of algorithm updates and try to plan ahead whenever possible. In most years, Google rolls out two core updates in the spring and the fall as well as several regular updates throughout the year. These updates are tracked by search engines themselves as well as other well-known trusted sources of SEO information. Monitoring news sites like Search Engine Journal or Google's blog is a best practice for staying informed of algorithm updates.

Table 2.2 can serve as a guide and includes key linking concepts of adding, reciprocating, and earning quality links for SEO purposes.

Other important ways to build links to your website are:

1 Create valuable content that others want to link to because it is compelling.

TABLE 2.2 Link Building 101

LINK BUILDING 101	
Add	Relevant links are added to websites
Reciprocate	Websites share relevant links creating authority and backlink strength for each site
Earn	Organic search rankings improve over time

2 Submit your site to as many quality directories as possible. Examples include Yahoo Directory, Yelp, and YP.com. There are three types of directories:

a. paid or featured web listing

b. free or regular web listing

c. reciprocal regular web listing

3 Use social media shares of content that ultimately generate links. Facebook, Twitter, and LinkedIn are examples of high-authority websites, as are popular news sites including *The New York Times*, *Wall Street Journal*, Reuters, and *Washington Post*:

a. Google provides Search Quality Rater Guidelines, which can be valuable when considering how and where to share content for maximum SEO authority building.

b. Try using a link checker like the one offered by WC3 to determine the best strategy for building quality backlinks.

c. Outreach with emails to influencers in your industry that will ultimately link to you.

4 Research guest blog or post opportunities on sites related to yours. These guest posts will have links back to your site:

a. Consider the people in your organization who are subject-matter experts and develop a guest post strategy for them. This could include a monthly spotlight on an industry website, for example.

b. Use sites like LinkedIn and Medium to amplify your content and remember to include links back to your website.

3. SEO Content

As the saying goes: content is king. This is especially true when it comes to search engine optimization. In SEO, we must think about our content and our keywords as an extension of our brand and fundamental to our marketing. We need to focus on both quality and quantity of content on our owned, earned, and paid properties. In Chapter 6 we will do a deeper dive into SEO-friendly content.

Content that incorporates keywords will be rewarded by search engines. There are several ways to keep SEO in mind when writing content for web pages:

- Consider shrinking attention spans: Most people scan pages looking for key ideas, concepts, and ideas. Use the billboard style, which helps users find what they are looking for without unnecessary burdens or cognitive loads.
- Deliver headlines using the "who, what, why" formula; this guides users to the most important information in the shortest amount of space.
- Remember that call-to-action (CTA) words draw attention. Test words that pull people in. When appropriate, words like free, easy, try, test, buy, ship, save, and earn can inspire action with users.
- Numbers and statistics also grab attention. Within headlines, lists, body content, or image notes, numbers look different and thereby garner attention from the eye and the user.
- Visuals are another useful tool to attract attention. This includes icons, photos, sketches, comics, infographics, datagrams—anything visual will differentiate your content.
- People are drawn to quotes that are visually or contextually interesting. People notice quotes in a similar way to how they notice images and numbers—it is visually different and thus eye-catching.

Table 2.3 includes content ideas based on the stage in the buyer's journey. It is helpful to consider the customer journey and how the website content aligns. Remember that users and customers carry the greatest importance when it comes to content creation. Search engines will value high-quality content that creates engagement with users.

It is increasingly important to know what your customers are typing into Google and to use that to your marketing advantage. Developing a content

TABLE 2.3 Customer Journey Cycle With Content Recommendations

Buyer Cycle Stage	Content/ Web Page Recommendations
Awareness	Blogs, images, videos, social posts, research reports, infographics
Consideration	Articles, white papers, case studies, comparisons, podcast, industry expertise and reports, about page
Purchase	eBooks, webinars, product demonstrations, calculators, testimonials, product pages
Loyalty	How-to guides, email, thought leadership, explainer videos, customer pages, exclusive content

strategy with keywords in mind is a win-win for both your company and your customers.

The "keys" to keywords are brainstorming and collaborating. Invite members of different stakeholder groups to brainstorm sessions. Consider main keywords—called core keywords—which can encompass larger categories, products, etc. Brainstorm helper keywords, think about geographies, descriptors, specific words to your industry or products. Also, research competitors. Try and find gaps in their use of keywords.

Because SEO is increasingly competitive, it can be less effective to choose keywords that competitors already dominate within search listings. Study keyword volume by doing simple searches on a search engine to gauge how many searches take place for those keywords. There are tools that can assist with keyword research and brainstorming. Keywords vary by industry, so brainstorm all variations of your keywords and develop a "keyword universe" with a research-backed strategy in mind. Which keyword categories will deliver highest value for lowest competition and maximum volume? The Step by Step offers a path to your ideal keyword universe.

STEP BY STEP

Utilizing keywords for strategic SEO content

- Brainstorm keywords—core keywords and helper keywords:
  - Don't dismiss indicators like geography and behaviors (e.g., used books in Chicago).

- Understand volume and value of keywords:
  - o Use a tool or Google to check volume for search phrase combinations.
- Reverse-engineer competitors' keywords:
  - o View page source, look for "title, description, keywords."
- Use keywords in site content and blogs universally.
- Spread the word across teams including sales, marketing, technology, human resources, and executives. The whole organization should consistently use the agreed-upon keywords in all of their communication.
- The Lookout box provides a list of helpful tools for keyword research and analysis.

There are countless tools to assist in the keyword research process. The Lookout box offers tools and how they can work toward developing a strategic keyword universe.

LOOKOUT

Use tools to brainstorm and expand your keyword universe:

1 **Google Keyword Planner:** keyword suggestions and volume

2 **Ahrefs Keyword Explorer:** research and metrics

3 **Google Trends:** visualizes search popularity over time

4 **AnswerThePublic:** questions, prepositions, comparisons, alphabetical, and related searches

5 **Keyword Sheeter:** autocomplete suggestions

6 **SpyFu:** competitive search and keyword information

Timeline for SEO

The three-pronged approach to SEO includes many steps which require time, resources, tools, or all three. Because of this, the number-one ingredient for SEO is patience. No two websites are the same, so optimization and results can vary greatly by industry, brand, search engine, and site. Other marketing tactics can also impact SEO; things like paid search or SEM, social media marketing, and reputation management can impact results. Outside factors like compliance, security, penalties, technical issues, and internal cooperation can also slow things down. A good rule of thumb is that with effective on-page SEO, off-page SEO, and content creation, most websites will start to see results within approximately six months. When beginning the work of search engine optimization, a timeline with priorities and goals can be beneficial. This keeps everyone rowing in the same direction and creates realistic expectations for successful outcomes.

Month 1

The first month should be dedicated to research. The research will include keyword research, website audits, content assessments, and resource allocation. Alongside the keyword research, it will be beneficial to conduct a thorough competitive SEO analysis looking at which competitors are aggressively pursuing SEO. Once those have been identified, try to determine campaign goals and objectives and which keywords are most important to them. It is also useful to explore their content and social media marketing strategies as part of the competitive analysis. Finally, the first month is a good time to identify the team of individuals who will oversee SEO, keeping in mind that there will be decision-makers, managers, and individual contributors, as well as partners like agencies, consultants, and freelancers. Who will manage the day-to-day and who is responsible for which outcomes? Who are the decision-makers when it comes to budget and resource allocation? Who will create reports, who will find insights, and who will review reports? What software, tools, and agencies are needed for SEO success? These are key decisions to make in the first month of SEO.

Month 2

Once audits and assessments are complete, it's time to implement the changes. Technical audits will typically deliver large quantities of website changes and work to be done. This is the time to focus on on-page SEO implementation. This is also a time to develop and implement the content-creation strategy. Use of tools like a shared content calendar and image repositories will assist in the content-creation initiatives. Content should be unique, original, and varied. The best content represents a balance of quality and quantity. Including diverse authors and unique perspectives contributes to that balance and gives freshness to the content, regardless of the topic.

Month 3

Next, the existing content should be analyzed and revised based on new keyword and competitive research findings. New and improved content like blogs, FAQ pages, and articles can enhance the content strategy while also attracting search engines to crawl and index those particular pages. This is also the time to begin off-page SEO work, including link-building, directory submissions, blog outreach, social bookmarking, and content-sharing.

Month 4

Now is the time for maintaining and optimizing the SEO work that has been done. It is still a good time for off-page SEO as well. It is not uncommon to start seeing some benefits of the SEO work around the fourth month, but it's also important not to give up. Keeping track of indicators like organic search traffic, number of backlinks, and content quantity can help track the progress of SEO at this stage.

Month 5

Implementing additional supporting digital marketing efforts is helpful at this stage. Focused social media posts and content-sharing plus additional digital ad opportunities will drive more traffic and increase the authority of the site, which are good SEO indicators. Consider how your content can reach the right audience and deliver value to those users.

Month 6

Maintenance and optimization are key for an ongoing SEO campaign to be and stay effective. Tracking metrics and continued audits will help identify areas of success or concern. Broken links, errors, tag issues, and other on-site SEO factors can and do happen at any time. Also, remember to vocalize your strategy across your organization, different departments, partners, and vendors. As you add or remove products, content, pages, and properties, be sure that SEO stays at the forefront. It should be as important as the design and functionality of the website.

Hiring for SEO

Hiring for any role can be tricky, let's face it. Hiring for SEO can be especially difficult for a few reasons. First, SEO in and of itself can be intimidating, and many hiring managers and human resources representatives don't fully understand it themselves. Some fear sounding ignorant or uninformed. SEO can also vary in terms of where it lands in an organization. Although there are technical components, it also carries the weight of marketing and sales. With the focus also including content, there are various and often unrelated skill sets that seem to fall under the SEO umbrella. The first thing to remember is that SEO is not a one-size-fits-all department or position. The best SEO will come from multiple people bringing specific expertise to the table, combined with useful tools that can help with audits, automation, and other non-manual tasks. Here are some key aspects to consider and questions to ask when hiring for SEO.

Communication

Many SEO campaigns break down not because of a lack of technical acumen, but rather a communication breakdown. Therefore, communication is a key area of focus when hiring for SEO. This rule is true across the board, whether the hire is internal, an agency, consultant, or freelancer. The people doing the work must be able to communicate in the form of regular updates, reports, collaboration, asking questions, asking for help, working cross-discipline, and excellent writing skills. Questions to consider asking include:

- How have you communicated your SEO work in the past? Please be specific.
- What is a good cadence for working with a team on an aggressive SEO campaign?
- Who was your target audience and how did you communicate to them effectively?

Technical Skills

Technical skills for SEO include familiarity and experience with crawl and audit tools like SEOcrawl or Screaming Frog. It is important to see experience with Google tools like Search Console and Google Analytics, if your company uses these. Many SEOs will also bring experience with tools like

Ahrefs, Moz, Semrush, seoClarity, and others. Experience working with cross-functional teams and different groups or teams that may include agencies or consultants is also nice. Many SEOs have experience in either on-page or off-page SEO and some have experience with both. To find out more, consider asking the following questions:

- What is your process for keyword research?
- How would you align content and backlinks to keywords?
- What is an example of a report that you use and how would you present it?
- Describe a tool you rely on, how you use it, and what it provides.

Critical Thinking

SEO professionals must be able to do vastly different tasks, all pointing to the goal of optimizing a site for search engines. This could include a multitude of disparate things like running reports containing massive amounts of data, thinking from the customer/user perspective, fixing errors and broken things, creating or overseeing the creation of content, running meetings with different groups of stakeholders, and more. Giving the candidate an SEO problem and seeing how they respond can be a way to gauge critical thinking skills.

Data Analysis

Data drives much of the work and decision-making in search engine optimization—not unlike other areas of digital marketing. Proficiency with data analysis tools, spreadsheets, and large number sets is important for those working successfully in SEO. The right individuals will be able to gather, analyze, and find insights in large datasets. They should also be able to turn the data into something meaningful for a wider audience. Compiling SEO data and presenting it to a candidate would make for an interesting discussion about what they would recommend.

Marketing Mindset

SEO should not be thought of simply as technical because it is ultimately responsible for driving growth. Therefore, coworkers with a marketing mindset make good SEO professionals. They must understand the overarching goals and objectives for the organization and how SEO fits into that with consistent messaging and a customer-centric mentality. Asking a few hypothetical questions can help determine a marketing mindset:

- What role does SEO play in an overall marketing (or digital marketing) strategy?
- How does SEO contribute to growth of the overall business and how do we track that?

CASE STUDY
Hill Laboratories and ExpandTheRoom Optimize a Website Redesign

Introduction

Hill Labs manufactures state-of-the-art customizable chiropractic and medical tables. Over the past 75 years, the quality and innovation of their products has continued to grow, making them a global player in the medical table market. However, their online digital experience had not kept pace with the changes in web design, usability, and e-commerce best practices. Their website was visually dated, text-heavy with a lot of industry jargon, and poorly optimized for today's search-focused user. Digital design agency ExpandTheRoom (ETR), part of Infinum, was hired to redesign HillLabs.com and help them launch an industry-leading product configurator and website.

Goals

It was clear that SEO would need to be at the forefront of the content website redesign strategy. The team at Hill Labs needed to completely transform their e-commerce abilities. Their existing model only allowed for online sales to happen through a dedicated salesperson, as opposed to directly to the consumer. Optimizing for users to find Hill Labs products through organic search and ultimately delivering conversions were primary goals for Hill Labs. Additionally, their content was dense and not consumer-friendly. Rewriting the content with proper attention to keywords would be crucial. Focusing on content and SEO would drive more visibility and sales for the site. Tracking key performance indicators (KPIs) using Google Analytics would provide metrics and measurement for organic search traffic and conversion increases over time.

Strategy

The discovery process conducted by ETR included a comprehensive SEO-focused content audit to better understand the current state of the website content. An initial site crawl performed by Screaming Frog determined the exact amount of content that existed on the current site. This helped understand the full scope of the website. It was discovered there were 133 pages on HillLabs.com. Using Google Analytics; they further identified the top 10 pages getting the most organic traffic. ETR also learned that these 10 pages were responsible for a whopping 50 percent of the organic traffic leading to HillLabs.com. The data proved that 8 percent of the pages on HillLabs.com accounted for 50 percent of the traffic and indicated huge gaps on how pages are optimized. It was clear to ETR that they needed to evaluate the content and keywords on those 10 pages so they could use similar strategies on the many other important pages on the site that were not being indexed. A comprehensive keyword strategy became a focus of the SEO priorities. Additionally, ETR wanted to understand what new search opportunities existed by evaluating competitors and popular search terms in the medical table category. This strategy would ultimately deliver new pages to search listings and help attract new customers.

Actions

To understand how best to optimize the website, the next step in the SEO-focused content audit was keyword research. Keyword research was done primarily in Semrush and focused on identifying non-branded keywords. The goals of the research were as follows:

- Understand what is currently driving search traffic (preserve).
  - ETR looked at top keywords on HillLabs.com, rank, and average search volume. The search volume helped inform overall popularity of these search words within the medical table category.
- Learn what is currently driving traffic to competitors (emulate).
  - By evaluating the same categories, ETR could see how competitors were ranking for different or more popular search terms.
- Identify new search opportunities (gaps to fill).
  - By cross-referencing Hill Labs' keyword rankings with those of competitors, ETR was able to create a list of keyword gaps that could be filled with an SEO-focused content strategy.
- Develop a consolidated list of keywords.
- Segment keywords into topic themes.
- Incorporate topic themes into product and category page planning.

The keyword research helped inform content and technical decisions for nearly every aspect of the site, including page titles, meta descriptions, product descriptions, URL naming conventions, navigation labels, on-page headings, and hyperlink text.

Optimizing the content in these areas to best match what was discovered in the keyword research could drastically improve organic traffic from search and improve page rankings overall.

Based on the keyword findings, ETR made many content strategy recommendations, including:

- Prioritize optimizing product and category pages, as those are most likely to lead to conversion, as opposed to the "about" page, for example.

    o With the Hill Labs goal of optimizing for direct-to-consumer e-commerce, it was more strategic to spend time and budget prioritizing the keyword content, headings, and usability of the product pages as opposed to lower-traffic content pages like the about page.

- Incorporate language that customers are using to search to describe products and write product descriptions that incorporate those keywords.

- Avoid jargon or internal product names.

    o The current site was using table names like "HA90C" as opposed to more colloquial terms that aligned with how users search, such as "Traction Massage Table." ETR recommended all internal codes be removed from any headings or descriptions about the tables.

- Include ways to search and filter products to make it easier for users to find the right products.

    o This was a UX-focused recommendation to incorporate search and filter functionality. In general, focusing on improving the user experience of a site helps improve the site for SEO too.

- Include links to related products on every page. If a user arrives on the page and the product is not what they are looking for, provide other options to keep them on the site. Avoid dead ends:

    o Incorporating internal links between pages within the same website helps communicate to search engines which pages and products are related to each other, overall improving SEO.

- Create more user-friendly URLs. This often requires setting up redirects.

    o Internal product codes and the brand name "Hill" were being used in product page URLs as well as page titles and headlines. ETR recommended that URLs be changed to use plain language and remove the internal product codes altogether. These recommendations were captured in a content specification sheet which was used as a guide for setting up all of the redirects for any URLs that changed.

Figure 2.8 shows URL and page heading titles adjusted to focus on target keywords by removing internal jargon like "HA90AM" and focusing on user-friendly language.

FIGURE 2.8 Hill Labs Content Specification Sheet

Current URL (Desktop)	New Site URL	Target Keywords
	Existing URL should 301 redirect to this URL	
https://hilllabs.com/chiropractic/Hill-Automatic-Flexion-Table.php	https://hilllabs.com/chiropractic/automatic-flexion-table-with-manual-drops/	automatic flexiontable
https://hilllabs.com/chiropractic/Hill-DNFT-Chiropractic-Table.php	https://hilllabs.com/chiropractic/dnft-chiropractic-table/	dnft chiropractic
https://hilllabs.com/chiropractic/Hill-HA90AM-HiLo-Activator-Table.php	https://hilllabs.com/chiropractic/elevation-table/	elevation table
https://hilllabs.com/chiropractic/Hill-HA90C-Chiropractic-Table.php	https://hilllabs.com/chiropractic/chiropractic-drop-table/	chiropractic drop table
https://hilllabs.com/chiropractic/Hill-Hilo-Table.php	https://hilllabs.com/chiropractic/hi-lo-treatment-table/	hi lo treatment table

Results

The HillLabs.com website needed a comprehensive redesign including content, navigation, art direction, UX, user interface (UI), and SEO. While good design and functional UI are essential for enhancing a user's experience, it cannot work in a vacuum. Content is the key driving force behind findability, discoverability, and search optimization. ETR made SEO and keyword development a primary area of focus to meet the goals and KPIs of Hill Labs and ensure current and prospective clients could find what they needed through organic search as well as right on the Hill Labs website. These SEO efforts led to increased crawlability and indexing of the primary product pages, which ultimately led to increased conversion and revenue.

After the launch of the new HillLabs.com website, the results were a clear indication of success.

Key metrics

- a 75 percent faster return on investment (ROI) than expected
- a 38 percent lift in website revenue
- a 500 percent lift in new web orders
- a 48 percent increase in page views from organic traffic

- a 33 percent increase in the number of keywords ranking in top three positions on Google in the two years since launch

Insights

- When developing an SEO strategy, research which includes internal metrics, competitive analysis, and focus on keywords will drive new optimization opportunities.
- Oftentimes very few pages deliver most of the traffic. Identifying new pages to optimize and new ways to create content for both users and search engines is critical for SEO.

Wrapping Up

SEO as a concept requires technique, time, resources, and patience. It is a long-term pursuit that delivers outcomes in both quality and quantity. High-performing and -converting website traffic will ultimately result in revenue growth. Using the three-pronged approach to SEO covers bases by incorporating crucial on-page elements like site structure, naming, tagging, and descriptors as well as off-page link-building and SEO-friendly content creation. In addition to the three-pronged approach, creating realistic expectations and a credible timeline helps the organization align in terms of expectations. Finally, keeping certain things in mind and asking applicable questions when hiring SEO professionals can lead to better hires and thus better SEO results in the future.

CHAPTER SUMMARY

1 SEO is a continuous process designed to improve the quality and quantity of web traffic. It can lead to increased visibility on search engines for specific queries or keyword searches by internet users and potential new customers.

2 SEO typically results in higher metrics than other digital tactics, as measured by click-through rates, conversions, leads, and sales from traffic coming from organic search. It is usually the highest-performing traffic source outside of direct traffic.

3 When executed effectively, SEO can contribute across the different stages of the CDJ, including awareness, consideration, purchase, and post-purchase.

4   A comprehensive focus on the three-pronged approach to SEO delivers the best results. The three prongs include on-page SEO, off-page SEO, and content. When companies pay close attention to each of these three, the best results are possible.

5   On-page SEO includes all of the elements that we can control within our website, such as site structure, naming, tagging, descriptions, and other technical elements.

6   Off-page SEO is about building authority outside of our website through linking, directory submissions, social bookmarking, and more.

7   Content that utilizes keywords and other best practices for SEO can impact the ranking of our site on search engines while providing a positive user experience for our customers.

8   On average, aggressive SEO campaigns can take up to six months to see results. There is work to be done throughout those six months and on from there.

9   When hiring SEO professionals, it is imperative to consider technical skills, communication, critical thinking, data analysis, and a marketing mindset.

Reflective Questions

1   Is our organization in alignment in our understanding of and commitment to search engine optimization?

2   Are we considering SEO as a valuable and integral part of our overall marketing due to its importance at each stage of the customer decision journey?

3   Are we taking a holistic approach to SEO by having comprehensive knowledge and focus on both on-page and off-page SEO elements?

4   Do we have a thorough, robust, and researched keyword universe that all stakeholder groups align with?

5   Does our content marketing strategy support our SEO strategy by incorporating keywords and best practices?

6   Do we have a realistic understanding of the techniques, time, and resources needed to implement SEO and are stakeholder groups all united on expectations?

7   When we hire SEO professionals, are we working under the appropriate guidelines, looking for the proper skill sets, and asking applicable questions?

3

The Functionality of SEO

WHAT TO EXPECT

- The History of SEO

- Why SEO?

- How SEO Works

- Search Algorithms

- Search Ranking Systems

- E-E-A-T Guidelines

- Technical SEO

- Local SEO

- Case Study: AMA Chicago

- Reflection Questions

OBJECTIVES AND KEY RESULTS

- Recognize the position of SEO as a foundational digital marketing tactic.
  - SEO is a vital component of earned media in the digital marketing trifecta (paid, earned, and owned).
- Learn and understand the key benefits of how organic search listings can drive uniquely qualified traffic.
  - Increase digital marketing conversions including sales, leads, and other growth metrics.

- Examine the way search algorithms and ranking systems work and how to use this knowledge.
  - Emphasize crawlability, indexing, and serving of search results within the context of existing, new, and updated web pages.
- Analyze influential systems within search engines including automated ranking and algorithms and how these impact SEO.
  - Focus on E-E-A-T guidelines and content creator questions for self-assessment of core SEO content analysis.
- Learn about specific technical SEO factors influencing search rankings.
  - Audits and analyses identify key issues and areas of opportunity with technical SEO.
- Understand the importance of local SEO in reaching an audience in specific geographic areas.
  - Focus on goals and action items to increase visibility for local website traffic.

The History of SEO

SEO is sometimes thought of as a special type of magic or snake oil, whereby search engines miraculously find certain websites and display their content, thereby driving exponential growth to those businesses. My early days on the sales team at AOL proved the value of those search rankings. Back in those days, America Online was like the internet's version of both a national and a local newspaper. Not only did AOL offer national news and information, it also included local entertainment content, classified ads, and a way for users to search and find relevant results.

In fact, Google only began displaying local listings in 2003. Local search was considered the new alternative to the 100-year-old Yellow Pages and classified newspaper advertising solutions. Yahoo was originally created by entrepreneurs Jerry Yang and David Filo to list their favorite websites back in 1994. From there, WebCrawler, Lycos, InfoSeek, AltaVista, and—one of my favorites—Ask Jeeves arrived on the scene. By 2000, Google launched in its first iteration with over 20 million sites indexed in 10 languages. 2005 was a big year for Google when they added weather and maps, which was quickly followed by mobile web search, translation services, and voice search in 2008. A few years later a new web indexing system called Caffeine was introduced, resulting in fresher results plus the ability for users to search for images rather than just text listings. Since then, many interesting and useful tools for local SEO have been announced, such as Google My Business, RankBrain, featured snippets, Discover, job search, Google Lens, AR features, dictionary pronunciation, multisearch, and more.

As Google and other search engines continue to invest in their product and the AI and algorithms behind it, businesses continue to embrace SEO. The little-known secret all along has been that SEO is not magic and it's not snake oil and it's certainly not easy. Quite the opposite, in fact: SEO is diffi-cult, competitive, and demanding. For many businesses, SEO has its own department. Some companies also have outside partners, consultants, and freelancers working on SEO. Often time, the more visible SEO is within a business, the more resources it gets.

I have been teaching on the topic of SEO since those days at AOL when I was approached at a business conference by an academic leader at DePaul University after my keynote presentation on search engine optimization. His simple question to me was, "Would you teach SEO to our students?" I went ahead and created one of the very first SEO courses at a major university. Since that day, I haven't looked back. My courses continue to evolve and I continue to build out my approach to teaching this fascinating topic.

SEO was and is an essential marketing tactic and can be even more powerful when combined with a strong digital marketing strategy incorpo-rating the digital trifecta of paid, earned, and owned media. In this chapter we will explore why SEO is important and how it works, taking a deeper look at the important areas of algorithms and ranking systems, guidelines for content, and conducting a technical SEO audit.

Why SEO?

Before we examine the functionality of SEO, it's important to understand the importance of SEO. Marketers are typically aware of the trifecta approach to media, which includes paid, earned, and owned. These three components make up a digital marketing strategy. Paid media includes advertising in the form of display, social media, retargeting, influencer marketing, and more. Owned media quite simply includes any property owned by the business, such as a website, emails, podcasts, webinars, and mobile apps. Earned media can be more complicated because businesses are hoping to gain media attention through compelling content, links, shares, and more. Earned media can include organic posts on social media and organic rankings on search engines (SEO). Other examples of earned media include online reviews, and shared or reposted content. Earned media can be amplified by shares, and the more content is amplified, the wider the audience reach.

In Figure 3.1, the digital marketing trifecta—the relationship between paid, earned, and owned media—is highlighted. Because earned media cannot simply be bought, it is often considered the most significant, most difficult, and best-performing method of digital marketing. Hence, the importance of SEO. Many search engine users place higher trust in organic (earned) ranking content than the content that they recognize as sponsored or a paid advertisement. Thus, organic search traffic typically performs at a much higher rate—as evaluated by click-through rates, conversions, purchases, and leads generated—than other types of traffic such as paid advertising.

FIGURE 3.1 The Digital Marketing Trifecta: Paid, Earned, and Owned Media

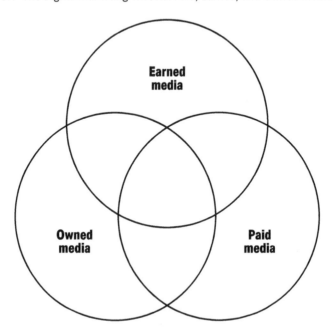

THE DIGITAL MEDIA TRIFECTA

- **earned media:** organic search listings, likes, shares, reviews
- **owned media:** website, mobile app, press release, webinar, email, event
- **paid media:** paid search, social media ads, sponsored content, retargeting, sponsorships

One of the most effective driving forces of earned media is a combination of strong organic rankings on search engines and content distributed by the brand. First-page rankings and good content are typically the biggest drivers. Rankings on the first page of the search engines place your owned media sites and links in a position to receive higher engagement, clicks, and shares, which is why a robust SEO strategy is essential. While many marketers dismiss SEO as difficult to execute or hard to measure, SEO, when thoroughly understood and diligently managed, can be a leading indicator in an overall marketing plan while being cost-effective and data-driven. In the most simplistic terms, traffic coming from organic search rankings is typically high-quality traffic that drives conversions, leads, and sales. Thus, the more a website is optimized for search, the more value, growth, and ultimately revenue will be driven. Therefore, higher rankings on search engines deliver valuable marketing and sales prospects.

How SEO Works

Figure 3.2 is a graphical representation of the way SEO works. The goal is to deliver the most relevant and reliable information for users in the most useful way. There is a rigorous process in place using both automated systems as well as human quality raters (more about this later in the chapter) to help provide the best possible outcomes.

Essentially, this initial process consists of three specific stages. When a user types in a search query, search engines will deliver the best content with the highest-ranking positions on the results page. First, bots, also commonly referred to as spiders, crawl the web to identify and save text, images, and video content that match the user's search query. Then the search engine will analyze and index those pages by storing the information in a massive database. Finally, the search engine will serve results based on the user query or combination of keywords entered into the search bar. Search engines determine the best matches based on quality and relevance to the user query. Let's take a closer look at each stage of this process to better understand how they work.

Crawling

Search engines are constantly looking for new and updated web pages to add them to a list of known pages. The process is often referred to as "URL discovery" and takes place during the crawl stage of search. Some pages cannot be crawled by search engines for various reasons, for example a robots.txt file is preventing access to the page (more about this later in this chapter) or there are problems with the server or the network making the page inaccessible. Blocked pages are a main reason site content is not crawled and can easily be remedied.

Indexing

Once a page is crawled, the search engine needs to understand more about the page and what it is about. During the index stage, search engines process and analyze the content and tags within a page to determine if that page is relevant to searchers. Additional collected information may include languages used within the page, locality of the page, or the usability of the page. Indexing depends on the content within the page as well as the metadata, which is used to help search engines capture the most important information about a page of content. Indexing can also be controlled with specific methods to help search engines locate new and relevant content. These methods include many aspects of technical SEO, which we will uncover later in this chapter, such as XML sitemaps, use of Google Search Console and Bing's Webmaster Tools and IndexNow (see the Step by Step), crawl budgets, and more. Indexing is an essential part of achieving search engine rankings and many aspects are within the control of the marketer.

Serving Search Results

Finally, after pages have been crawled and indexed, they are ready to be served to users based on search queries. Search engines identify pages that match keywords entered by users and return results with the highest level of quality content and the most relevance to the user's search. Many factors

FIGURE 3.2 The Process for How Search Engines Work

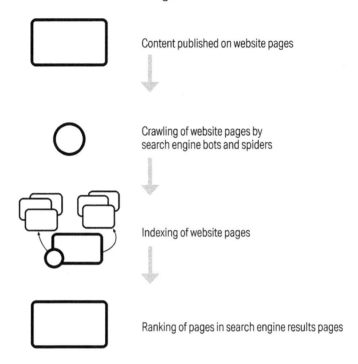

Content published on website pages

Crawling of website pages by
search engine bots and spiders

Indexing of website pages

Ranking of pages in search engine results pages

influence relevance for search engines. For example, location, device type (mobile or desktop), language, keywords, and other comparable factors can affect relevance. Website pages may be indexed but not show on search results. This can be caused by irrelevant content, low-quality content, or other factors.

STEP BY STEP

IndexNow is an indexing protocol tool that alerts search engines about new or updated content as it is added to a website. Microsoft announced the open-source protocol as an option for all search engines. However, only Bing and Yandex are currently using it. This is useful because the alert will lead to the swift indexing of that new or updated content. It notifies search engines when a URL has changed to prioritize crawling and indexing those changes. There are several ways to implement IndexNow; below are a few options:

1 Developers can generate a key by using a free online key generation tool provided by Microsoft, which will then allow them to submit URLs when they are added, updated, or deleted.

2 Businesses can use a widely available plugin for a content management system like WordPress, Wix, or Drupal.

3 Content delivery networks like Cloudflare and Akamai also have integrated solutions to provide their partners and customers with resources to support the use of IndexNow.

4 SEO companies like Botify and Yext have integrated IndexNow in their proprietary software suites.

Search Algorithms

Most marketers consider the algorithms used by search engines mysterious. It can feel like a random concoction or formula that determines the quality and relevance of a search result. Algorithms can affect a paid ad or an organic ranking, and determine if or where a listing will fall within the results and rankings. It should be noted that while there are countless formulas that exist within an algorithm, there are also various precise algorithms focused on fulfilling specific functions that are core to the overall way that search engines work.

For example, Google's Panda algorithm, launched in 2011 to combat misuse or "black hat" SEO (see Sidebar: Panda update), focuses on analyzing and filtering content based on specific parameters. The use of this algorithm leads to rewarding or penalizing sites for the proper use or misuse of the guidelines. There have been many other publicly announced updates to the Google algorithm including Penguin in 2012 and Hummingbird in 2013. Similarly, in 2018, a system update called "Page Speed" was announced to signify the importance and relevance of page load time for mobile users and within mobile search results.

Search Ranking Systems

Automated ranking systems include indicators about web pages and content that help in the manner of presenting the best-matched listings when users perform search queries. There are several systems that combine into the core ranking system. In Google's ranking system guide there are additional details about how these indicators work. Understanding the ranking systems helps to better prepare and implement SEO effectively.

Below are a few of these systems. For a comprehensive overview, visit Google's Search Central—Guide to Google Search ranking systems.

- BERT: Bidirectional Encoder Representation from Transformers. BERT is an artificial intelligence system, or natural language processor (NLP), that Google developed in 2019 to understand and process word combinations based on meaning and intent as opposed to just content or keyword matching.
- MUM: Multitask Unified Model. This AI system provides the capability to both comprehend and produce text and language. It is used to help improve specific searches based on language understanding and processing. MUM can also understand distinctive modalities like text, images, and videos.

- RankBrain: Launched in 2015, this is an AI system that determines how words and concepts relate to each other. It helps to better understand what users are looking for when they type in certain complex queries.

- Exact match domain systems: Words within a domain name are considered as a factor to determine relevance to a search query.

- Freshness systems: Content that has been released recently can be considered higher quality for certain searches. This can include news articles or recent reviews, which may be more timely than older information. An example could be weather-related searches.

- Crisis information systems: Systems that help by providing timely updates and information during a crisis. This could include natural disasters like floods or earthquakes, health-related crises such as Covid-19 policies, or personal crisis information like violence or drug addiction, for example.

- Product review systems: Higher-quality reviews will exemplify content that is insightful, useful, and original. These reviews will be rewarded based on page-level analysis.

E-E-A-T Guidelines

In 2014 Google released a new and helpful guideline commonly referred to as E-A-T, which stood for: expertise, authoritativeness, and trustworthiness. This automated system's core purpose is to identify and prioritize the most helpful and relevant content. In 2022, E-A-T was updated and another E was added, for experience. Google provides publicly accessible guidelines with useful details about the framework. The E-E-A-T guidelines describe trust as being the core value at the center of expertise, experience, and authoritativeness. E-E-A-T is not a ranking factor; it is an important way to determine the effectiveness of web content for search placement and relevance. Many marketers and SEO professionals use self-assessment questions when considering new content for search engine optimization. Figure 3.3 illustrates the E-E-A-T guidelines for content creation.

- **Experience:** Quality content creators must demonstrate the necessary experience with the topic of the content. A wealth of personal and professional experience leads to extensive and valuable knowledge of a topic.

- **Expertise:** The creator of any quality content must also have the skills that are relevant to the topic. This is established through proficiency and demonstrated dexterity with a particular topic.

- **Authoritativeness:** The content creator or website should be considered a dependable source on the topic. While this may not be an official designation, the source must be considered reliable, accurate, and truthful for their understanding of the topic.

- **Trust:** This is the extent to which the content is accurate, honest, safe, and reliable. This can be established through security measures, reviews, as well as informational and definitive pages that describe why the source is trustworthy.

According to the guidelines—and also considered an SEO best practice—content creators should first and foremost consider their users when generating content. Content should not be created with the sole purpose of trying to achieve search engine rankings. Google relates to this as a people-first approach to content, meaning that the content was created with users and customers in mind, not search engines. Using different tools and formulas, search engines can identify spammy content or content created for the purposes of search engine rankings rather than users. This results in manual actions, penalties, and even removal from search engine indices for substantial breaches of confidence.

FIGURE 3.3 The E-E-A-T Guidelines for Content Creators

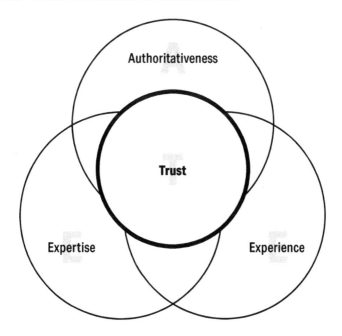

LOOKOUT

The questions below can serve as a self-assessment for following Google's E-E-A-T guidelines.

- Does the content provide original information, insights, research, or analysis?
- Is the content complete, substantial, or comprehensive?
- Does the content provide considerable value as compared with other similar content that may be available to users?
- Is the content able to provide an insightful analysis or information that is beyond what might already be obvious?
- Is the content written by an expert or enthusiast who clearly knows and understands the topic at a deep level?
- Is it easy to verify that the content is factual and accurate?
- Are there any errors within the content, such as spelling, grammar, or inconsistent tenses?
- Is the content well produced and at a high-quality level?
- Does the content display well across different devices, browsers, and operating systems?
- Does the content leave a user looking for additional information that was not included or received?
- Is this content providing a summary rather than new information?
- Is the content automated or copied from another source?
- Are the topics important only because they are timely or trending, or are the topics things of interest that would be written about even if they were not timely or trending?

Technical SEO

Search engine ranking systems draw on the E-E-A-T guidelines as well as technical SEO. Because SEO is such an important driver of qualified traffic, businesses must pay close attention to the crawlability and indexability of their website pages. There are other fundamental components of SEO that we will explore in subsequent chapters, such as keyword research and link-building. However, this process is often called technical SEO and, when done effectively, makes it easier for search engines to find and rank the right content that matches with the user queries.

There are several important concepts within technical SEO that a solid team or agency should understand. A website can have a beautiful, modern design and the most cutting-edge technology features, but if no one can find it, the design and technology are for naught. Technical SEO incorporates many components ranging from simple things like purchasing the domain name and linking it to an IP (internet protocol) address to more complex things like sitemaps, structured data, canonical tags, and rendering.

Technical SEO starts with an audit. Seasoned SEO professionals will have experience conducting technical SEO audits using specific software, tools, and concepts that work for them. There are certain elements of a technical SEO audit that are standard and are based solely on ranking factors within search engine algorithms. Becoming familiar with these elements ensures that the technical SEO audit is thorough and closely related to search engine ranking factors.

Audits help marketers and SEO teams determine the crawlability and indexing for a website. Google Search Console and Bing Webmaster Tools are free tools offering a variety of critical reports and data points for search engine optimization purposes. The Step by Steps below demonstrate how to use Bing Webmaster Tools and Google Search Console for technical SEO.

STEP BY STEP

Bing Webmaster Tools

Bing Webmaster Tools (BWT) and its help center provide steps to improve website performance in Bing search. BWT is usually used by webmasters, developers, digital marketers, and SEO professionals. It is required to open a Webmaster Tools account to get started. From there, here are the steps to use BWT:

1   Add a web property to the Webmaster Tools account and verify the ownership of your site.

2   Create and upload sitemaps. Bing supports sitemaps in multiple formats:

   a. XML sitemaps

   b. Atom 0.3 and 1.0

    c. RSS 2.0

    d. text files

3 Create a search optimization plan using Webmaster Tools to help identify relevant and important SEO tasks, such as:

    a. backlinks

    b. keyword research

    c. analysis of SEO errors

    d. IndexNow

    e. URL inspection

    f. site scan

    g. crawl control

    h. Verify Bingbot

    i. user management

    j. Microsoft Clarity tool

4 Utilize the Notification Center to receive alerts and messages about various issues, including:

    a. administrator

    b. crawl errors

    c. index issues

    d. malware

5 Read and learn about Bing's content guidelines:

    a. make sitemaps available and easy for Bing to crawl

    b. appropriate use of redirects

    c. use of JavaScript and dynamic rendering

    d. remove content receiving error message

    e. inclusion of robots.txt file to inform Bingbot which pages to access and which to remove from index

    f. SafeSearch specifies how to handle explicit images, videos, or websites in search results

    g. images and videos should be original and include descriptive titles, filenames, and text. They should also be in supported formats, high quality, and include subtitles or captions

h. Bing uses three key parameters to rank pages in search results:

    i. relevance

    ii. quality and credibility

    iii. user engagement

6 Learn about Bing's best practices with schema markup, 404 pages, and MRSS video feeds.

7 Peruse the FAQs of Bing's Webmaster Tools for helpful answers to common questions, such as:

    a. Why is my site not in the Bing index?

    b. How can we remove pages on my site from Bing's index?

    c. How do Bing crawlers access my site?

STEP BY STEP

Google Search Console

Google Search Console (GSC) is an important learning and implementation tool that will help improve search engine optimization. GSC is used by webmasters, developers, digital marketers, and SEO professionals. The only requirement is a Google account. Once that is in place, here are the steps to use GSC:

1 Open Search Console and verify the ownership of your site.

2 Read the guide for basic usage.

3 Learn about important reports and dashboards, such as:

    a. Property dashboard: shows critical issues such as security issues or manual actions, which are penalties, as well as charts showing indexing, performance, and more.

    b. Google performance: web search, news search, and Discover.

    c. Security issues: site hacking, violations of spam policies, acceptable site behavior, omitted content, and more.

    d. Indexing: which pages have been found on the website.

    e. Site usability: reports describing mobile usability, site and page load time, and other metrics affecting ranking of the site.

    f. URL inspection report: how Google views the page if there is a problem.

4 Learn important key terms within Search Console (these are also commonly used in web analytics and other tools):

   a. Property: a website that has been added to Search Console.

   b. Verify ownership: proving ownership of a property so that you can manage it within Search Console.

   c. Click: number of users who click on a link, image, or video in Google Search.

   d. Impression: number of times your link or listing was displayed, but not necessarily clicked.

   e. CTR (click-through rate): clicks divided by impressions.

   f. Googlebot: the web crawler that requests web pages as different device type based on search results for users on those device types.

   g. Render: the ability for search engines to display the indexed pages in the way the user will view them.

   h. Manual action: a penalty for pages in violation of one of the quality guidelines. For example, pages using spam content will be assigned a manual action and thus demoted or removed from search results.

Here are some of the important elements of a technical SEO audit:

- Sitemap: Helps users and search engines find and navigate a website.
  - An HTML sitemap is written for users, helping them understand the information architecture of a site.
  - An XML sitemap is written specifically for search engines and serves as a guide for bots and spiders to properly crawl and index a website.
- Robots.txt: Excludes certain parts of a website from being crawled using a disallow command.
  - Validation tools are available online to help find and maximize the use of the robots.txt file.
- Site structure: The way a website is organized, including how content is grouped together and how easy it is for users and search engines to reach deep, interior pages of a website. Good site structure includes:
  - URL structure that is clean and consistent, does not include long strings of unused characters
  - no parameters that are useless or unnecessary, such as session IDs

- o no broken links
- o use of breadcrumb navigation
- o use of internal linking to help users find deep, interior pages
- o navigation that is intuitive and easy for users
- o limited number of clicks for users to find what they need—three clicks is ideal
- Canonical tags: Multiple pages within a site containing the same content or "duplicate content" can be problematic for SEO. Canonical tags provide the opportunity to tag the best representative page from a group of duplicate pages which sends a signal to search engines, thus eliminating duplicate content from indexing. Canonical tags best practices include:
  - o use of only one per page
  - o use of correct domain protocol, typically HTTPS
  - o only tag duplicate content, not merely similar content
  - o different pages with the same content point to the same canonical URL
- Structured markup: While structured data—the markup that helps search engines gather information and display content—is not itself a ranking factor, if it is used effectively, it can help search engines understand the content within pages of the site better, which leads to better indexing and displaying on results pages. Best practices for structured markup include:
  - o Understand the types of structured data that Google supports, including books, breadcrumbs, Covid-19, events, FAQ, how-to, recipe, video, and more.
  - o Code structured data using in-page markup and describe the content of the page.
  - o No empty or blank pages should be used to hold structured data.
  - o Check vocabulary on schema.org or Google Search Central documentation for required, recommended, and optional properties of structured data.
- Content: Search engines like Google publish Search Essentials (formerly called Quality Guidelines) to demonstrate the important factors that determine if website content will appear on search results pages. These fall into three core parts, important for SEO:
  - o technical requirements: the bare minimum of what is needed from a web page for it to be displayed on a results page

- spam policies: the tactics that can lead to a page either being ranked lower or not ranked at all

- key best practices: the things that can be done to have the greatest impact on web content ranking, such as crawlable links, tagging, and helpful relevant content

- Things to avoid: There are many disruptive techniques used by websites that will interfere with user experience and thus search engine rankings:

  - Flash: pages using Flash will be ignored by most search engines.

  - Iframes: iframes often interfere with load time and create issues for search engines.

  - Heavy ads or interstitials: mobile-friendliness and page load speed are impacted by heavy ads or interstitials.

  - Infinite scroll: use paginated loading, which means the URL changes as the visitor scrolls down a page, rather than infinite scroll, even if the design is impacted.

  - Triggering Chrome SafeSearch filters: millions of users access the internet with Google Chrome's SafeSearch filters, a browser extension, to eliminate explicit content from search results. Sometimes a site can be flagged for explicit content when none actually exists. Manual checks using the SafeSearch filter can help identify any flagged content.

  - Broken page links: linking to a page that contains a 404 error creates a frustrating user experience and stops the flow of link equity, which can negatively impact search rankings.

  - Slow load time: web analytics tools can report on page load time to ensure speed performance is part of the technical SEO process.

Local SEO

Many businesses will focus on attracting local customers within specific geographies. By incorporating certain SEO elements, businesses can work toward optimizing their site for local search results, directories, and map listings. The goals of local SEO are to improve local visibility, increase local website traffic, boost foot traffic, establish local authority, and enhance an online reputation.

To accomplish these goals, marketers should focus on local SEO action items, as follows:

1 Claim and optimize Google My Business (GMB) listing:

   o Claim and verify the business on GMB.

   o Optimize the listing with accurate business information, including name, address, phone number (NAP), hours of operation, and website URL.

   o Choose relevant categories and add high-quality images.

   o Encourage customers to leave reviews on the GMB listing.

2 Local keyword research and on-page optimization:

   o Research and identify local keywords and phrases that are relevant to the business and target audience. Local keywords often include geographic modifiers.

   o Optimize website content, meta tags, headings, and URLs to include local keywords.

   o Create location-specific landing pages with unique and valuable content.

3 Online directories and citations:

   o Submit the business information to relevant online directories and citation sites, such as Yelp, Yellow Pages, and industry-specific directories.

   o Ensure consistent NAP information across all directories.

   o Encourage customers to leave reviews on directory listings.

4 Local link-building:

   o Build relationships with local influencers, bloggers, and businesses for potential link-sharing opportunities.

   o Seek out local sponsorships, events, and partnerships to earn backlinks.

   o Create valuable local content that attracts natural backlinks from local websites.

5 Online reviews and reputation management:

   o Encourage customers to leave reviews on platforms like Google, Yelp, and Facebook.

   o Monitor and respond to reviews promptly, addressing both positive and negative feedback.

   o Implement strategies to generate positive reviews and manage customer feedback effectively.

6 Mobile-friendly and fast-loading website:

- o Ensure the website is optimized for mobile devices, providing a seamless browsing experience for local users.

- o Optimize website loading speed by compressing images, minimizing code, and utilizing caching techniques.

7 Local content marketing and social media:

- o Create and promote locally focused content, including blog posts, articles, and infographics, to engage the local audience.

- o Utilize social media platforms to share local updates, promotions, and events.

- o Encourage social sharing and engagement from local customers.

8 Local SEO analytics and iteration:

- o Set up tracking and analytics tools to measure local SEO performance and monitor key metrics such as local organic traffic, conversions, and rankings.

- o Analyze data to gain insights into customer behavior, preferences, and local market trends.

- o Continuously refine and optimize local SEO strategies based on data-driven analysis.

CASE STUDY
AMA Chicago and Be Found Online Implement Local SEO
for Increased Visibility

Introduction

AMA Chicago is a local chapter of the American Marketing Association (AMA). The AMA is a professional association for marketers with 76 professional chapters, 250 collegiate chapters, and over 30,000 members. Local chapter performance is based on membership and engagement with the goal of building a local audience and membership base of engaged marketers. Unfortunately, AMA Chicago competes online with the main office of the organization, which is also located in Chicago.

AMA Chicago was having difficulty achieving organic search results for their local area, with decreased visibility and outranking by their main organization's website. Chicago-based digital agency, Be Found Online (BFO), created a six-month local SEO campaign to increase organic search traffic by focusing on the number of keywords ranking on page 1 of local search results.

Goals

AMA Chicago wanted to build and maintain visibility around news and networking for the marketing industry. In addition to concerns around visibility in search results, the job listings and member directory areas of the site were seeing low traffic volumes and were areas of concern. After reviewing the site's performance, BFO identified that engaging with a targeted local SEO campaign would be the best approach. They established two primary goals and subsequent key performance indicators (KPIs) for the local SEO campaign, and a six-month timeframe for completion.

BFO aligned KPIs directly with the two goals of the campaign:

1 Increase traffic and keyword rankings for AMA Chicago:

   a. growth in organic search traffic by 5 percent

   b. increase page 1 keyword rankings by 20 percent

2 Increase traffic to job listings and member directory sections of AMA Chicago:

   a. increase job listings traffic by 25 percent

   b. increase member directory traffic by 25 percent

Establishing KPIs is an integral part of the SEO strategy. BFO first developed a benchmark report from existing web data. For AMA Chicago, this included data from Google Analytics, Google Search Console, and Google My Business. Reviewing trends over the last several years, BFO identified points of seasonality in site traffic and located specific high-value pages that lost organic search traffic over the years. Of particular note was the decrease in year-over-year organic search traffic to the site. AMA Chicago saw a 57 percent decrease in organic sessions year over year. However, SEO takes time, so setting an attainable KPI was important. BFO determined that growing organic search traffic to the entire site by 5 percent over six months would indicate success.

Based on AMA Chicago's goals and data, BFO also determined that the job listings board and the member directory were areas of focus, and thus created a KPI that focused on increasing organic search traffic to these areas by 25 percent over six months.

Strategy

BFO developed a list of 116 keywords that were applicable to AMA Chicago through keyword research. Based on search intent, the list of keywords would help drive visibility for AMA Chicago events and membership. Of the list of 116 keywords, AMA Chicago was ranking on page 1 for 20 keywords. A 20 percent increase in page 1 rankings would be an indicator of success for this campaign.

TABLE 3.1 Keyword Volume and Ranking

Keyword	Average Search Volume	Position March 30
Chicago digital marketing events	10	8
Chicago marketing	260	35
Marketing events near me	10	Not ranking
Marketing agency directory	10	54
Chicago networking events	390	Not ranking
Marketing events	170	6
Marketing directory	170	Not ranking
Marketing workshop	10	Not ranking

Search intent is one of the primary factors when determining factors for an SEO campaign. Ranking for terms that connect with the target audience who will ideally complete the conversion is a critical measurement of successful SEO. Intent can be coupled with average monthly search volume to bring a more complete picture of the best keyword opportunities. Table 3.1 includes a list of the highest focus keywords for AMA Chicago with average monthly search volume (SV) and ranking position at the beginning of the campaign.

During the initial site review, several hurdles were identified that would impact the success of the campaign. Hurdles with AMA Chicago:

- Low domain authority (DA): AMA Chicago started with a DA of 28. DA is a metric that rates the likelihood of a site to rank in the number 1 position of search engine results pages (SERPs). Ranked on a scale of 1–100, 28 is a low starting position.

- Competition: Job listing sites are notoriously competitive—large sites like Monster and Indeed dominate most search engines, even for local listings.

- Support: Limited web developer support was available to implement changes for AMA Chicago, which led to choosing the most impactful items and prioritizing accordingly.

- Seasonality: AMA Chicago hosts events that boost traffic throughout the year that could cause fluctuations in website traffic.

- Time: Six months is a very short SEO campaign. Typically, SEO is at least a one-year engagement to provide time for the recommended changes to be fully accepted by Google and to start seeing results.

Actions

BFO developed a comprehensive local SEO strategy that comprised three key components:

- **Audit:** A series of audits helped identify what AMA Chicago was currently doing for on-page and off-page SEO, as well as content marketing. The top focus was technical SEO and Google My Business, an invaluable resource for any local organization. Top audit findings included technical elements that impacted user experience and the functioning of the site, search rankings, and relevance. Audits also revealed opportunities with content creation around particular keywords.

- **Research:** After the audits, the research phase began. BFO identified and researched top competitors and which keywords, backlinks, and structured data were focal points.

- **Optimizations:** The audits and research culminated in specific optimizations, including several important SEO elements:
  - keyword targeting—specific focus on metadata and headers
  - on-page content optimizations, including header optimizations and keyword integration
  - interlinking recommendations
  - alt tagging optimization
  - customized structured data, also known as schema markup
  - technical troubleshooting and optimizing

Halfway into the local SEO campaign for AMA Chicago, a new challenge arose. BFO discovered that the job listings board was run by a third-party partner, making SEO work nearly impossible. This made the first KPI of goal 2—increase job listings traffic by 25 percent—null and void. BFO adapted the strategy and recommendations to AMA Chicago for how to better connect the job listings board to the main domain and refocused work into the first KPI of goal 2.

Results

Goal 1: Increase traffic and keyword rankings for AMA Chicago. The first KPI attached to this goal was to increase organic search traffic by 5 percent. At the end of the six-month campaign, organic search traffic was trending at a 24 percent increase, far exceeding expectations. Additionally, the primary target pages saw a significant increase, specifically with the marketing events page seeing a 147 percent increase in sessions and the weekly networking page seeing a 145 percent increase.

There was also an increase of page 1 keywords by 60 percent. The campaign began with 20 targeted keywords on page 1. By the end, there were 32 targeted and highly relevant keyword phrases on page 1.

The second KPI attached to goal 1 was to increase page 1 keyword rankings by 20 percent. At the beginning of the campaign, AMA Chicago had 20 keywords ranking on page 1. To reach the goal of a 20 percent increase, AMA needed 24 keywords ranking on page 1. They ended with 32 keywords ranking on page 1, achieving a 60 percent increase in page 1 keyword rankings. There was also a significant increase in rankings on page 2 and pages 3–10. This is depicted in Table 3.2, a comparison of search results at the beginning to the end of the campaign. Similarly, Table 3.3 indicates the keyword volume and ranking for specific keywords and phrases targeted in the campaign.

Goal 2: Increase traffic to job listings and member directory sections of AMA Chicago. The first KPI for goal 2 was originally to increase traffic to the job listings board by 25 percent. However, that goal was removed since no SEO work was

TABLE 3.2 Search Results Comparison

SERP Position	March 30 Rankings	September 6 Rankings
Page 1	20 keywords	32 keywords
Page 2	7 keywords	8 keywords
Pages 3–10	12 keywords	26 keywords
Not ranking (past position 100 or page 10)	77 keywords	50 keywords

TABLE 3.3 Keyword Volume and Ranking

Keyword	Average Search Volume	Position March 30	Position September 6
Chicago digital marketing events	10	8	5
Chicago marketing	260	35	9
Marketing events near me	10	Not ranking	3
Marketing agency directory	10	54	3
Chicago networking events	390	Not ranking	9
Marketing events	170	6	1
Marketing directory	170	Not ranking	1
Marketing workshop	10	Not ranking	5

possible on the platform. The second KPI was to increase member directory organic search traffic by 25 percent. This goal presented challenges, resulting in a yearly increase in traffic of 14.63 percent to the member directory page.

BFO identified the three main challenges faced with this part of the SEO campaign:

- **Technical formatting difficulties:** During the SEO technical audit for AMA Chicago, it was identified that the member directory page template had formatting issues in the form of multiple H1 headers and improperly configured H2s. The H1s were a primary concern. Having more than one H1 on a site is problematic for SEO. It took months to resolve the error with the page template.

- **Content:** Content presented a challenge as it could not be easily added to the platform. Google needs to crawl content to understand the page. Lack of optimized content is a hindrance to an SEO campaign.

- **Time:** Six months is a very short timeline for SEO results. The above issues caused delays, resulting in less time to see results. A 12-month campaign would have been preferable.

Insights

1 SEO takes time. Campaigns running for less than 12 months can be difficult for driving aggressive results.

2 Technical SEO is critical. Performing strategic audits delivers impactful action items and delivers strong value.

3 Content is an essential SEO component. Without strong content, achieving visibility in search rankings is much more difficult.

4 Challenges present themselves at different times and marketers must always be prepared to adapt, pivot, and provide additional strategic direction in the presence of unforeseen hurdles.

Wrapping Up

Appreciating the history and value of SEO leads to a more comprehensive understanding of its significance. Similarly, examining the ranking systems and algorithms used by search engines helps marketers see the complexity of SEO in a new light. A technical audit is a critical step in SEO. As they say, it takes a village, and in the case of SEO, that usually includes higher-level decision-makers, managers, and individual contributors across departments, including marketing, sales, and technology, as well as trusted partner agencies, contractors, and freelancers. For SEO to truly be successful, there must be understanding and buy-in, both from the value standpoint and the technical perspective. Finally, local SEO can be an important strategic direction for businesses with a geographic or localized strategy.

CHAPTER SUMMARY

1   Marketers must recognize the history and value of SEO as a foundational digital marketing tactic. Because SEO is a vital component of earned media, in the digital marketing trifecta (paid, earned, and owned), it should be a marketing focus in any organization motivated by growth through digital marketing.

2   As a component of earned media, organic search listings can drive uniquely highly qualified traffic and thus increase digital marketing conversions, including sales, leads, and other growth metrics.

3   Understanding the way search algorithms and ranking systems work and how to use this knowledge with an emphasis on crawlability, indexing, and serving of search results for existing, new, and updated web pages will deliver growth from organic search traffic.

4   The analysis of systems within search engines, including automated ranking and algorithms and how these impact SEO, helps marketers focus on content creation. Using the E-E-A-T guidelines and content creator questions for self-assessment of core SEO content analysis will assist in this arduous process.

5   Learning about technical SEO factors that influence search rankings will lead to identification of key issues and areas of opportunity.

6   Local SEO provides an opportunity to attract customers in specific geographies and involves various elements to ensure that businesses appear in local search results.

Reflection Questions

• Do the team members involved in SEO understand its history and the value it provides? This includes all stakeholder groups: decision-makers, managers, and individual contributors, plus third-party partners, agencies, and contract workers or freelancers. It also includes marketing, technical, sales, and creative coworkers.

- Does the team truly recognize the value that organic search traffic can deliver? Do we have data and reporting to prove it?

- Is it apparent that SEO is a valuable part of the digital marketing trifecta: earned media?

- Do stakeholders have a comprehensive understanding of ranking systems, algorithms, and technical SEO and how these factors influence ranking on top search engines?

- Are we using important tools like IndexNow, Search Console, and Webmaster Tools to increase indexing and deliver critical reports about technical issues that can hinder SEO performance?

- Is local SEO important for our business and, if so, are we incorporating it into the strategy?

4

A Winning SEO Framework

WHAT TO EXPECT

- Marketing Frameworks
- The STMO Framework
- Case Study: Qualitest
- Reflection Questions

OBJECTIVES AND KEY RESULTS

- Understand marketing frameworks which deliver structure to the marketing process.
  - Porter's Five Forces and AARRR provide a blueprint for the work that goes into marketing within an organization.
- Recall the digital marketing framework, providing marketers with a way to organize and prioritize efforts in a meaningful way.
  - SEO is fundamental to an overall digital marketing strategy; drawing upon each step of the STMO process, it can deliver powerful business growth and results.
- Comprehend and apply SMART goals within the STMO process.
  - SEO goals should be specific, measurable, attainable, realistic, and timebound.

- Define specific campaign tactics and plan for implementation.
  - Considerations must include team, technology, and timing as well as budgets and resources.
- Outline metrics, KPIs, and equations to evaluate success of efforts.
  - Apply analysis and ongoing optimization to continuously improve results.

Marketing Frameworks

Developing messaging and communication with customers can be one of the biggest challenges in modern business. Marketing frameworks help companies, departments, and individuals by providing a blueprint for the rigorous effort that goes into marketing, advertising, and communication strategies for businesses. Frameworks also provide context and details about the execution and delivery of marketing plans for specific audiences. Improving the strategy, clearly communicating roles and responsibilities, and clarifying expectations are some of the benefits of using marketing frameworks. Further, because marketing involves an increasingly complex dynamic with creativity, analytics, and project management at the forefront, frameworks create a sustainable process, rather than an ad hoc environment.

Key Benefits of Marketing Frameworks

- clearly communicating strategies and tactics
- organizing tasks into specific steps
- creating workflows with approval processes
- clarifying roles and responsibilities
- creating efficiency and eliminating overlap of duties
- consistent messaging and communication
- documenting content, guidelines, tools, assets for marketing

Studying examples of marketing frameworks can help contextualize these ideas. Three well-known marketing frameworks are Porter's Five Forces, STP, and Pirate Metrics (AARRR). Understanding these fundamentals at a closer level can help us appreciate the power of a good framework.

Porter's Five Forces

A thorough and detailed understanding of the competitive landscape is an important tool in the marketer's arsenal. This longstanding model—originally developed by Michael E. Porter out of Harvard Business School—is often used in conjunction with a SWOT (strengths, weaknesses, opportunities, threats) analysis to study competitors and understand market conditions.

- supplier power: potential to raise prices and lower profitability
- buyer power: consumers' effect on price and quality
- threat of substitution: how easy it is for consumers to switch to a competitive product
- threat of new entry: how easy or difficult it is for new competitors to enter the market
- competitive rivalry: how intense the competition is in the marketplace

STP (Segmentation, Targeting, and Positioning)

Marketing efforts are known to be most successful when the market is clearly segmented into the right groups, products are effectively targeted, and services are well positioned. Developed by Phillip Kotler—a distinguished professor of marketing at the Kellogg School of Management at Northwestern University and author of several essential marketing books—STP is used as a tool to help businesses identify a clear customer segment prior to creating a plan. Every business faces the challenge of understanding their customers and how to reach them effectively. Using the STP model, a clear direction for marketing and messaging can be produced.

These three criteria are:

1 Segmentation: Divide the market into distinct groups using criteria such as:

- o demographic: age, gender, income, education, occupation, etc.
- o psychographic: lifestyle, hobby, activity, attitude, opinion, etc.
- o geographic: country, region, state, province, city, neighborhood, etc.
- o behavioral: payment, loyalty, usage, past purchases, etc.

2 Targeting: Determine the commercial factors to reach each segment, such as:

- o size: segment size and ability to grow
- o profitability: payment opportunities and lifetime value
- o ease of reach: ability to reach audiences and cost to acquire

3 Positioning: Map out the variables to position products in the marketplace:

- o functional positioning: solving a problem or delivering a key benefit
- o symbolic positioning: enhancing image or ego with a luxury product
- o experiential positioning: focusing on product features that connect emotionally

Pirate Metrics (AARRR)

Companies focused on tracking the right metrics will succeed long term, according to the Silicon Valley investor and serial entrepreneur Dave McClure, who developed the AARRR framework. This method provides companies with a framework for narrowing their focus on the most important metrics that impact the health of the business and determine the success of their product management and marketing efforts.

- Acquisition: How are people discovering our brand and products?
- Activation: Are those people taking the right actions?
- Retention: Are those people continuing to engage and take actions?
- Referral: Do those people like us enough to tell others?
- Revenue: Are our customers willing to pay for the products?

The STMO Framework

In Chapter 3 we studied the digital marketing trifecta, which is based on a marketing framework that considers paid, earned, and owned media. Taking a closer look at digital marketing, we know that there are many strategies and tactics at the disposal of the modern marketer. In the early days of digital marketing, there were few choices and even fewer platforms.

In the modern era of digital marketing, a marketing plan can include display, search, social media, retargeting, affiliate, mobile, and more. Similarly, platforms can include Google, Amazon, Bing, Facebook, Instagram, YouTube, Snapchat, and TikTok. This does not even scratch the surface of the marketing technology tools and software that exist, such as customer relationship management, marketing automation, content management, data management, and web analytics, just to name a few.

To organize digital marketing efforts, we turn to the digital marketing framework in Figure 4.1. This framework offers a roadmap for digital marketers to organize and prioritize while ensuring that we don't put the cart ahead of the horse. The STMO framework (or SiTMO) is effective for any type of digital marketing, and it provides order for developing campaigns, whether that is an SEO campaign, paid search, social media, retargeting, or anything else. The STMO framework can be examined through the lens of both digital marketing and SEO.

The first step is strategy, which includes high-level goals, tighter marketing objectives, resources, and budget. Next are tactics, which involves selection of channels and platforms. Then comes measurement for aligning metrics back to goals and objectives. Finally, there is optimization for refining work based on the insights coming out of measuring effectiveness. Let's explore each of these in closer detail. But first, let's take a close look at a methodology for creating goals that align with strategy.

FIGURE 4.1 STMO: A Framework for Digital Marketing Success

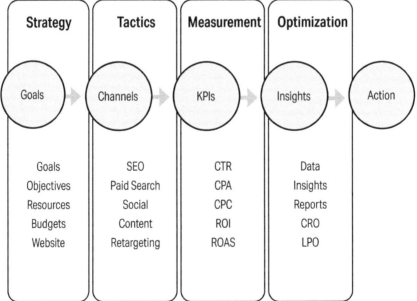

SMART Goals

In the context of the digital marketing framework, we will be analyzing and agreeing upon business and campaign goals. For this, we turn to a framework commonly referred to as SMART goals. SMART is an acronym that stands for: specific, measurable, attainable, realistic, and timebound. Figure 4.2 demonstrates the dos and don'ts of SMART goals through the lens of digital marketing efforts.

The S stands for "specific," which means that the goals include actual numbers that are associated with deadlines. The M is for "measurable," to ensure that the team is aligned on which metrics will be tracked, analyzed, and used to gauge success. Next comes A for "attainable," meaning that although the work may be challenging, it can be done. R is "realistic" and indicates the actuality of the work that must be completed. Finally, T is for "timebound." Without precise timelines and due dates, things can go on indefinitely.

SMART Goals and SEO

SMART goals can be used at any company or business, large or small. For SEO purposes, SMART goals help to accurately define and measure the impact of the SEO efforts. To apply them to the SEO process, think critically about what the most important and relevant results are for measuring successful outcomes.

SPECIFIC
Start by being specific and tying the SEO metrics back to goals and objectives. Specific metrics can be impressions, clicks, organic search traffic, conversions, or others. Be sure to clarify how these metrics tie in with the overall business goals and how SEO will deliver.

MEASURABLE
Next, for measurable, there are many options for tracking and analyzing web data, such as Google Analytics, Adobe Analytics, and Mixpanel. We will take a more in-depth look at digital analytics and measurement in Chapter 6. Setting benchmarks ahead of time will make it easier to measure against previous timeframes. Always compare annual, monthly, or weekly data against a similar timeframe. For example, benchmark monthly impressions, clicks, organic search traffic, and conversions for the previous year leading up to the SEO campaign and measure against those benchmarks.

ATTAINABLE

For goals to be attainable, they must be focused on specifics such as keyword research, competitive analysis, and site auditing. These processes, as well as overall traffic trends combined with the rigor and work going into SEO, will help determine what is achievable and truly possible.

REALISTIC

To build a realistic set of goals, it's important to remember that SEO is a work in progress. It does not happen quickly, and results can be uncertain. Therefore, realistic expectations should be at the forefront of SMART goals. Taking a full year before expecting major changes can be a good step toward realistic goals. It's always better to overdeliver than underperform.

TIMEBOUND

Finally, results for SEO should be bound by specific time parameters. This means that there is an established and agreed-upon timeline for tracking impact. Many companies have regular monthly or weekly reporting of results for SEO for a small team and quarterly or annual reporting of results for a bigger group of stakeholders. Daily and weekly reporting should not be used for analyzing SMART goals or overall results. Seasonality and internal and external factors can all influence SEO results. Therefore, an adequate amount of time should be given, typically 6 to 12 months will work.

When SMART goals are used and agreed upon by teams involved with SEO, everyone should be in alignment on the goals, objectives, and metrics for successful outcomes. Figure 4.2 offers a description of each component within the SMART goal framework.

Here are a few examples of applying SMART goals to SEO:

- Increase organic search traffic by 10 percent from January to January.
- Increase organic search traffic by 5 percent in the fourth quarter this year, as compared with the fourth quarter last year.
- Maintain at least 20,000 monthly organic visitors, starting in January and for one full year.
- Increase revenue from organic searches by 5 percent for the next 12 months, as compared with the previous 12 months.
- Grow the number of e-book downloads by 10 percent for users coming from organic search, year over year in 2025.
- Expand organic newsletter signups by 30 percent year over year.

FIGURE 4.2 The SMART Goal Methodology

Smart	Measurable	Attainable	Realistic	Time-bound
Do include precise numbers that have real deadlines	**Do** make sure that goals are trackable	**Do** work towards a goal that is challenging, but possible	**Do** be honest and up front about what the team is capable of considering the resources and budget it has	**Do** agree on timelines and deadlines
Don't say we need more website traffic	**Don't** track only generic things like influence or sentiment; be sure to track key performance indicators	**Don't** try to take over the world in one night	**Don't** forget about barriers or hurdles that could impede success	

Now that we have a window into other marketing frameworks and a starting point and methodology for creating goals, we can go further into the processes for successful digital marketing and SEO. First, let's examine how the STMO framework applies to digital marketing. Then we can apply it directly to search engine optimization.

Strategy

Strategies for digital marketing campaigns must be built on a solid foundation. Marketers often want to skip strategy and go straight to tactics. Without agreed-upon goals, expectations, and funding, these campaigns are doomed to fail. The first step is to outline and gain agreement around the overarching goals of the digital plan. Goals are high level and impact the entire business. Examples include awareness, engagement, and sales. Once the business is in agreement about the high-level goals, it's time to assign marketing objectives and metrics. Marketing objectives can be considered the action we hope our customers will take, such as clicking, viewing, or converting in some way. From there, the metric to track success must be assigned. This is typically a key performance indicator from web analytics, such as traffic, click-through rate (CTR), e-commerce revenue, or conversion rate.

RESOURCES

Once we have goals and objectives, we must consider everything required to execute against those goals and objectives. This should be revisited frequently, and it should also be part of the initial digital marketing strategy. In terms of digital marketing, we have a simple framework called the three Ts: teams, technology, and time. During the strategy phase, we must lay out the plan, including the team members who will be involved, the software tools needed, and what the timing and cadence will be.

Below are a few questions to consider about the three Ts:

1 Teams:
   a. What can the existing people on the team accomplish and what is outside of their expertise?
   b. Who do we need to hire?
   c. What will we outsource?
   d. Will we hire an agency?
   e. Do we need contract or freelance help?
   f. What are the costs involved?

2 Technology:
   a. What role will technology play in our digital marketing initiatives?
   b. Do we already have technology that we can leverage?
   c. Are there existing licenses within the organization that we can leverage, like Microsoft, Google, Adobe, or Salesforce?
   d. What can technology do that people cannot?
   e. What are the primary goals of the software: management, creative, data analysis, reporting, etc.?
   f. Is our website and/or app ready for our digital marketing? Do we need to add landing pages or improve UI/UX?

3 Timing:

   a. When do we hope to have our plan up and running?

   b. How long will it run for?

   c. Will there be seasonality, i.e. holiday, back to school, Super Bowl?

   d. Who will oversee the timing of our digital marketing and who is ultimately responsible for it running on time?

BUDGET

Once we have a sense of the resources needed for an effective digital marketing plan, we can move on to the budgeting exercise. Again, this is an area that can be revisited but should be planned out in the early stages. There is no golden rule for digital marketing budget allocation. Many factors influence the decision of how much to allocate to marketing, including industry, competition, market conditions, and other costs. Some businesses follow a rule of thumb indicating that businesses should allocate 7–10 percent of their revenue to marketing. From there, about half of that budget can be allocated to digital marketing. The budget Step by Step offers insights into the budgeting process and how to tackle it head on.

STEP BY STEP

Digital Marketing Budget

1 Understand the sales funnel.

2 Outline fixed costs.

3 Revisit goals and objectives.

4 Review previous results—budget allocation and customer acquisition.

5 Determine costs for marketing activities and estimated budget:

   a. media
   b. people
   c. technology
   d. website
   e. other costs

6 Consider what competitors have done and are doing.

7 Make data-driven decisions:

  a. Calculate costs to acquire customers.

  b. Calculate return on investment.

8 Run models with different budget levels.

Table 4.1 illustrates the progression from business goal to marketing objective plus a metric for specific SEO components. There is an example for each: business-to-consumer (B2C), business-to-business (B2B), recruiting, and non-profit.

TABLE 4.1 Examples for SEO Strategy Success

B2B Example				
Business Goal	Marketing Objective	Metric	SEO Component	Example
Awareness	Traffic	Organic Traffic	Generic Keywords	U.S. Travel
Engagement	Clicks	CTR	Relevant Keywords	Disney family vacation
Sales	e-commerce	Conversion Rate	Bottom funnel Keywords	Book hotel near Disneyland holiday 2023
B2B Example				
Business Goal	Marketing Objective	Metric	SEO Component	Example
Awareness	Traffic	Organic Traffic	Generic Keywords	Accounting software
Engagement	Clicks	CTR	Relevant Keywords	Best accounting software for small business
Sales	e-commerce	Conversion Rate	Bottom funnel Keywords	Purchase 5 user license Intuit accounting software
Recruiting Example				
Business Goal	Marketing Objective	Metric	SEO Component	Example
Awareness	Traffic	Organic Traffic	Generic Keywords	Digital Marketing jobs
Engagement	Clicks	CTR	Relevant Keywords	Social Media Marketing Manager Jobs

(continued)

TABLE 4.1 (Continued)

Sales	e-commerce	Conversion Rate	Bottom funnel Keywords	Apply for jobs as social media marketing manager in Chicago
Non-Profit Example				
Business Goal	**Marketing Objective**	**Metric**	**SEO Component**	**Example**
Awareness	Traffic	Organic Traffic	Generic Keywords	Donations near me
Engagement	Clicks	CTR	Relevant Keywords	Donations pick-up near me
Sales	e-commerce	Conversion Rate	Bottom funnel Keywords	Donation pick-up winter clothes in Evanston, IL

Tactics

The novel model of the "marketing mix" originated in the 1950s through Harvard Business School and drew on the idea that marketers and executives needed to use factors based on situation, rather than a predefined recipe for marketing. Soon thereafter, the concept of the four Ps was introduced as a reliable marketing framework, consisting of four noteworthy components: product, place, price, and promotion. The four Ps remain an important framework today for marketing success by essentially placing the customer at the center of the strategy. Delivering tactics to provide customers with what they need, when they need it, at an accessible cost, and making it easy to access is what makes the four Ps the baseline for all marketing efforts.

In terms of digital marketing, the playing field has become crowded with different tactics, approaches, tools, and platforms. When we think of digital marketing tactics, social media often comes to mind. Placing image or carousel ads, short-form videos or organic posts on networks like Snapchat, Facebook, YouTube, Instagram, LinkedIn, or TikTok can be a valuable way to reach a particular audience segment. Similarly, email marketing, paid search, and retargeting can be important tactics for delivering a message to a specific group of users, prospects, or customers.

AUDIENCE
Therefore, the first step with tactics is to identify the audience. There are many ways to work through this step, including the development of customer

personas, which can be a useful exercise where marketers create definition around their audience groups using demographic, psychographic, behavioral, and geographic identifiers, thus leading to answers about where those users spend their time online. From there, marketers can identify the proper channels for their digital marketing efforts. In the Step by Step below, marketers can consider several specific customer aspects to build out personas for marketing purposes.

STEP BY STEP

Marketing Personas – Considerations

- name, age, job title
- organization type, industry, and size
- geographic location—specific place or rural vs. urban, for example
- social networks
- job responsibilities
- preferred communication methods
- family
- education
- preferences, likes/dislikes

DIGITAL CHANNELS

The tactics of digital marketing include the process of deciding how to go about the online placement of messaging. For example, Google is an important channel for many marketers, but it must be considered in two distinct tactics: SEO and SEM, organic and paid. As we have learned, both are important and effective but include different skills to execute, different strategies, timelines, and metrics. Channels typically refer to the source and medium of a digital marketing campaign. The best digital channel for marketing is the one preferred and used by your customers. For example, Facebook may be an important marketing channel for a business. That business can leverage Facebook with organic content posts as well as paid advertising and other tactics to reach their primary audience with messaging and communication.

Paid channels can include different pricing and cost models. Some include auctions, self-service platforms, or third-party partners to execute. There are many elements involved in paid advertising on digital channels. In terms of SEO, because it is considered earned media rather than paid, the channel strategy is straightforward in that it will be an organic listing on search engines like Google or Bing. Using these methods, marketers can determine the proper tactics for their digital marketing efforts. It is safe to assume that SEO makes sense for all marketing efforts, regardless of industry.

Measurement

One of the best things about digital marketing is that unlike its traditional marketing brethren, digital is decidedly measurable. We will take a closer look at the topic of measurement in Chapter 6. With the right tools and focus, marketers can use data to drive insights and action in their digital marketing efforts, which delivers better outcomes than a static marketing effort without a focus on results. Most companies use Google Analytics or a similar web analytics application. Some companies develop their own proprietary measurement tools or use a combination of tools for analytics. When utilizing web analytics, the first step is knowing what to measure.

FUNDAMENTALS

There are three fundamental areas of focus for digital marketing measurement:

1 Acquisition: How is website traffic acquired? Where do users come from?

2 Action: What actions do we want users to take once they arrive on our site?

3 Results: What are the results of those actions?

KPIs

To track and measure these three key areas, we must assign each of them the appropriate key performance indicators (KPIs) that will determine the effectiveness of each. A KPI is a metric that shows effectiveness against our objectives. For example, with SEO our objective is to increase the traffic coming to our site from organic search. We will use the simple metric of percentage increase in organic traffic over time to understand the effectiveness of our new traffic acquisition from SEO efforts. Taking it a step further, to track the actions, we must return to the objectives. If we are promoting a specific content item—like a video or an article—for thought leadership, we can track how many users complete the task of watching the video or downloading the article. That KPI will help us understand the effectiveness of SEO in driving the preferred action on the website. Similarly, if we want to increase the website traffic coming from organic search, we can track that KPI using our web analytics software.

EQUATIONS

We can continue this process by tracking further metrics, like return on investment (ROI) or return on ad spend (ROAS), which we will examine more closely in Part 3 of this book. Simply stated, these help us understand if we made more money than we spent and can be useful in making future decisions about budgets and ad spending. It is important to keep in mind that costs can include more than just media.

For example, SEO incurs no media costs but often incurs fees, such as monthly software licensing, agency fees, new hires, and technical costs. A best practice with digital marketing measurement is to identify targets up front. Targets align expectations for campaigns by giving us a sense of what we accomplish with our efforts. Without targets, there can be varying opinions and definitions of success. To avoid confusion and possible conflict, set realistic targets up front and then measure efforts against those targets. Here is the simple equation for tracking return on investment:

$$\frac{\text{Return (Benefit)}}{\text{Investment (Cost)}} = \text{ROI}$$

Optimization

Once we have developed and agreed upon a strategy, selected the right tactics, and assigned the right metrics, we move into the optimization phase. This is an area that often does not receive enough attention in digital marketing but can provide the best opportunities for improvement of efforts and streamlining budgets. A smart approach to optimization is to look at the KPIs and metrics for success against the targets. Then determine what has worked best and why. From there, make changes to the strategy and tactics to increase the effectiveness of the digital marketing efforts. Reporting is an important ingredient in the recipe for optimization because good reports lead to improved outcomes. Quite simply, marketers want to focus their energy, resources, and budgets on the best-performing tactics that will deliver the highest results. We get to those decisions through data-driven, insightful reports. Also critical to the optimization process of SEO is testing and experimentation, which affords the opportunity to test variables and make data-driven decisions.

SEO TESTING AND EXPERIMENTATION

A successful SEO experimentation process is similar to the scientific method that most people are already familiar with. It starts with an observation, leading to a hypothesis or question. From there data is gathered and analyzed, drawing a conclusion which drives new action. SEO experiments can get very technical and can include code and database updates. For our purposes, we will review less technical, more intuitive opportunities for SEO testing. Figure 4.3 represents the experimentation process.

Tests should run for long enough to measure results. This usually means at least one to two months but could be shorter or longer, depending on the website and the element being tested. Experiments should also be well documented using a template that tracks the data on the experiment and exactly what is being tested.

FIGURE 4.3 The SEO Experimentation Process

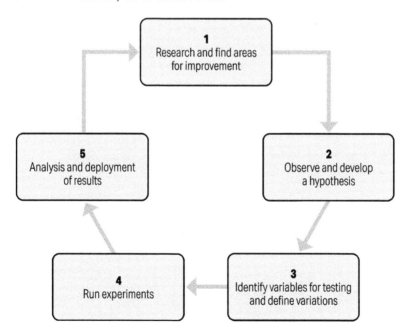

One area that is useful for testing purposes is landing pages or content pages. SEO professionals will often test elements like word count, use of visuals, on-page SEO elements, URLs, linking, headlines, call to action, and other aspects of either landing pages or content pages. Updating processes, templates, and standards for SEO is important. Hence, testing these elements is a useful exercise to continue enhancing the SEO strategy.

EXAMPLE OF AN SEO EXPERIMENT

1 Observation: My website is not visible on page 1 of search results for an important key phrase.

2 Hypothesis: Meta descriptions and tags are outdated. If we update them and include keywords and phrases more strategically, will that impact visibility?

3 Gather data: Make the required changes and track any changes over time in ranking positioning or traffic coming to the website from organic search.

4 Analyze data: Create reports and visualizations to understand the relationship between the changes made and new traffic patterns and trends.

5 Conclusion: How did our changes impact our results? If it was successful, we can implement similar site-wide changes. If it was not successful or inconclusive, we can go back and alter a different variable, such as nofollow tags or load time, following the same steps.

Possible SEO experiments include:

1 Test use of nofollow links.

2 Test social signals impact:

   a. Are social networks driving organic traffic?

   b. How can they be used more intentionally for SEO purposes?

3 Test keyword intent:

   a. What keywords are being used and are they effectively capturing user intent?

   b. Are there other semantic search words for content creation and optimization?

4 Test the impact of load time, which is an important ranking factor.

5 Test impact of meta descriptions and tagging by updating them and utilizing keywords.

6 Test the use of schema markup to see if it improves rankings.

7 Test landing page or content page optimization.

8 Experiment with use of original images:

   a. Add images throughout the site.

   b. Use keywords in file names and descriptions.

   c. Change formatting—use JPEG for larger file sizes and PNG to preserve a transparent background.

   d. Compress file sizes whenever possible.

   e. Test responsiveness in mobile and desktop searches.

   f. Include descriptive alt text with keywords.

LOOKOUT

Tools for SEO Experimentation and Testing

   1 Optimizely

   2 BuzzStream

   3 SiteSeer

   4 Ryte

CASE STUDY
Managed Services Provider Qualitest Drives Leads with SEO

Introduction

Qualitest, provider of AI-led quality engineering and testing solutions, helps brands make the transition through the digital assurance journey, from functional testing to adopting new innovations such as automation, AI, and crowdsourced UX testing. At Qualitest, organic traffic to the website is the most valuable marketing asset. Previously, the website did not rank well in Google and the website was not converting visitors into customers.

Goals

Qualitest needed to increase visibility in Google search results and achieve ranking for as many relevant keywords as possible to appear in the top 10 results. Data showed that increasing visibility in organic search results would drive leads and ultimately new customers. Qualitest needed an updated website focused on driving organic search traffic.

The website strategy and technology presented challenges. The design was outdated and not fully mobile optimized, using an older WordPress template and content management system that limited flexibility. Similarly, the team was not staffed and budgeted to give this the required attention, and there were technical issues that needed to be addressed. Technical issues hindering SEO included:

- inconsistent URL structure
- cross-device compatibility
- broken links were prevalent
- site lacked authoritative backlinks
- website tracking was missing
- site lacked keyword strategy
- low-quality content
- lack of on-page SEO elements on key pages

Strategy

SEO became a priority for Qualitest and the marketing team created a strategy that included:

1 team optimization and ongoing learning

2 audience and industry research

3 keyword research

4 on-page optimization

5 off-page optimization

6 content development

7 website technical optimization

8 metrics and measurement

9 optimization

Actions

Research was a critical component, and a starting point for SEO at Qualitest. This included several key steps:

- Identify the top industries representing strategic opportunities for the company.
- Analyze target keywords, content, technical SEO, and website UX for competitors.
- Examine where competitors primarily do business.

These steps determined the next formation of the SEO strategy. Keyword research is a foundational element of SEO. Strategic keyword research was directed by solutions on offer and industries served. Keywords needed to go deeper into the long tail by focusing on more specific and targeted opportunities.

The original keyword list only included the highest-volume keywords, such as:

- software testing
- software testing companies
- quality assurance
- quality assurance companies
- best software testing companies
- best quality assurance companies
- software QA companies
- QA companies

Over time Qualitest learned that high volume did not always determine the best quality. These general keywords were attracting the wrong audience. People looking for "software testing" could be looking for technical information, searching for academic reasons, or looking for a job.

The updated keyword list became much more specific and included long-tail keywords, such as:

- quality engineering services
- digital engineering services
- blockchain testing services
- medical device testing services
- AI testing services
- salesforce ERP CRM testing
- DevOps testing services

- digital transformation consulting
- drone testing

These keywords did not have the highest volume of searches, but they are high quality and deliver prospects expressing intent to learn about services offered by Qualitest.

The team and tools were another important area of focus. Qualitest hired specific talents to improve all aspects of SEO performance. This included technical writers with SEO experience, and an SEO specialist to oversee and manage on-page and off-page activities. Qualitest also partnered with new referral domains and website owners to list the website name and descriptions, such as softwaretestinghelp.com, clutch.com, techcrunch.com, and others. Additionally, new software tools such as Ahrefs, Semrush, Yoast SEO plugin, and Similarweb were acquired to monitor and optimize performance.

On-page SEO meant that Qualitest optimized various front-end and back-end components of the website to increase indexing and ranking. On-page SEO components included content elements, site architecture, and HTML elements, such as:

- page titles
- meta descriptions
- image alt text
- headers
- internal linking
- cross-device compatibility
- URL structure

URLs were inconsistent on important solutions pages. Different words had been used to describe the same concept, which led to customer confusion. For example, several pages used the word "technology" while others used "initiative" or "solutions." Qualitest identified the word "solutions" and added "solutions" to all solution pages and "industries" to all industry pages, and brought consistency into the URLs. The WordPress CMS templates were updated to include necessary fields on each page. Google Analytics tracking was set up with defined goals. Ahrefs was used to perform regular website SEO audits and ongoing analysis.

Equally important to on-page optimization is off-page optimization. Regular analysis of competitors' backlinks on high-authority and high-traffic websites informs this process. Backlinks can include guest blogs, business directories, and social bookmarking websites. For referral marketing, a list of websites which are ranking highly on specific keywords is useful for additional listings and linking opportunities.

Qualitest focused on building a strong technical SEO foundation, by fixing website issues and making the website error-free, indexable, and compatible.

Technical optimization included:

- broken link checks
- identifying and fixing 404 errors
- checking load time performance
- identifying and fixing orphan page issues
- server performance
- redirection errors
- optimization of large image file size
- tracking backlinks and competitor performance with Ahrefs

Content also played a large part in the strategy. After finalizing the strategic keyword universe, Qualitest focused on building out the SEO content strategy, with focus on key pages to drive crawlability, indexing, and rankings.

A few key things helped create high-quality content and achieve organic traffic:

- discussions with industry-based subject matter experts (SMEs)
- strong on-page optimization of content
- research-driven approach
- relying on authoritative information

Focusing on specific areas of expertise, content was created in two main ways:

1 content hosted on external assets to help build authority—this included guest blogs, articles on public sites like Medium and LinkedIn, and a PR strategy

2 content hosted on internal owned assets, including the company website

The external content was heavily focused on strategic keywords, while the internal content was more focused on thought leadership, still incorporating keywords whenever possible.

The internal, thought leadership content was also created using two main strategies:

1 **industry-focused:** gathering TIPS (trends, implications and possibilities, solutions) information from the industry sector heads about each industry

2 **keywords-focused:** creating a list of strategic keyword categories, with short- and long-tail keywords for each

When setting out to create new thought leadership content, Qualitest relied on those two sources to guide topics, either by creating a content item that focused on a specific industry, a specific set of keywords, or ideally pairing keywords with a specific industry to cover both areas in one item and save time and effort. Focusing on content not only helps produce content that ranks better in search results and generates more quality traffic, but it also aligns with our sector teams. The unexpected benefit is that by creating higher-quality content, it is more relevant to the target audience.

Tools

To get a full picture of the SEO work, Qualitest uses many tools to track, measure, and analyze SEO. The following tools drive the SEO work forward:

- **Google Tag Manager (GTM)**—When web pages incorporate multiple tags, it can increase load time. Tag Manager is an important tool for optimizing tags. GTM is used to add, edit, and manage all tags and pixels to improve page load time, which is critical for SEO.
- **Google Analytics (GA)**—Google Analytics helps analyze website traffic data and is used to understand where users are coming from and how they behave. These metrics, combined with the bounce rate, help to improve website content, user experience, and compatibility.
- **Hotjar**—Hotjar is a tool that provides heat maps for web pages. A heat map shows how users behave when they access a website, what they click on, where they spend their time, and how they interact with various widgets. This leads to better understanding of which pages are delivering the most value for users.
- **Ahrefs**—This site audit tool can audit the website for common SEO issues and monitor the SEO health over time. It is used to analyze the backlink profile for Qualitest and their competitors.
- **Similarweb**—Similarweb provides analysis of competitors' traffic sources, including referring sites, social traffic, and top search keywords.
- **Leadfeeder**—This intelligence platform helps identify anonymous visitors coming to a website. It provides analysis of users at a closer level.

Along with the tools included above, Qualitest found that there were a few key areas of focus to advance their SEO work. The continued focus on content has been a large driver for both users and search engines. Several key initiatives go into this ongoing strategy:

- **Quality content:** Content fuels the SEO engine. Qualitest works with SMEs throughout the organization to create quality content focused on keywords, trends, and industries.

- **Keywords:** The list of strategic keywords informs the content-creation process. Keyword rankings are checked twice per month for key regions around the world.

- **Industries:** Industry SMEs are utilized to marry keywords with a specific industry language to catch two objectives with every content item—the target keywords and a specific industry. This helps make the content more specialized, providing added value to users.

- **Thought leadership:** SMEs craft insightful and valuable content that resonates with the Qualitest target audience.

- **Diversity of content:** Creating different formats of content, including text as well as visual, is key. Blogs, white papers, infographics, case studies, webinars, podcasts, and videos are all useful and beneficial formats for Qualitest.

Results

- Organic traffic improved by 459 percent.
- Page views increased by 446 percent.
- Bounce rate increased by 2.4 percent.
- Sessions showed a significant growth of 487 percent.
- Number of sessions per user increased by 5.12 percent.

Insights

- SEO is a long-term marketing strategy. Investing in the proper team, tools, technology, and education will pay dividends in the long run.
- The combination of research and content with on-page and off-page SEO delivers real results. There are no shortcuts.

Wrapping Up

Marketing can be complicated. Useful frameworks help provide structure and guidance for marketers. SEO is also complicated and can involve very detailed, technical work, including on-page elements like site structure, naming, tagging, and URLs. However, SEO also includes higher-level, sometimes ambiguous, work like off-page SEO: link-building, social-sharing, and authority-building. Throw in the need for fresh, original, and unique content, and SEO is a lot to manage. To organize and prioritize, the STMO framework is a useful tool.

This framework, combined with the SMART goal methodology, can help marketers plan, implement, and improve their SEO work. Within STMO, we can focus specifically on each stage: starting with strategy—developing goals and objectives; then tactics—the channels and platforms; then measurement—an important set of targets and metrics for tracking success; and finally, optimization—using data-driven insights to drive future actions. Actions can include changes, tests, and experiments with SEO campaigns. When SEO is organized this way, it can be an essential and cost-effective marketing technique.

CHAPTER SUMMARY

1 Marketing frameworks provide structure and blueprints for marketers.

2 Frameworks like Porter's Five Forces and AARRR are respected examples of marketing frameworks.

3 SEO can be complex and time-consuming. Organizing and prioritizing is important.

4 The STMO framework can be used generally for digital marketing and specifically for SEO.

5 The first step in STMO is strategy. Using the SMART goal methodology helps to develop goals and assign objectives while considering budgets and resources that will be needed for successful outcomes.

6 Next, we must agree on the tactics. Considerations include on-page and off-page SEO as well as content. Building out the plan for SEO includes people and tools.

7 From there, measurement is key. Assigning specific metrics and key performance indicators helps with understanding the effectiveness and results of SEO efforts.

8 Finally, optimization allows for analysis of results, using KPIs and data-driven reporting to discover insights and future actions to improve our SEO work.

9 Testing and experimentation are results of the optimization phase and provide a chance to observe SEO work, develop hypotheses, gather and analyze data, make changes, and draw conclusions. This critical step in the SEO journey focuses on the revising and refining of SEO efforts.

Reflection Questions

- How can marketing frameworks be utilized in our company strategy?
- What is the overall strategy for our company marketing efforts? How does that translate to digital and to SEO?
- What are the overall business goals for our marketing? How is that being tracked across the organization?
- What are the specific goals for SEO and how will we measure them?
- How can we apply the SMART goal methodology?
- How are different channels, platforms, and tactics used for our digital marketing efforts?
- What are the resources needed for success: teams, technology, and timing?
- What is the budget and how will we go about getting approval?
- How will we measure outcomes? What are the fundamental metrics, the KPIs, and the equations we will use?
- In terms of optimizing, who will be responsible for the data, the insights, and the recommended actions? How will we gain approval or buy-in from key stakeholders?
- How will testing and experimentation be utilized as an optimization strategy?
- What tools will we need for success?

5

Publishing SEO-friendly Content

OBJECTIVES AND KEY RESULTS

- Recognize the role of content for overall marketing and SEO benefits.
  - Content plays a significant role in general awareness for a brand, as well as specifically for SEO purposes.
- Learn the function of semantic search and keyword research with respect to content and SEO.
  - Development of a keyword universe with semantic search in mind will deliver SEO-driven results.

- Distinguish content across styles, structures, and authors to be applied for user engagement and SEO benefits.
  - A rich and distinctive content landscape incorporates many different types and formats of content.
- Understand content workflow which provides organization and prioritization across teams and coworkers.
  - Align teams on the process, tools, and timing of content creation.
- Use content calendars for collaboration and inclusion opportunities across the organization.
  - Teamwork across departments and perspectives delivers better content and a more robust and inclusive viewpoint.
- Application and inclusion of SEO-friendly elements will increase likelihood of indexing, crawling, and ranking by search engines.
  - Considerations and tools for SEO friendliness include many factors.
- Knowing and following specific guidelines, such as using an SEO-friendly template and writing for users first, will lead to more authentic content creation.
  - Consistent content creation must follow best practices and guidelines.

Content is King

In the world of marketing, content is the backbone of messaging and communication. Without thought leadership and content, businesses lose credibility and individuals risk reputations. Content marketing is a valuable and strategic marketing asset whereby businesses and individuals create and distribute relevant information to attract and retain customers. Companies across the world of various sizes and industries invest heavily in the practice of content marketing as an opportunity to connect with customers and demonstrate the knowledge and expertise they bring to their industries.

Although content is a significant component in the SEO three-pronged approach, it is also a vital part of the user experience with a brand. Most importantly, content should provide value. It should also softly promote the brand, products, and services when applicable. It should directly connect with the audience, and it should move them along through the customer decision journey. The very best content will promote engagement and advocacy through liking, commenting, and—most importantly—sharing.

Overall Benefits

Content marketing is a fundamental part of a strategic marketing plan. There are countless benefits that can influence customers along their journey. The brand benefits of content marketing can be distilled into four key elements:

- Delivers brand affinity: Evergreen content provides customers with access to information that connects the brand to their products, categories, and industry.
- Creates and establishes trust: Audiences will connect to a brand that is delivering high-quality content and thought leadership. This allows the brand to communicate their values and knowledge in a meaningful and compelling way.
- Increases stickiness: Customers will stay longer and come back more frequently if there is fresh and valuable content to consume.
- Drives other marketing initiatives: Marketing—including social media, SEO, PR, demand generation, email marketing, sponsorships, and more—are all initiatives that connect back to quality content.

SEO Benefits

Beyond the high-level benefits of content marketing for the brand, it is particularly central to a search engine optimization strategy. In fact, its importance can't be overstated. Recall the three-pronged approach to SEO from Chapter 3, which includes and equally values on-page SEO, off-page SEO, and content. There are numerous vital factors of content that drive SEO results when done effectively. Businesses that invest in high-quality and high-volume content will see more organic search traffic as a result.

Below is a list of the content benefits specific to SEO.

1 Gain authority and visibility: Fresh content attracts bots and spiders.
2 Increase organic search traffic: Content delivers value to users.
3 Identify search intent: Data provides customer insights.
4 Obtain rich results: Rich results signal thought leadership.

5 Afford linking opportunities: Credible content will bring links.

6 Signal search engines to crawl and index pages: Add and refresh content regularly.

7 Use across customer decision journey: Different types of content drive different types of engagement.

    a. awareness: blog, social posts, infographics

    b. consideration: case studies, reviews, webinars

    c. purchase: demos, free trials, promotions

    d. post-purchase: how-to videos, testimonials, VIP content

For content to have SEO value, it must be useful for users and searchers. When companies create content solely for the purposes of SEO, there can be problems. Websites can receive penalties or be removed completely from search engines. Making sure that content provides value for users and customers can be done by following the "UCHIE" method.

UCHIE Method for SEO-friendly Content

Before developing SEO-friendly content, there are several things to keep in mind. Best practices include creating a set structure that includes a beginning, middle, and end for each post and also includes keywords and related words. The length of the content is another consideration, as search engines appreciate longer articles, but users can get scared off when a blog post is too lengthy. Ideally, blog posts are a minimum of 300 words, up to 1,000 words. Articles and white papers are expected to be more in-depth, longer pieces. My UCHIE framework helps marketers and content creators ensure that SEO friendliness is a priority when developing website content.

- Unique: Content should be different than what others are providing. Offer a distinctive perspective, voice, opinion, or slant.

- Credible: Including testimonials, credits, citations, guest experts, reviews, and original research will indicate that content is authoritative and trustworthy.

- High quality: Outsourced or copied content will deliver a poor user experience and can also lead to penalties by search engines. See the Sidebar regarding use of chatbots and AI for content creation.

- Informative: Compelling and useful content will provide users with valuable information.

- **Engaging:** Making content enjoyable, entertaining, and appealing will encourage sharing.

Semantic Search and Keyword Research

Semantic keywords are all the rage in the world of SEO. This terminology refers to keywords that are conceptually related to topics or categories. For example, SEO is semantically related to digital marketing. Keyword research helps marketers identify the semantic keywords that will help drive organic visibility on search engines while also creating content around topics of interest to customers. While researching keywords for semantic search, keep in mind there is more to this process than meets the eye.

Creating a Keyword Universe

Start by doing research about potential keywords and categories. Also, try using Google's related search suggestions, which shows up at the bottom of search results pages and can include additional keyword considerations. Figure 5.1 shows a screenshot with an example of related searches.

The next step is identifying core keywords. These can be brand, industry, category, and product-related keywords plus semantic search ideas. Core keywords—sometimes called primary or head keywords—are typically high in search volume but also higher in competition. Consider them broader in definition and typically comprising two to three words. From there, incorporate helper keywords—sometimes called secondary or body keywords—which contain more descriptive words. Ideas for helpers include geographies,

FIGURE 5.1 Example of Related Searches on Google

Related searches :

running **trainers** womens **sale**	**asics** running **trainers women's**
best running **trainers women's**	womens running **trainers black**
womens running **trainers uk**	**new balance** running **trainers** womens
nike running **trainers women's**	**women's road** running **trainers**

NOTE Screenshot of Google search, 2023, keyphrase: womens running shoes. Google and the Google logo are trademarks of Google LLC.

adjectives, descriptors, and more specific product and category keywords. These helpers are usually lower in search volume but also lower in competition. The final category of keywords are the long-tail keywords—sometimes just called the tail—these can be 10+ words and are closer to the searcher's intent. Long-tail keywords have lower volume but tend to be more qualified and lead to higher conversions and better results.

The Step by Step offers a guide for creating a keyword universe.

STEP BY STEP

Keyword Universe Spreadsheet

1 Research with tools like Google's Keyword Planner, Semrush, BrightEdge, or Moz.

2 Create a spreadsheet with columns to track search volume, rankings, and competition.

3 Divide keywords into groupings based on brand, non-brand, category, industry, product. Use the head, body, tail framework if it helps.

4 Choose destination URLs for keywords.

5 Revise and update frequently.

There are other ways to get new ideas for keyword research, including social monitoring tools, web analytics, and paid search data. Using this type of data will help acquire more knowledge about user behavior with keywords, search intent, and semantic search. Also, be sure to share the keyword universe across departments and teams within the company. Content may be created in other departments outside of marketing and the message and keywords should be consistent. Further, including sales, product, technology, and other teams may lead to additional research, brainstorming, collaboration, and stronger results.

Considerations for keyword research include:

- **Volume:** Analyze the search volume, or number of searches, associated with specific keywords to determine if it is worthwhile to include those keywords in the keyword universe.

- **Long tail:** Be sure to include long-tail, specific keywords in the strategy. Top-level or basic keyword searches are often too vague and won't deliver real value or conversions in the long run.

- **Competitive nature:** Determine how competitive keywords are by doing searches and examining the quantity and quality of results. For example, Figure 5.2 shows the difference between a generic search for "seo companies near me," which returned 321,000,000 results, versus a more specific search for "seo companies in Glenview IL," which returned a measly 561,000 results.

- **Trends:** Use a tool like Google Trends to highlight the trends around certain keywords while generating ideas for other keywords to include in the universe, such as geographies, related queries, and related topics.

- **Competitors' strategies:** Identify the content being created by top competitors and examine the headings, naming, and URLs to reverse-engineer their keyword universe.

- **Impact:** Measuring the effectiveness of keywords by running ads on search engines can prove whether those keywords deliver true SEO value.

FIGURE 5.2 Search Results Volume

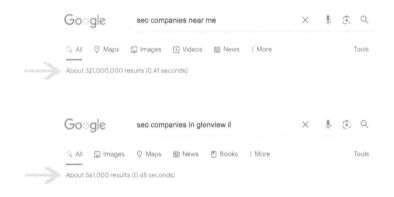

NOTE Screenshot of Google search, 2023, keyphrase: seo companies near me. Screenshot of Google search, 2023, keyphrase: seo companies in glenview il. Google and the Google logo are trademarks of Google LLC.

Content Audit

Now that there is a keyword universe, a content audit will provide an inventory of all the content that is indexable within a website or domain name.

The purpose of a content audit is to organize and analyze content using SEO performance metrics to better determine which content to keep, which to improve, and which to remove. This process has many benefits for businesses as well as for SEO:

- Identify or avert a content-related penalty.
- Improve content quality by revising copy or editing.
- Update content that has become outdated.
- Consolidate overlapping content.
- Remove content that is irrelevant.
- Prioritize editing and removing content.
- Identify content gaps as opportunities for the future.
- Track how content ranks for keywords.
- Identify the strongest SEO pages.
- Due diligence when redesigning a website.

The first step in a content audit is to create an inventory of all existing content that is indexed by search engines. This is called a content repository. Documenting the content to create an inventory is the next step of the audit. A useful automation tool, like Screaming Frog, can automate the process and perform a full crawl. The crawl results in gathering on-page SEO metrics like URLs, titles, descriptions, meta tags, word count, and more.

Additional useful information to gather in a content audit includes internal links, external links, organic search traffic, uniqueness, publish date, and more. This data can be automatically obtained using a tool like URL Profiler. Screaming Frog and URL Profiler both have integration capabilities and can be combined to provide all the data in one report. Once the content audit is complete, there is a chance to analyze the results, identify issues, and pave the way forward.

Content Issues

The four biggest issues that typically arise regarding content are:

1 **Not enough content:** Many businesses report that the biggest challenge with SEO is creating enough content. There are many opportunities to repurpose content in a way that helps users access content in different

formats that are useful for them while also signaling to search engines that new, fresh content exists. A blog post can easily be turned into an infographic and a slide deck. Each of these pieces can be used in different places. The blog can go on the website while the infographic can be posted on social media sites and the slide deck can be used in presentations and turned into a video.

2 **Too much content:** Many issues can arise from having too much content. Duplicating content and posting it in many places can lead to pages being removed from search engine indexing or, even worse, a manual action penalty from Google. The right amount of content should be aligned with the user experience just as much as with the SEO goals and objectives.

3 **Low-quality content:** Content must be useful and relevant. These factors influence the customer purchase process as well as search engine indexing. Maintaining the highest level of quality should be at the forefront of the strategy. This includes authority, trust, and brand building, as well as spelling, grammar, and focus. Measuring content engagement metrics and asking customers with surveys, quizzes, or informally for feedback are ways to ensure content is hitting the quality mark. This is especially important when using AI or automated tools like chatbots for content creation.

4 **Discoverability:** Unfortunately, many marketers and content creators are developing the right amount of content at the highest level of quality. However, because neither the audience nor search engines are able to find the content, there is no benefit. Ensuring that the SEO best practices for content are being followed and creating backlinks are important ways to protect against this issue.

SIDEBAR

Generative AI tools can assist in the content process and increase productivity in many ways. However, AI is not a replacement for human creativity, expertise, and experience. Be sure to include manual reviews and editing of any content generated using AI.

Ideas for Using AI or Chatbots for Content Creation

1 Ideation: Generate new and creative ideas for content.

2 Social media posts: Refine messaging for posts, ads, and campaigns.

3 SEO: Provide guidance for keyword inclusion, meta descriptions, etc.

4 Editing: Make sure to proofread and edit to check grammar and spelling.

5 Repurposing: Format content in new and unique ways.

Types of Content

Content comes in various types and formats. Marketers must consider their audience when determining the right content to create. Not all content types will work for all brands and products. Below is a list containing several ideas for types of content.

- *Blogs*: Blogs are a cost-effective way to consistently add new and fresh content to the website. Blog posts' average length is 1,500–2,500 words and they provide search bots with updated opportunities to crawl and index them while providing users with original new ideas.

- *Case studies and testimonials*: Having customers tell the story is a great way to create word of mouth and directly impact sales and leads. Case studies and testimonials allow customers to become brand ambassadors.

- *Articles and white papers*: Longer and more formal than their blog post brethren, articles and white papers can go deeper into subject matters while also promoting stickiness through downloads, shares, and saving.

- *E-books*: Creating authority and trust with customers can be done using long-form text in the e-book format. These deeper dives often showcase a mix of text, visuals, charts, and graphs. Often e-books are downloaded, providing a lead-generation email-capture opportunity as well.

- *Videos*: Videos can be used across social media sites and websites to increase visibility and views. Many users prefer to watch a short video rather than read an article or post. Consider creating video versions of text content types like blogs, articles, white papers, and e-books. Videos can also provide how-to guides, demonstrations, interviews, and other useful tools for customers.

- *Checklists*: Audiences appreciate lists that help them organize, consolidate, or prioritize. *The Checklist Manifesto*, a bestselling book by Atul Gawande, shows how simple checklists can create meaningful behaviors. Use them for guiding customers through simple or complex processes.

- *Listicles*: People like listicles, also known as list-posts, because they are easy to read and digest. Listicles can apply to any topic and can deliver an engaging content and SEO opportunity. The listicle Step by Step demonstrates how to create them.

- *Infographics and data visualization*: Delivering data in a visual and interesting way provides customers with easy access to often complicated information. Infographics, graphs, and charts are eye-catching and attention-grabbing forms of content.

- *How-to guides*: In-depth guides allow companies to showcase their knowledge while providing valuable product or industry material for users.

- *Visuals*: The days of stock images are long gone. Creating original, fresh, and interesting visuals will deliver brand affinity and create engagement opportunities.

- *FAQs*: Customers often have questions about products, brands, processes, and more. Summarizing these in an FAQ section minimizes frustrations for customers looking for answers.

- *Podcasts (with transcripts)*: Audio marketing has been booming and podcasts are more popular than ever. Sharing stories, interviews, and audio clips through podcasts provides a different and unique type of engagement. Transcripts are significant for users who prefer reading to listening, while also giving search engines access to the full content contained within the audio.

- *Social media posts*: Social media sites like Facebook, LinkedIn, and Instagram provide high-quality links and should be considered a vital part of the content marketing strategy.

- *Quizzes and polls*: Technology allows marketers to create a dialogue with customers. Quizzes and polls create engagement and showcase creativity. Brands can also gain valuable insights by giving their customers a voice and listening to them.

STEP BY STEP

Creating a Listicle

1 Select a topic that is relevant to your brand and valuable to your customers.

2 Decide on the angle.

3 Include keywords.

4 Write the listicle content points.

5 Include engaging images.

6 End with a conclusion.

SIDEBAR

Brainstorming Content Topics

Use tools to find trending topics and keyword patterns. Tools like ChatGPT, Jasper, Google Trends, AnswerThePublic, Ubersuggest, and HubSpot's Blog Ideas Generator can help with writer's block. New ideas can also be found when doing social media research, looking at competitors' blogs, or surveying customers.

Reuse, Recycle, Repurpose

Keep in mind that reusing, repurposing, or recycling content in different formats is one of the best ways to increase discoverability and sharing. Written content such as articles, white papers, and blogs are easy to create and post. Visual choices are a way to attract backlinks. This methodology is also important for user engagement. People learn in different ways and prefer different methods for consuming content. Some enjoy reading a long-form article while others prefer a short video or a summary in a visual chart or graph. One important caveat to consider is that while repurposing content is a best practice, it is important not to simply include the exact same content in multiple places. There can be penalties for use of what Google calls "appreciably similar" content. The solution is to focus on repurposing content in a way that best suits the user and search engines. Below is a list of great ways to repurpose content.

1 Create a video: How-to or informational posts convert well to videos. Consider writing a script and utilizing a diverse and interesting group of people to deliver the message via video.

2 Create an e-book: This option works well for longer-form content with educational value. E-books include imagery, lists, statistics, and other important information that can be highlighted visually.

3 Design an infographic: Statistics and data can be represented visually using an infographic. This can be designed using a simple free tool like Canva or a more advanced tool like Figma or Adobe Illustrator.

4 Consider audio: Many people enjoy listening to information that interests them, as opposed to reading or viewing it. This can be accomplished by extracting quotes, statistics, and other valuable nuggets from a written piece. Then a script can be created and recorded using free podcast

software like GarageBand or AudioDirector. MozPod provides AI tools for audio content creation.

5 Turn transcripts into content: Videos and webinars provide excellent content when transcribed into text. This is also a useful tool that increases the accessibility of content for different people and can be posted as a blog or article after the event.

LOOKOUT

AI Tools for Audio Content Creation

1 IBM Watson: Converts written text into natural-sounding speech.

2 Lyrebird: AI voice synthesis that generates voiceovers.

3 Descript: AI-powered audio and video editing tool.

4 Wavve: Creates social media-friendly audiovisual content.

5 Speechmatics: Automatic speech recognition tool that converts spoken language to written text.

Create a Killer Content Workflow

What is a content workflow? Content marketing is a team sport, meaning that it crosses over the organization and can include many teams and individuals. Consider involving not just writers and editors to create content but also including members of cross-functional teams like product, sales, marketing, executives, technology, and other thought leaders in or outside of the organization. To coordinate the tasks involved in content, we need a content workflow. This is a series of tasks that are performed by the team to take content from the idea phase all the way through to publishing in an efficient process.

Content workflow involves the people, tools, and resources needed for creating meaningful and SEO-friendly content. While it can be adapted based on each organization's internal processes, it ultimately serves the purpose of organizing the team, promoting collaboration, increasing productivity, and creating efficiency. Projects will stay on track and on schedule when everyone knows what the plan is and what their role is within that plan. The workflow will also increase the quantity of content while reducing duplication of efforts. The Step by Step lists the stages for creating a killer content workflow and Figure 5.3 illustrates the process.

FIGURE 5.3 Content Workflow Chart

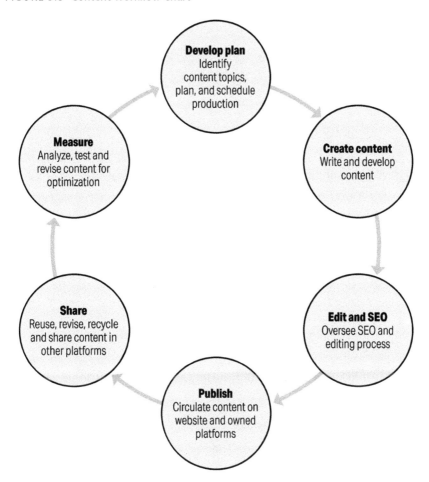

STEP BY STEP

Content Workflow

1 Strategize content: What is the content topic, type, and angle, and who is responsible?

2 Develop content plan: Create a content calendar that tracks the process.

3 Create content: Writers, creatives, thought leaders, and software.

4 Edit and QA the content: Proofread and review for quality assurance.

5 SEO it: Check for keywords, structure, calls to action, URLs, etc.

6 Publish it: Approve and publish the content.

7 Share it: Share and/or repurpose content across channels, platforms, media.

8 Measure: Analyze and measure content performance and future planning.

Content Calendars

Content calendars—also called editorial calendars—are great tools to align teams while collecting and organizing valuable information in a shared document. Content calendars help keep track of different teams, agencies, and individuals and their roles within the content-creation schedule. Calendars can come in many shapes and sizes. Typically, a basic spreadsheet that can easily be shared is the best option. There are also free templates or paid software tools depending on the level of sophistication for the calendar. The Lookout lists tools for content calendar creation.

LOOKOUT

Tools for Content Calendar Creation

- **CoSchedule**—includes timelines and categorization
- **Trello**—project management tool
- **HubSpot**—free editorial calendar template
- **Smartsheet**—dashboards and automation
- **Google Sheets**—shared spreadsheet, fully customizable

There are three key elements of a useful content calendar:

- The first is editorial. The pieces that will be published are the editorial. This can include blog posts, podcasts, social posts, articles, and videos as the editorial pieces. The goal of the content calendar is to create a process so that editorial pieces can be created, managed, and published.
- Next up is the team. Content calendars organize those who are involved in content creation and what their roles will be in the process. It is a mistake to limit content to a finite number of contributors. Unique voices provide diverse viewpoints and deliver a richer experience.

- The final element is the publishing consideration. This refers to where the editorial will be posted. The obvious choice is the company website, but there may be opportunities to post it in other places or to repurpose content for use in other formats. A good content calendar provides structure and planning for the publishing of editorial content while also ensuring that unique perspectives are included in the voice and tone of the organization.

Before creating the calendar, there are a few key questions to ponder. These questions will help address the issues that could arise and can potentially be solved with a content calendar.

- How frequently will content be published?
- What types of content will be created?
- Who will create, edit, approve, and publish content?
- What are the stages for content to go through prior to being published?
- What is the best format to use for organizing a calendar?

SEO-friendly Content

Creating content with SEO best practices in mind will result in greater likelihood of crawling, indexing, and ranking by search engines. Approaching content creation with users at the center while incorporating SEO best practices helps focus on achieving organic search traffic, consistent messaging and building trust with your audience. Some experts find that pages that rank well are at least 1,800–2,000 words, but there are no specific guidelines. Posts that are written well for users will typically be the right length for SEO purposes as well.

There are a few significant ways to keep SEO at the forefront when creating content for websites.

Remember the Keyword Universe

Keywords should be incorporated within the content as well as in meta descriptions, URLs, page titles, headings, and anywhere else that makes sense. In SEO content it is a good idea to select a primary keyword which denotes the main focus of the content. Selecting secondary keywords can help build out the use of the keyword universe within the content piece. Keywords should be used naturally and not overused. Also, keeping the audience in mind, modification to keywords is fine. Content should be organic and should not sound redundant or superfluous.

This is achieved by monitoring keyword density, or the ratio between the number of words in the content and the number of keywords. For example, if five keywords are used in a post that is 100 words in total, the keyword density is 5 percent. The ratio is a loose guide, but it's important to be purposeful about keyword usage in content. Some SEO experts believe that keyword density should be, on average, around 3 percent. Each organization and team will identify the right usage of keywords in their content.

Match Search Intent

Search engine algorithms evaluate search intent as a leading indicator. This encourages content publishers to identify and answer questions from their audience or target customers. Understanding search intent will help create content in a more SEO-focused way.

There are four types of search intent which should be considered when creating content. When researching content topics and building the keyword universe, think about how you can speak to the user and their search intent, through your content. Below are the four types of search intent.

- Informational: User is searching for information on a topic.
- Navigational: User is looking for a specific website.
- Commercial: User is researching options for a product or service.
- Transactional: User is searching for a specific product or brand.

Create User-friendly Content Structure

If users don't like content, search engines won't either. A simple way to increase readability is to break text into digestible chunks. This can be done in several ways, such as use of bullet points or numbered lists, and including visuals such as images, graphs, and charts whenever possible. Also, headlines should be short and to the point; use subheadings to go into more depth or detail. Establishing user-friendliness content guidelines plus an SEO template for all content creators to follow will deliver consistency and efficiency.

Guidelines should indicate the overall structure for content. This points to aspects such as word count, use of images, and formatting. Below are two examples.

Blog post guidelines could include:

- catchy title including a specific benefit: 40 words or less
- subtitle: explains the topic more clearly: 100 words or less
- keywords: posts should include natural and useful keywords when applicable
- introduction, body, and conclusion: 1,500–2,000 words total
- tags: keywords that are relevant to this post
- one or two supporting images, charts, or graphs to be included in the post plus alt text to describe them

Case study guidelines could include:

- catchy title with a specific benefit: 40 words or less
- subtitle: explains the topic more clearly: 100 words or less
- total post word count: 1,500–2,000 words
- introduction: set up the case with the problem statement
- actions: details of implementation plan
- results: outcomes based on steps taken
- one or two supporting visuals to be included in the post plus alt text to describe them
- quotations, references, links, and supporting documents

An SEO template helps by proving recommendations for content topics, analyzing competitors, optimizing content, and suggesting SEO-friendly elements to include. Other important metrics for SEO templates include readability, word count, keywords, title, tone, paragraph length, and tags.

Consider investing in an SEO content tool like Yoast or Semrush, which can provide helpful guidelines and templates while also delivering useful tools like related keywords, backlink ideas, and readability scores.

Include Visual Content

Visuals provide engaging ways for users to access information. They can include images, infographics, templates, and more. Not only do visuals improve the user experience, but they also create SEO value by creating sharing and linking opportunities to build authority. Images and videos that are indexed by Google can also show up in the image and video search results, as an added benefit. Be sure to include unique alt text for all images, remembering that alt text should be under 125 characters and should include keywords when relevant. There are a few factors to consider when including visual content:

- Format: Select the right file type based on the quality and quantity of images. PNG files are higher quality but also larger file sizes, which can slow down the site load speed. JPGs are lower quality but can usually work well for websites when edited and adjusted properly.

- Compression: Images can be compressed using tools like Adobe Photoshop or TinyPNG. This will provide the benefit of reducing the file size of the image without sacrificing the quality of the image.

- Uniqueness: Using images that are unique to your site will add originality and freshness to your content. Stock images are overused and often looked over or skipped entirely.

- Naming: Use keywords and creative descriptions for all visual elements to increase accessibility and alert search engines to precisely what the visuals represent.

- Mobile-friendly: Create responsive visuals that scale based on the device type of the user.

Consider SEO Ranking Signals

Load speed, URLs, naming, tagging, and linking are important SEO ranking signals. The content that is created should follow a template to ensure that these ranking signals are consistently included, whether content is developed by the marketing team, an outside vendor, the sales team, or a chatbot. Using keywords when appropriate and following best practices for on-page SEO will help.

For example, URLs should be lower-case and short—fewer than 60 characters, or three to five words. They should not contain unnecessary characters and should not include stop words such as to, but, an, and or. Hyphens should be used to separate words and the URLs should be simple and relevant to the page. Other SEO signals to consider are metadata, image optimization, schema markup, mobile rendering, shareability (include social media share buttons), and freshness of content (update content regularly).

Linking is also an important way to increase SEO friendliness for content. This can include linking to information, such as citations or endnotes. It can also include links to other websites with high authority and valuable content. Steer clear of linking to anything that could be considered controversial or spammy. It is also a good idea to have anything linked externally open in a new window or tab, to keep users on your site when possible. Finally, amplify content by posting it within social media sites. Consider where your target audience will find the content most easily; this could be Facebook, Twitter, Reddit, or LinkedIn—or all of the above. Sharing buttons also spread the access to the content and create a high-quality link opportunity.

LOOKOUT

Tools for Creating, Editing, and Publishing SEO-friendly Content

1 **Hemingway Editor, Read-Able:** readability, synonyms

2 **Grammarly:** editing, spell-checking

3 **Help.plagtracker, PaperRater:** plagiarism tracking

4 **Keyword Density Checker:** keyword usage

5 **KWFinder:** keyword suggestions, volume, and competition

6 **Jasper:** AI-powered copywriting and formatting

7 **Surfer:** content optimization for SEO

8 **Clearscope:** AI-powered content optimization

9 **Ginger:** grammar and translation

10 **Airstory:** researching, organizing, and publishing

Content Marketing Checklist

- Write for users, not search engines.
- Answer questions.
- Incorporate search intent.
- Know the competition.
- Utilize the keyword universe.
- No keyword stuffing.

- Always structure posts.
- Good headlines are short and to the point.
- Keep it simple.
- Lose the jargon.
- Avoid plagiarism.
- Consider SEO ranking signals.
- Include visuals.
- Compress large files for fast page load.
- Incorporate links and SEO-friendly URLs.
- Amplify with social media and linking.
- Use tools to automate the process when possible.

CASE STUDY
Home Health Care Provider VNS Health Rebrands with SEO Redirect Strategy

Introduction

VNS Health is one of the nation's largest nonprofit home and community healthcare provider. In 2022, the organization rebranded from The Visiting Nurse Service of New York, and with that rebrand, a new WordPress website was launched with all-new content. Digital design agency ExpandTheRoom (ETR), part of Infinum, had been working with the organization since 2015 and came in to redesign this newly rebranded VNS Health website and to focus on strategic SEO as a marketing strategy.

Goals

Because of the complete content overhaul along with the organization name change, VNS Health knew that a significant site restructure was needed, which would include the URLs changing. Therefore, a key goal of this project was to not lose any SEO value as part of this process. For ETR, this meant that setting up a solid redirect mapping plan was a critical step and that post-launch monitoring of organic traffic and total top-ranking keywords would be required for evaluating success.

Strategy

To set up a redirect mapping plan, ETR first gathered a list of all the existing site URLs and put them into a spreadsheet. Then they identified which new URL each would need to redirect to on the new website and entered the new URLs into the spreadsheet in a second column. Because so much content was reconfigured and consolidated, often there were multiple old URLs that all made sense to redirect to a single new URL. For any pages where there was not a good one-to-one match, ETR redirected those to the new home page. All redirects were then entered into WordPress and in place when the new website launched.

Even with a solid redirect mapping plan being implemented, it is still common to see an organic traffic dip after a significant website relaunch. After a couple of months, VNS Health asked ETR to evaluate how the current site was performing from an SEO perspective, as compared with the previous website, which had enjoyed solid search rankings. ETR focused on evaluating organic traffic, leveraging Google Search Console to track metrics such as total impressions, total clicks, and click-through rate, as well as the total number of top-ranking keywords, leveraging Semrush.

Usually ETR would rely on Google Analytics for organic traffic metrics evaluations; however, there were factors that made it more challenging to rely on Google Analytics data for comparisons for this project. One factor was that the old site had used Google Analytics Universal, and the new site was set up to use GA4, which tracks metrics differently. The other factor was that Google Analytics was removed from the site entirely in January 2023 for business reasons. Because of these factors, ETR decided to focus on keyword ranking position changes over time and to use Google Search Console metrics for organic traffic comparisons.

The overall number of keywords ranking in the top positions on Google had declined as compared with the previous site. Some pages that had ranked highly for certain keywords on the previous site were no longer ranking for those same keywords, or had significantly lower positions than before. The number of total impressions and clicks to the site had declined as compared with the previous site. With this high-level knowledge, ETR dug deeper to look for five specific pages where there was significant opportunity to further optimize the page's content for search.

Table 5.1 shows the total number of keywords that were ranking on the old website and the total number of keywords that were ranking two months after the new website was launched in May 2022. This data was sourced from Semrush.

Table 5.2 shows the total number of clicks and impressions for the old website compared with the new website two months after the website was launched in May 2022. This data was sourced from Google Search Console.

TABLE 5.1 Comparison of the Number of Keywords in Top-ranking Positions

Ranking Position	vnsny.org (April 2022)	vnshealth.org (July 2022)
#1	184	66
Top 3	480	186
Top 10	1,100	344
Top 20	2,000	537
Top 50	5,500	1,000

TABLE 5.2 Comparison of the Impressions and Clicks

Google Search Console Metrics	vnsny.org (April 2022)	vnshealth.org (July 2022)
Total Clicks	29,000	9,600
Total Impressions	1,060,000	287,000

Actions

Two main factors went into how ETR identified five priority pages to optimize. In-depth research was key to the strategy and the outcomes of this project.

1 **Learning about and understanding the importance of key services for VNS Health helped focus the SEO strategy toward dominant categories.** ETR had learned about which areas of the business were top priority for VNS Health to raise awareness during the discovery phase of the project, where they spoke with over 50 stakeholders across the company. Hospice care and behavioral health care were two priority areas for the business, so ETR looked to identify pages related to those two areas specifically as candidates for further optimizing for search.

2 **Good search volume combined with achievable scores for relevant keywords would give VNS Health the best chance to improve rankings for those pages by optimizing for the proper terms.** For this project, ETR looked for keywords with a search volume of over 50 searches per month and a difficulty score of 70 or less (out of 100). The difficulty score is a proprietary metric provided by Semrush to give a sense of how much effort it would take to rank for any given keyword given the competition. In general, the lower the difficulty score, the less effort it will take to create content to rank for that keyword.

One of the five pages ETR identified was the "Hospice Care at Home" page. At the national level, this page was ranking number 84 for "hospice in the home" as of July

2022. Semrush data showed that this keyword had an average monthly search volume of 210 and a difficulty score of 67.

Once ETR identified this as a good candidate page to invest in further optimizing, they recommended specific ways to optimize that the VNS Health team then implemented. Specific optimization actions that were taken included:

1   Incorporate the primary target keyword and variations into the page copy, especially into headlines, H2s, and H3s where possible.

2   Include the primary target keyword in the page's meta description.

3   Expand on page's content to address additional information.

4   Add a video embed.

5   Add internal links to other related pages.

Because SEO is an ongoing marketing technique and a significant business driver, this process is repeated every quarter. Each quarter ETR finds four or five new pages to prioritize optimizing along with monitoring the progress of previously optimized pages, following the same process described above.

Tools

- Semrush
- Google Analytics
- Google Search Console
- Google Search

Results

Over the course of six months, significant ranking gains were achieved for the "Hospice Care at Home" page on both a local and national level, which generated a 157 percent increase in organic visits to the page. Due to Google Analytics being removed from the website in January 2023 for VNS Health's business reasons, ETR needed to rely on Google Search Console data to approximate organic traffic growth instead of Google Analytics data. ETR evaluated the difference between the total number of clicks to the page between Q3 2022 (108 clicks) and Q1 2023 (278 clicks), as illustrated in Figure 5.4.

Local to New York, New York, per Semrush data, they saw this page go from ranking number 38 for the keyword "hospice care in the home" to number 1 over the course of six months. Similar increases were seen for similar keyword variations as well, as seen in Table 5.3.

The data shown in Table 5.3 was sourced from Semrush.

FIGURE 5.4 Google Search Console Data for the Hospice Care at Home Page

☑ Total clicks	☑ Total impressions	☐ Average CTR	☐ Average position
278 —	**64.5K** —	**0.4%**	**35.2**
1/1/23 - 3/31/23	1/1/23 - 3/31/23	1/1/23 - 3/31/23	1/1/23 - 3/31/23
108 ---	**29.3K** ---	**0.4%**	**48.9**
7/1/22 - 9/30/22	7/1/22 - 9/30/22	7/1/22 - 9/30/22	7/1/22 - 9/30/22
⑦	⑦	⑦	⑦

On a national level, they saw this page go from ranking number 68 to number 3 for several keywords.

Sitewide, the total number of top-ranking keywords began to surpass the previous website.

Table 5.4 shows the total number of keywords that were ranking on the old website and the total number of keywords that were ranking 10 months after the new website was launched in May 2022. This data was sourced from Semrush.

These are exceptional results, and this level of improvement this quickly cannot always be expected. Typically, ETR sets expectations that it can take up to a year before significant traffic gains are achieved due to SEO improvements. SEO is a long game, and ETR has been working with VNS Health for over five years, building the foundation of content strategy and user research. At the heart of a good SEO strategy is high-quality content.

In terms of the full website, ETR is seeing the new site surpass the previous site in terms of total number of search terms ranking number 1 and in the top 10 on Google. Based on Google Search Console data, ETR is seeing a 187 percent increase in the

TABLE 5.3 Local Ranking Position Changes Over Time

Keyword	Rank Q3 – 2022	Rank Q4 – 2022	Rank Q1 – 2023
home hospice services	17	8	1
hospice at home	28	24	1
hospice care at home	18	3	1
hospice care in the home	38	27	1

TABLE 5.4 Comparison of the Number of Keywords in Top-ranking Positions

Ranking Position	vnsny.org (April 2022)	vnshealth.org (March 2023)
#1	184	200
Top 3	480	485
Top 10	1,100	959
Top 20	2,000	1,766
Top 50	5,500	4,130

FIGURE 5.5 Comparison of Data for the Entire Website

☑ Total clicks	☑ Total impressions	☐ Average CTR	☐ Average position
55.4K —	2.59M —	2.1%	29.5
1/1/23 - 3/31/23	1/1/23 - 3/31/23	1/1/23 - 3/31/23	1/1/23 - 3/31/23
30.4K ---	903K ---	3.4%	31
7/1/22 - 9/30/22	7/1/22 - 9/30/22	7/1/22 - 9/30/22	7/1/22 - 9/30/22
⑦	⑦	⑦	⑦

total number of organic search impressions and an 82 percent increase in the total number of organic search clicks. Optimization work and new content development is ongoing, and the continuation of strategic SEO is delivering a positive trajectory of organic search traffic growth for this website.

Insights

- Website redesigns and relaunches often lead to dips in organic search traffic. This must be countered with an aggressive SEO strategy that focuses on redirects, specific keywords, and pages to regain rankings and build organic traffic.
- Research and knowledge of the importance of products and services, combined with optimization data such as difficulty scores and search volume, drive positive SEO outcomes. An acute focus combined with consistent evaluation is key.

Wrapping Up

The three-pronged approach to SEO denotes content as a significant component in SEO success. The creation of fresh, timely, and compelling content is a benefit for users as well as search engines. There are numerous benefits for the overall brand as well as for SEO. In order to reap those benefits, marketers must develop and implement a strategy for content that starts with keyword research and semantic search, leads to development of a content workflow and calendar, and features different and engaging types of content. All the while, SEO must be considered an essential part of the process, following best practices and accounting for ranking signals. Use of templates, unique voices, and the right tools will lead to SEO success while providing a rich user experience, building trust, and establishing thought leadership.

CHAPTER SUMMARY

1 Content marketing is a fundamental effort that establishes brand affinity, trust, and stickiness while driving additional marketing efforts like SEO.

2 Specifically, content benefits SEO by increasing authority and visibility, providing link-building opportunities, promoting shareability, signaling search engines to crawl and index pages, and more.

3 Semantic search and keyword research lead to a more strategic and nuanced approach to SEO.

4 There are numerous types and formats for content, and all should be considered when creating, editing, and repurposing content for users as well as SEO benefits.

5 Content workflow and calendars will organize and prioritize tasks, align teams, and increase collaboration and inclusivity across the organization.

6 SEO friendliness must be implemented for all content creation to afford consistent and purposeful elements that drive organic traffic.

7 Best practices and rules of thumb like using templates and writing for users first help keep content creation consistent and effective for both users and search engines.

Reflection Questions

• What is our existing content marketing strategy?

• Are we creating and publishing an interesting mix of content types and highlighting unique voices and perspectives?

- Who is involved and what is our process?
- Are we embracing SEO best practices in an efficient, consistent, and effective way?
- Are we using an aligned workflow and calendar to keep things organized and prioritized across teams?
- Are the company's internal teams and any outside partners aligned on our keyword universe and are we utilizing semantic search?
- Do we have the proper tools and AI for SEO and content success?

6

Measuring Successful SEO Outcomes

OBJECTIVES AND KEY RESULTS

- Measuring results leads to better campaign insights and optimization.
  - o Digital analytics solutions provide data that help marketers define outcomes and track results.
- Website metrics help determine effectiveness of search engine optimization campaigns.
  - o Specific metrics can be used for measuring both the quality and quantity of website traffic.

- Benchmarks serve as documentation of a baseline, with which future results can be compared.
  - Indexed pages and organic search traffic are just two of the critical metrics to include in a benchmark report.
- Using reports for data-driven insights drives future opportunities.
  - Consistent reporting must incorporate data, insights, and actions for forward-thinking momentum.

Measurement Overview

Marketers are increasingly prioritizing the significance of data and analytics. Their jobs are becoming more scientific, and they must rely on data as the starting point for solving business issues. Many organizations face internal and external challenges such as data privacy concerns, siloed information, technology integration, cross-platform tracking, and others. Successful digital marketing efforts like search engine optimization can deliver business results such as sales, new customers, and leads generated. These are considered bottom-of-the-funnel business metrics. SEO can also deliver at the top of the funnel by increasing brand recognition and consideration, resulting in awareness, new website visitors, engagement with content, or other indicators.

The first step in understanding measurement is going back to strategy and goals. To accurately track and concisely summarize complexities like user experience, tools and software are required. From there, metrics and key performance indicators (KPIs) from digital analytics or other solutions help create a uniform tracking system. Equations can help to better understand the return from budgets invested into programs. Benchmarks provide a window into a moment in time and give marketers a comparison of metrics and equations over time. Finally, reporting helps connect the dots by using data to find insights, leading to action and optimization. Measuring SEO follows all the same steps. In this chapter we will learn the fundamentals of measurement for digital and how that specifically applies to SEO.

Digital Analytics

Understanding the effectiveness of digital marketing and the behavior of website visitors is critical for many reasons. Budget allocation and campaign decisions are made based on this data. For this, companies use many different analysis tools.

Digital analytics, also called web analytics or web stats, should be at the top of the list because it is the most common and the best solution for collecting, synthesizing, and analyzing website data. The goal in analyzing website data is to understand how users are finding and using web properties, while also identifying areas for improvement and optimization in digital campaigns, technology, and the user experience.

This data-driven process is used for websites, web applications, mobile apps, or other web-based products. Many teams and individuals across an organization can use digital analytics to expand understanding of user behavior and enhance the overall experience. When selecting the best solutions for digital analytics, there are several important considerations.

Understanding who, how, and why digital analytics will be used is the first step. While some solutions are more user friendly and turnkey—offering customizable widgets and dashboards—others can be highly technical, requiring certain processes and procedures to deliver what is needed. Integration with other solutions is also an essential consideration. Many marketers and technology teams invest in large and complex technology stacks that integrate across multiple platforms. Digital analytics may need to integrate with other systems and technologies. Finally, the features and benefits of the digital analytics solution should be examined and agreed upon up front. Some tools offer more in-depth features and others may be more high level. Similarly, some tools are highly technical while others are designed for marketers. Review websites like G2.com offer helpful information, reviews, and ratings for digital analytics and other software solutions. The Lookout offers common reasons for using digital analytics solutions.

LOOKOUT

Some of the most common reasons to use digital analytics are:

1 Understand web traffic patterns.

2 Examine how users enter and exit the website.

3 Learn about user behavior within the website.

4 Identify best- and worst-performing content.

5 Refine digital marketing efforts and campaigns.

6 Improve the user experience on the website.

7 Improve search rankings and SEO.

8 Increase sales, leads, and traffic to the website.

9 Find technical issues such as broken links, outages, or shopping cart abandonment.

10 Optimize digital campaigns.

11 Increase ROI across channels.

Google Analytics

Google Analytics is a standard web tracking and analytics tool that is used by many organizations to collect and analyze website data. Google Analytics (GA) is part of Google Marketing Platform and is free and easy to install. There are configurable widgets that can be dragged and dropped to create custom dashboards and reports, and GA integrates with Google platforms as well as Salesforce. Date ranges can be customized, and reports can compare similar timeframes, such as year over year or month over month comparisons.

Many essential features are included with Google Analytics. A few of those features are automation, reporting, advertising, exploration, data management, and integration. Let's explore each of these features in more detail.

AUTOMATION: MODELING CAPABILITIES

- Predictive: Create predicted audiences to drive conversions.
- Proactive insights: Automate detection of actionable insights.
- Answers to questions: Natural language model provides search capabilities.

REPORTING: UNDERSTAND USER INTERACTIONS WITH CUSTOMIZABLE REPORTS

- Real time: Monitor site activity as it happens.
- Acquisition: User and traffic reporting from paid and organic sources.
- Engagement: Understand what content drives actions, events, errors, conversions, pages, and screens.

- Monetization: Determine how much revenue is generated through e-commerce, in-app purchases, and advertising.

ADVERTISING: UNDERSTAND ROI OF MEDIA SPEND ACROSS CHANNELS

- Snapshot: Find insights into campaign performance.
- Attribution: Evaluate full funnel attribution across channels using machine learning, conversion paths, and comparison models.

EXPLORATION: ORGANIZE AND VISUALIZE DATA AND INSIGHTS

- Drag and drop: Create custom analyses with multiple variables to create data visualizations.
- Funnels and segments: Visualize user paths, segments, and journeys.
- Lifetime: Explore behavior and value of customers over a lifetime.

DATA MANAGEMENT

- Collection: Supports JavaScript, mobile app SDKs, and open measurement.
- Tag management: Supports all leading tagging systems.
- Custom definitions: Import customized data, dimensions, and metrics.
- Data import: First-party data imports securely.

INTEGRATIONS: SEAMLESSLY INTEGRATES WITH OTHER GOOGLE TOOLS AND PARTNER PRODUCTS

- Google Ads
- Display & Video 360
- Google Cloud
- Salesforce Marketing Cloud
- Google AdMob
- Google Play
- Google Search Console
- Data Studio

While Google Analytics is considered a standard digital analytics solution, it is important to recognize that the tool exists within the walled garden that is

Google. It works best when connected to other Google tools such as Google Search Console, Tag Manager, and Google Ads. The multitude of data points and seemingly infinite number of reports combined with a customizable and easy-to-use interface make this a very appealing option.

Adobe Analytics

Part of the Adobe Experience Cloud, Adobe Analytics provides the ability to analyze data from many different digital touchpoints and in many ways. This solution provides reporting like GA, plus ad hoc analysis that allows for creating numerous data visualizations and reports with drag and drop functionality.

Distinctive features differentiate this solution from others. For example, Segment IQ is a unique feature that helps automatically uncover specific segments of value using customizable metrics and dimensions. The open measurement protocol offers capabilities for collecting data from other sources like voice, video, connected TV, gaming consoles, CRM, and intranet, and Adobe offers additional opportunities for data integration. Creating, managing, storing, and sharing a range of powerful segments delivers compelling reporting through Adobe Analytics.

This digital analytics solution is a good choice for enterprise-level organizations that are already using other components of the Adobe Experience Cloud, which includes content management, customer journeys, marketing workflow, and commerce. Other products and applications include Real-Time CDP (a customer data platform), Marketo Engage (the marketing automation and account-based marketing toolkit), Target (AI-powered testing, personalization, and automation), Customer Journey Analytics (a tool for connecting touchpoints to obtain real-time insights), and Audience Manager (for customer segmentation), plus many others.

Mixpanel

An alternative to the digital analytics offerings from behemoths Google and Adobe is Mixpanel. Offering a basic free version as well as two affordable enterprise solutions, Mixpanel provides many of the features and benefits required to analyze website traffic. Standard interactive reports like funnels and retention help examine the quality and quantity of traffic. Additionally, there are customizable dashboards that update in real time, and deep segmentation capabilities.

A powerful differentiator is that while Google offers seamless integration with Google solutions, Mixpanel offers a wide variety of seamless integrations as well as the ability to integrate directly with any data lake or customer data platform (CDP) such as Segment, mParticle, or RudderStack. Integrations with tools like Optimizely, Figma, Marketo, Slack, Freshpaint, HubSpot, and Facebook Ads provide marketers with countless opportunities to take their digital marketing to the next level.

Similarly, data can be seamlessly exported from Mixpanel to data warehouses such as Amazon Redshift Spectrum or Snowflake, or to cloud storage platforms like Azure Blob Storage or Amazon S3. SDK integration includes JavaScript, iOS Swift, Python, Ruby, and others. This flexibility provides marketers with integration across the tech stack that may be more difficult with other digital analytics tools. This solution is an appealing one for companies looking to work outside of Google and to integrate seamlessly with other advanced tools for various purposes like marketing automation, AB testing, heatmapping, product development, surveying, business intelligence, data segmentation, CRM, and more.

Metrics Overview

No matter which digital analytics solution is selected, understanding the metrics and the data coming out of analytics is critical. Digital marketing programs and SEO deliver many things: eyeballs, clicks, customers, leads, and sales. The other thing that digital marketing delivers is data. To fully understand and best utilize our marketing data, we need a consistent set of metrics or KPIs to determine the success or failure of campaigns. Moreover, with a consistent set of metrics, we can perform creative tests, reallocate budgets, and optimize the strategy.

Typically, marketers will use a digital analytics solution such as Google Analytics to track campaign metrics. We can find high-level quantitative metrics like overall traffic and new versus returning visitors. However, to go in more depth, we also need to study qualitative metrics that help us understand engagement with our site, pages, or apps. Digital analytics delivers metrics across sources, mediums, campaigns, content, keywords, locations, devices, browsers, geographies, and more.

Website Metrics

We can identify and gather specific metrics about our website traffic using digital analytics. From there, the data goes into reports that include insights, analysis, and future recommendations. Google categorizes metrics into the following four categories:

- Real time: **What** is happening on my site right now? Metrics include locations, content, and events that real-time users are accessing.

- Audience: **Who** is visiting the website? This includes metrics like average session duration, ratio of new versus returning visitors, bounce rate, mobile devices, and user flow.

- Acquisition: **How** are visitors accessing the site? Traffic channels, sources, mediums, referrals, and ad campaigns are examples of metrics for acquisition.

- Behavior: **What** are customers doing on the site? Here we track content engagement, site speed, site search and experiments, and other metrics for understanding user behavior.

- Conversions: **Do** customers take action on the site? Setting up goals, e-commerce, and multi-channel funnels provide access to deeper-level data such as revenue and return on investment.

Below are common website metrics and KPIs specific to evaluating digital analytics data; it is critical to examine for insights.

Pageviews: The total number of times a particular page on the site was viewed or loaded by a browser. Pageviews can provide an idea of how popular a page is, but it is also a limiting metric because it is possible that a small group of visitors could be accountable for many views of a page.

Unique pageviews: The total number of times a page was viewed by users within a single session. This is the aggregate of pages viewed by the same users within a single session. This metric eliminates the times a user reloads a page, thus making it a more useful indicator of how popular a page on the site is.

Sessions: A session is a group of interactions including pageviews, clicks, and events taking place on the website within a given amount of time. The timeframe varies depending on the analytics tool. A website user session usually ends after 30 minutes by default, meaning that a session ends. A new session begins when a user has been inactive for 30 minutes and then becomes active again or the user leaves the site and comes back using a new traffic source different than the original session. For example, a user arrives on the site from a Facebook ad. The user clicks around and eventually leaves. Later, the user arrives back on the site from a Google search. This would be considered a new session. Another example is a user arrives on the site and leaves it open but performs no actions, meaning the user is inactive. That session will end after 30 minutes and a new session will start if and when the user becomes active again.

New visitors: This can also be called new users or unique visitors and refers to the number of unique visitors to the website. This can be an important metric when campaigns are geared at driving new prospective customers and traffic to the website. It is important to remember that new visitors can have multiple sessions and pageviews. Also, unique visitors is not always a completely accurate metric because of cross-device usage and other similar factors.

Returning visitors: The number of visitors (or users) that have visited the site before and have returned. In some cases, comparing the new visitors and returning visitors is helpful to determine what type of visits a campaign is delivering. This comparison can be influenced by many factors but is often something to consider.

Traffic by source: Where users were immediately before coming to the site. This can include several sources; some are listed below. This can also be tracked further to see which social networks, search engines, or referral sites users visited prior. The traffic source organic search is critically important for SEO measurement.

- Direct: Users typed in the URL or bookmarked a page and came directly to the site.

- Organic search: Users performed a search then clicked on an organic or non-paid listing.

- Paid search: Users performed a search then clicked on a paid or sponsored listing.

- Social: Users were on a social network like Facebook, Instagram, or LinkedIn.

- Referral: Any other sites that are sending traffic or users to the website.

- Email: Users subscribed to email campaigns, newsletters, or other similar sources.

Bounce rate: The percentage of visitors who left the site without clicking on any additional links or pages. Bounce rate indicates a "single page session." Bounce rate helps us determine the engagement or "stickiness" of our website. Usually, we don't want a user to leave our site without clicking around first. A high bounce rate can indicate that users are not having a good experience on the site, not finding what they need, or landed in the wrong place. Bounce rate can be used as a site-wide metric or a page-specific one. In general, a bounce rate of lower than 40 percent is considered good, and anything above 70 percent is considered high.

Exit rate: The percentage of sessions that ended on a particular page. It can be helpful to examine the patterns of exiting the site to get a sense of overall flow and whether users are able to find what they need within certain pages.

Pages per session: Indicating the number of pages viewed within a session, this metric can provide insight into user experience. Understanding if users are viewing more pages when coming from specific traffic sources and the average number of pages per session can be helpful when considering effectiveness of content and pages within the site.

Average session duration: Also called time on site or time on page, this metric can indicate the engagement of visitors by understanding the time spent within a session.

Conversions: When users complete a specific action such as purchasing a product, filling out a form, or watching a video. This metric helps us align our campaign goals with customer actions.

Demographics: Identify age groupings, gender, and interests, as well as geographic locations, behavior, and technology. Demographic information provides insights about how marketing efforts are reaching our core and prospective customers.

User flow: Defines how users move throughout the site, where they enter, how they browse, where they exit, and more.

Site content: Which content is performing best, how users are interacting with landing pages, which blog posts they are reading, which pages are underperforming. Studying site content helps us understand what is working and what isn't within the website's content. For example, if we are tracking performance of blog posts, we can optimize the frequency and content for future posts.

SEO Metrics

Understanding the fundamental digital analytics metrics affords a closer look at the metrics for SEO. Reporting allows for a gathering of many different data points, including both fundamentals and campaign-specific metrics plus equations to deliver additional insights. SEO-specific metrics will help align the team on what is working while also providing areas of opportunity and optimization. SEO metrics are often not easily attainable through digital analytics tools but may require additional SEO-specific tools to gather a deeper level of data.

Organic traffic: Organic traffic, the non-paid search engine traffic that arrived on the website, is the central measurement for search engine optimization. As SEO is implemented, the organic search traffic should grow. Organic traffic can be tracked in digital analytics as well as through Google Search Console. More advanced tracking can be implemented by filtering out branded search traffic—when users search for the name of your company or brand. This provides a clearer view of organic searches that include keywords like categories, products, and more. Similarly, the KPIs for all website traffic discussed in the above sections can all be applied specifically to the organic traffic source, providing advanced learning about engagement and actions within SEO-driven traffic.

Keyword rankings: Tracking positions in search results for keywords delivers information about overall keyword performance. This is a significant step in monitoring SEO success based on the keyword universe and the three-pronged approach to SEO success. Keyword rankings can be tracked using solutions such as Ahrefs Rank Tracker or other tools available for purchase.

Search visibility: This is the percentage of clicks for the keywords being tracked. Using the keyword universe, visibility will be the percentage of keywords that are visible on search engines. To take this further, measuring share of voice delivers perspective on the overall percentage of traffic that your site receives compared with competing sites for those keywords.

Share of voice: The fraction of a market's total organic search traffic that is going to your website, compared with competitors.

Indexed pages: Tracking the number of pages and the specific URLs for pages that are being indexed is an important way to determine successful SEO work. The number of indexed pages should grow as SEO work is being completed and content is being added to the site. Larger and more complex websites especially need to focus on this metric to ensure that new and updated pages are in the search engine index. This can be tracked with tools like Google Search Console, which offers a coverage report that specifically details site and page indexing while also delivering useful information about errors, sitemaps, removals, and more.

Referring domains: Backlinks are an imperative SEO ranking factor and there is a clear association between referring domains, websites that link to your site, and organic traffic. Keeping in mind that search engines value quality, not just quantity, tracking each domain that is linking back to the website provides vital data.

Website health score: Site audits provide insight into the overall state of the technical SEO within the website. Tracking this metric regularly helps identify any issues, like errors or broken links, that may arise while also providing a metric that can be tracked over time for improvement. There are many free basic tools available for monitoring website health. More advanced tools can be purchased and will provide a deeper level of data plus integration with other tools. The description below offers a free and simple way to monitor the website health score using Website Grader.

Website Grader for Rating Website Health

SEO relies on many specific ranking factors. Website Grader helps marketers understand the overall performance of the website by providing insight into performance, SEO, mobility, and security. There are also recommendations provided in the next steps section.

- **Performance optimization** will increase traffic and improve conversions. This includes page size. Pages should ideally be below 3MB so that they load quickly. Page requests, page speed, browser caching, redirects, image sizes, JavaScript, and CSS are all indicators of performance and are tracked in this section.

- **SEO** drives organic traffic to the website by enticing both users and search crawlers. Indexing is the first and most important key to SEO. Other factors being tracked here include meta descriptions, content plugins, and descriptive link text.

- **Mobile** device usage continues to increase over time. Optimization for mobile devices is an important component of website health. Legible fonts, tap targets, and responsiveness are tracked here to ensure mobile devices are provided a valuable user experience.

- **Security** involves delivering a safe experience for users, free from vulnerabilities. Using HTTPS, a secure SSL certificate, and secure JavaScript libraries are indicators that are tracked here.

Now that we have a better handle on the metrics and KPIs for digital marketing as well as SEO, we can start to calculate the effectiveness of our overall digital marketing efforts. There are different measurements based on platforms, campaign type, or objective. A straightforward measurement for digital marketing is often click-through rate (CTR), which indicates the number of clicks on a given search result, display ad, or listing. Some other important ways to measure digital marketing success are by tracking either return on investment (ROI) or return on ad spend (ROAS). However, for organic or unpaid campaigns like SEO or content marketing, we need to look at other ways to measure. For example, did we see an increase in overall brand sentiment when we launched a new content marketing effort? Were we able to drive more email newsletter sign-ups or Twitter followers with a branding campaign? These data points are the foundation for measurement of digital marketing success. To build on measurement best practices, creating benchmarks will help businesses see the correlation between SEO efforts and metrics over time.

Benchmarks

Establishing benchmarks is a best practice for SEO measurement and is an important first step in the measurement journey. Creating a baseline of trackable metrics before and after SEO implementation will allow a deeper understanding of the campaign's success or lack thereof.

Many different metrics can be tracked in a benchmark report, depending on the size of the business, the competition, and other factors. Here are some specific metrics to track within a benchmark report.

1 pages indexed by Google
2 organic traffic
3 click-through rate
4 landing page conversions
5 number of backlinks
6 number of ranking keywords
7 bounce rate
8 time on site
9 conversions from organic traffic
10 attribution

STEP BY STEP

Develop a Benchmark Report

1   Develop a template for the benchmark report.

2   Decide on the metrics to include in the benchmark.

3   Analyze those key metrics.

4   Do a competitive analysis.

5   Determine areas for improvement.

6   Monitor and update the benchmark regularly.

Reporting

After the hard work of digital marketing and SEO, the analytics and metrics come together, and reports are created. Reporting is where the rubber meets the road with SEO. To truly understand results, metrics and visualizations are combined with insights and future recommendations in elegant and user-friendly reports.

It is also worth mentioning that dashboards are different than reports. While dashboards—typically coming from digital analytics like Google Analytics—provide useful information such as key performance indicators, charts, and graphs, they are typically a snapshot rather than a longer-term view. Conversely, reports can include information from dashboards and can also combine data from other sources. In the case of SEO, tools such as Moz, Semrush or Ahrefs may be used for SEO-specific metrics which can integrate with digital analytics to deliver deeper opportunities for insights and future actions.

Reporting best practices help marketers develop insightful, meaningful, accurate reporting.

Tips for Reporting

1   SMART goals: Remember that reports should include specific, measurable, attainable, relevant, and timebound goals.

2 Accurate data: When data does not show large gains or the success of a campaign, it is important to focus on accuracy and report in a truthful and helpful manner. Sometimes failures lead to important insights and consequential changes.

3 Clean reporting: Include meaningful data and actionable results. Oftentimes, this involves removing information that is superlative or unnecessary. Carefully consider everything that is going into a report. Editing is usually a requirement.

4 Consider content: Content marketing and SEO are connected to one another. Therefore, content measurement is important to measure. Track how content performs related to page optimization, user engagement, keyword rankings, or other significant metrics. Reports are also useful for suggestions for future content ideas, fueled by data and analytics.

5 Tell a story: The best reports are not there to regurgitate data. Rather, they provide an analysis and a way forward. This does not mean defining data but finding insights within the data. The best stories have a beginning, middle, and end. The reports should as well.

6 Templates: Reporting is an ongoing component of digital marketing and SEO. When a team agrees with the overall structure and format of a report and what will be included, they can focus on the story. Generating a template with input from everyone who will access the report goes a long way in aligning expectations and increasing focus on the report itself, rather than the format.

Reporting templates can be created in many ways. For some companies, an Excel spreadsheet with different tabs containing data will do the trick. Other organizations use specific software that generates dashboards and visualizations. PowerPoint, Google Slides, and Keynote are also good tools for creating report templates. Typically, collaborators can come from a wide variety of backgrounds and departments. An up-front discussion about reporting, where different examples are provided, can be helpful. A best practice is to have dashboards and spreadsheets as appendices or backups but use some type of slide deck software for the reporting template, making it easy to copy and paste information into the slides while also providing opportunities for analysis, opinions, and written insights from collaborators.

Reports tell a story that comes together by combining the data with insights. To make recommendations, sometimes using statistics, charts, or graphs can help. Oftentimes, there are presentations to larger groups of stakeholders, which can include people from IT, marketing, sales, and even the C-suite. In all cases, following three defined steps can help.

1 **Visualization:** Don't assume the data will speak for itself. Visualizations and illustrations help people understand the meaning behind the data. Try something very basic to start, like a bar chart created in PowerPoint or Keynote, and gradually try more powerful tools such as Tableau or Power BI. Visualizations help answer the "what" behind the data. What are we looking for? What is the purpose of this? Many people learn visually and will pay more attention to colorful charts than bullet points.

2 **Context:** Different people viewing reports may not share the same understanding of the context of the data. Reporting helps provide context for stakeholders so they can easily digest the "why" behind the data. Use key insights to provide context. Why is this relevant? Why are we suggesting a change?

3 **Solution:** Actions should feel approachable and attainable. Rather than focusing on the huge mountain to climb, select bite-sized actions that help stakeholders understand the "how" component. How will we get where we need to go? How will this benefit the team and the organization? What is a realistic first step?

DIA Framework—a Data-driven Method

DIA (we do love our acronyms in digital) stands for data, insights, action. To create effective and engaging reports, the starting point is data. Therefore, looking at numbers, finding trends, and taking in the information is the very first step. Next, we must uncover insights in the data, which will ultimately drive actions, changes, and updates to our digital plan. Let's take a closer look at each of these in more detail. Figure 6.1 illustrates the DIA framework.

Data

Quite simply, data refers to numbers, facts, and information. Digital analytics tools like Google Analytics can provide a staggering accumulation of data about the quantity and quality of our website traffic. However, some of the data may not be important, useful, or applicable.

FIGURE 6.1 Data, Information, and Insights

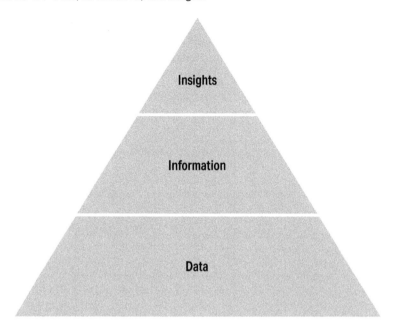

As marketers we must determine what data is important by going back to our metrics and KPIs. Then we study and examine that data to find trends and patterns. Is traffic spiking during holidays, weekends, certain times of the day? Do users come from specific geographic areas? Do they click on certain pages or stay longer on others? How many clicks before they leave the site? Where do they go when they leave?

It's a best practice to examine data over time, rather than looking at what happened yesterday; review trends last year compared with the year before or this quarter-to-date compared with the same timeframe last year. Customized reports can help us quickly and easily get to the data that matters most to us. Once we are comfortable with the data, we can start to pull out insights.

Insights

The data process is usually automated and gathered using software tools However, insights often require human thought processing. While artificial intelligence can be used for many tasks within digital marketing, humans can think through the "why" that leads to the most significant insights.

Asking why can help us better understand our customers' behavior and drive better outcomes from our campaigns.

For example, why are we seeing a spike in traffic during certain times of day? Should we increase our ad budgets and promotional messaging to try and sell more products during those times? If we see drops in traffic over specific holidays or device types, we may want to investigate which keywords are driving the traffic, and if they are also driving conversions like new sales, leads, video completion, article download, etc. The best reporting in digital marketing and SEO will incorporate strategic insights that are garnered from studying the data trends and patterns at a deep level.

Action

Using the data and insights, we can determine next steps for SEO in the form of actions that review, change, and revise our plan based on what we have learned. It is considered a best practice to let campaigns exist and run for a while, 6–12 months, before making sweeping changes.

However, small tweaks and updates are always made on a continuing basis for SEO. It is also key to use a data-driven approach—not using assumptions, gut feelings, or outside factors. Actions with SEO can include revising keywords, adding new ones, or updating on-page SEO elements. It can also include content creation around areas of interest within the data. We can react to timely events or new entrants by recommending changes to SEO strategic initiatives. Actions help us continually test and improve new SEO strategies and tactics while also considering outside factors like changes in the marketplace, industry, competitors, and more.

Using the DIA method, we start with data observation, form insightful opinions, and then make clear and specific recommended changes. Our recommended changes create a loop that goes from optimization back to strategy and tactics and make this a fluid and continual cycle of improvement. Data, insights, and action are important pieces of the reporting process.

When data leads to insights that inspire action, marketers can make meaningful change within the strategy and execution of campaigns.

Wrapping Up

SEO is only as effective as its measurement and metrics. Marketers must continually measure SEO with the goal of optimizing, testing, and improving upon results. Like any digital marketing strategy, search engine optimization relies heavily on the capability to use data to drive decisions. With digital analytics solutions like Google Analytics, we can measure the performance, results, and outcomes of our SEO work. Moreover, we can find new opportunities for SEO by analyzing our keyword and content performance, monitoring competitors, and finding patterns and trends over time. Share of voice and other essential SEO metrics may not be easy to come by with digital analytics, but should nonetheless be tracked for a fuller picture of SEO performance. Reports pull together the data and insights to provide a roadmap for the future.

CHAPTER SUMMARY

1 The capability to measure results with clear and concise data is what separates digital marketing from traditional marketing.

2 By assigning the proper metrics to SEO, we can measure both the quality and quantity of the website traffic it generates.

3 Digital analytics solutions like Google Analytics, Adobe Analytics, and Mixpanel provide businesses with the means to organize, synthesize, and analyze crucial data to inform future SEO decisions.

4 Website metrics help us determine who is on the site, how they got there, why they are there, and what they are doing.

5 We can also look at SEO-specific metrics to understand the overall effectiveness of the strategy.

6 Helpful tools like Website Grader and benchmarks make it easier to track patterns and trends over time.

7 When developing SEO reporting, we can apply the DIA framework, which includes data, insights, and actions.

Reflection Questions

• Does our organization have and utilize a digital analytics solution, such as Google Analytics, effectively?

• Are we as an organization tracking the right website metrics and SEO metrics, and do we have a benchmark for comparison?

• Are we tracking important things like search visibility, indexed pages, referring domains, website health, and share of voice?

- Is the data we are collecting both quantitative and qualitative and is it driving insights?
- Do we have a thorough understanding of the essential key performance indicators that provide guidance into the performance, results, and outcomes of our SEO efforts?
- Do we take data and metrics, and identify trends and patterns to drive future actions?
- Are we creating compelling reports that align with SMART goals? Do these help the business stakeholders to understand our performance, results, and future actions?

PART THREE

SEM

7

Overview of SEM

WHAT TO EXPECT

- The Definition of SEM

- Why SEM?

- Google Search Network

- Ad Auctions

- SEM Strategy

- Website Success

- Hiring an SEM Specialist

- Reflection Questions

OBJECTIVES AND KEY RESULTS

- Define search engine marketing in the context of general marketing and digital marketing.

  o SEM campaigns, when set up and managed effectively, drive high-quality traffic through a paid ad auction model.

- Maintaining control of the many aspects of SEM can deliver high-value returns.

  o SEM is predictable, cost-effective, and data-driven while providing immediate results.

- Understanding of ad auctions and the factors shaping the way SEM works is key for success.

- o There are several key factors involved in the auction outcomes including costs, Ad Rank, and ad quality.
- Interpretation of strategic SEM incorporates many elements.
  - o Impactful aspects are keywords, account structure, bidding, targeting, and ad text.
- Once an SEM campaign is running, website success ensures conversion of traffic into customers and leads.
  - o Navigation, copy, site speed, and other factors affect the user experience.
- Identify best practices and skills to look for when hiring SEM professionals.
  - o Hire SEM specialists with specific skills for successful campaign research, analysis, setup, management, and communication.

The Definition of SEM

Search engine marketing offers the opportunity to communicate directly with users who have typed in specific keywords to Google, Bing, and other search engines. As we have learned, SEO is how marketers build up organic listings on search results pages. On the other side of the coin, we have paid search or SEM. Paid search refers to an auction-based type of digital advertising where controlled messages are placed directly on search results pages. In contrast to SEO, which is based on unpaid, organic search results, SEM provides advertisers with a way to identify potential customers, using a host of different targeting options, and deliver a highly customized advertisement, which is indicated as a sponsored listing. Ad Rank, which we will explore in greater detail, consists of the factors that determine the ad position and costs for SEM. The look and feel of paid search ads can vary from one search engine to another or across different operating systems, devices, and browsers.

In some cases, the term SEM is used to encompass both organic and paid search (SEO and SEM). To make things even more confusing, SEM is also sometimes referred to as pay-per-click, or PPC, but that terminology can also be used for ads on Facebook, Snap, LinkedIn, and other auction-based digital platforms. SEM is often a digital marketing strategy that is used alongside SEO to deliver as much traffic as possible from search engines. While SEO and SEM might seem similar, they are entirely different, yet go hand in hand.

Google Ads is the most popular and widely used search engine self-service ad platform. Although Bing, Yahoo, Duck Duck Go, and others have ad platforms, we will use Google Ads as our baseline. Typically, other search engine ad platforms will follow Google's lead and use similar best practices. This is because Google has a dominant market position and is the leader in paid search advertising. We will use the term SEM to refer to paid or sponsored advertisements specifically on search engines.

Why SEM?

Unlike with SEO, marketers have much control over their SEM campaigns. In general, there are many key benefits of SEM within a digital marketing strategy. Search results listings deliver qualified traffic through organic and sponsored links. However, there are specific advantages with SEM. Here are a few of the benefits of SEM in an overall digital marketing plan.

- **Predictable:** Using tools from Google Ads or other sources, shrewd marketers can gauge most aspects of their SEM campaigns ahead of time. Doing keyword research and competitive analysis helps get a sense of the costs that will be involved. Calculating visitors, based on budget and costs, leads to forecasting the number of conversions and even revenue generated.

- **Customer intent:** Keyword exploration and focused targeting selections, like match type for example, help marketers deliver search ads to a uniquely precise group of users. Corresponding motivating search ads to user intent and keywords can lead to higher conversions and, thus, increased sales and lead generation for advertisers.

- **Cost-effective:** By participating in an online auction, marketers can set the bid they are willing to pay for each click. They can set overall budgets and control how and when that budget is allocated. In general, SEM is thought of as a more financially viable digital marketing tactic than others, such as display or social media.

- **Immediacy:** Unlike SEO, the effects of SEM can be experienced immediately, once campaigns are approved. Additionally, setting up and launching

SEM campaigns—for experienced professionals—can be done fairly quickly and efficiently. Paid search specialists with experience developing campaigns and writing strong ads will be effective at driving immediate results.

- **Flexible:** When developed properly, SEM campaigns allow for maximum flexibility. Marketers can turn campaigns, ad groups, and keywords on or off or pause them at any time. Landing pages, links, ad text, and extensions can easily be updated. There are various targeting options that allow marketers to identify and test many different ways of capturing the right audience.

- **Data-driven:** Using the data derived from SEM campaigns, marketers can find a wealth of opportunities to help drive other successful outcomes, like SEO, email marketing, and more. Google Ads integrates directly with Google Analytics and other systems and provides valuable information about elements such as keyword performance, landing pages, user behavior, and multi-touch attribution.

In the world of digital marketing, paid search is seen as driving less valuable traffic than organic, meaning it converts at a lower level. However, the average click-through rate (CTR) for paid search is over 3 percent, which is considerably higher than display or social ads, which can typically be less than 1 percent. Also, most brands indicate that PPC ads are a huge driver for business growth. While SEO takes time to see results and is extremely competitive, SEM shows immediate results. SEM campaigns give experienced marketers numerous controls, which allow ads to easily be edited, changed, paused, or turned off. Similarly, ongoing campaign management, testing, and optimization can and should be consistent with SEM. When managed effectively, data-driven SEM campaigns can deliver impactful results that inform the overall digital marketing strategy.

Google Search Network

The Google Search Network comprises search-related websites and apps where ads placed through the self-service Google Ads platform can be displayed. A search campaign is one of the types of campaigns available in Google Ads, along with other offerings, including display campaigns, video campaigns, app campaigns, local campaigns, shopping campaigns, and performance max campaigns. We will explore those other offerings later in this section.

Search campaigns are essentially text ads within search results that can drive leads, sales, or traffic to a website. These text ads can appear above or below organic search results on Google Search, Google Play, the Shopping tab, Google Images, and Google Maps. Ads may also appear near results from Google search partners, such as YouTube. When initially creating a campaign, search partners are included by default. Google Ads does not provide information detailing where ads were shown on partner networks. This means a lack of transparency for advertisers. Using "campaign settings," advertisers can easily opt out and remove search partners from campaigns running in the Search Network.

There are several different types of ads on the Search Network:

- **Text ads, dynamic search ads, responsive ads, and call-only ads:** the most common Search Network ads. These ads are displayed with a label indicating that they are a sponsored result. These ads often contain ad assets such as phone numbers or links within the ads.
- **Shopping ads:** linking to products that are for sale, these ads are also labeled as sponsored and also appear on search results pages, often in a line across the top of the page.
- **Image and video ads:** search partners can host image and video ads.

Also, there are two other ways to increase audience size within a search campaign on Google. Campaigns within the Search Network can be expanded to include the Display Network and can be managed with the same tools as the search campaign. Marketers can set their bids and targeting options and can implement automatic ad creation based on the search ads. Also, the overall budget cap of the campaign will be observed, meaning that only unspent Search budget will be used for display. Ads can appear across Google's Display Network, on relevant pages. Keep in mind that display ads typically convert at a much lower level, so this strategy is usually best for brand awareness, to grow an audience, or to use up extra budget from the Search Network campaigns.

The other way to potentially increase audience reach is with responsive ads. These are an all-in-one ad format that can serve across the Display Network. The text ad assets will be used to automatically create responsive ads in different sizes and appearances so that they can work across the network. Responsive ads provide broader reach and access to a larger audience without the work of creating many different ad sizes, types, and formats. However, using the exact same ad creative across various sites and networks can create a poor user experience. It is recommended that responsive ads be used sparingly and with smaller budgets to complement the strategy that is already in place. For bigger and broader display advertising campaigns, ads created specifically for certain platforms, networks, audiences, and sites tend to perform better than a one-size-fits-all approach.

Ad Auctions

Search engine ads are determined through an auction, taking place in real time online. This auction system is used by search engines to determine how ads appear for specific searches and in which order. The ad with the highest bid does not always win an auction because it is based on multiple factors, such as ad relevance and quality. Auctions are repeated each time there is a unique search. Therefore, there will often be fluctuation in an ad's position and price.

This is how the auction system works:

1 The user does a search, and the search engine finds all the ads with matching keywords to the user's search.

2 The system ignores any irrelevant ads, for example ads targeting a different geography or disapproved ads.

3 Of the remaining ads, those with a high Ad Rank may be shown. Ad Rank is determined by an advertiser's bid, ad quality, Ad Rank thresholds, context of user's search, and expected impact of ad format, extensions, etc.

There are five main elements within the ad auction that determine if and where an ad appears:

1 **Bid:** This is the maximum amount an advertiser is willing to pay for a click.

2 **Ad quality:** Relevance and usefulness of ads and landing pages is considered, using quality score, which is a metric that will be examined in detail later in this section.

3 **Expected impact:** Ads can include additional information such as phone numbers or links to other pages, which can impact ad performance.

4 **Ad Rank:** Minimum quality thresholds are set to help ensure high-quality ads. Ad Rank is further examined later in this section.

5 **Context:** The search terms, location, device type, and other factors are considered as signals for which ads fit the context of the user's search.

Pricing Models

Google Ads, for example, allows advertisers to determine bids based on how much they're willing to pay each time a user clicks on their ad. This fee model is called cost per click (CPC). The CPC model is different than other pricing models used in other digital ad buying, such as CPM, which is cost per thousand impressions, and CPA, or cost per acquisition. Although it's rare, there are some instances where a flat fee or percentage fee is charged. However, typically with digital ad campaigns, fees are based on one of these three models. Let's take a closer look at the three different pricing types, as illustrated in Table 7.1.

- **CPM (cost per mille)** = campaign cost / impressions
- **CPC (cost per click)** = campaign cost / clicks
- **CPA (cost per acquisition)** = campaign cost / conversions

CPM

The principle of CPM, or cost per thousand impressions, is that the advertiser is paying for impressions, rather than results. For example, if the CPM is $10, for every 1,000 ads viewed by users, a website will earn $10. The benefit of the CPM model is that it is affordable and delivers volume of

TABLE 7.1 Paid Search Cost Models

CPM	CPC	CPA
CPM is cost per mille or cost per thousand impressions	CPC is cost per click, also known as pay per click (PPC)	CPA is cost per action or cost per acquisition
CPM is the amount an advertiser pays per thousand impressions of their ad on a web page	CPC is a model where advertisers pay based on the number of times a visitor clicks on an ad	CPA is a model where advertisers pay every time a user completes a pre-determined action
CPM is more cost effective	CPC marketing is often more expensive	CPA marketing can be run with many ad formats
$$CPM = \frac{Ad\ Spend}{Impressions} \times 1000$$	$$CPC = \frac{Advertising\ cost}{Number\ of\ clicks}$$	$$CPA = \frac{Campaign\ cost}{Conversions}$$

inventory. However, CPM campaigns do not offer engagement or conversion metrics. They are also more often subject to fraud. CPMs can climb higher with increased targeting parameters, highly competitive keywords, and industries. These types of ads are often used to drive awareness and can be suitable for new product launches, branding, or large businesses that desire broad exposure. CPM models are common with programmatic, video, and display campaigns.

CPC

Advertisers using CPC, or cost per click, ad models are often tracking performance based on the number of new site visitors or similar metrics. Because this is a performance-based pricing model, the ad will be shown as often as necessary to deliver the clicks for the advertiser, based on their budget. The CPC model is often used to target the middle of the customer journey, where users have familiarity with the brand or the product but are seeking additional information to inform their purchase decision. Hence, it is considered more cost-effective and measurable than CPM. CPC campaigns are used in ad campaigns with interaction opportunities, such as paid search, affiliate marketing, and sponsored social media posts.

CPA

Cost per acquisition (or action) (CPA) campaigns are based on predetermined actions such as conversions, subscriptions, installs, views, or downloads. Although actions can be measured separately, they are all viewed as actions within the confines of a campaign. Costs for these desired actions are typically much higher than either paying for clicks or impressions. However, CPA also delivers the highest level of value in many ways, focusing on high-quality traffic which can generate revenue and leads for advertisers. Because it can be expensive and unpredictable, it is most suitable for motivating immediate action in campaigns geared toward revenue- or lead-generation.

Ad Rank

Going a step further, we can explore Ad Rank. Ad Rank, a key element of the ad auction, is calculated for every ad, and, generally, determines the order, position, and cost for ads. Ad Rank consists of six main factors:

- **Bid**: the maximum amount an advertiser is willing to pay for each click on an ad.

- **Quality of ads and landing pages:** relevance and usefulness are assessed in quality score, which can be monitored for improvement over time.
- **Ad Rank thresholds:** location and device type and many others, as described in detail below.
- **Competitiveness of auction:** two ads competing for the same position with similar Ad Ranks will have the same opportunity to be displayed. Gaps in Ad Rank will drive competition, with the higher-ranking ad being more likely to win the auction, but also having a higher cost per click.
- **Context of the search:** context is an important factor with the ad auction. Ad Rank will consider the keywords of the search, the location, time of day, and other contextual factors.
- **Expected impact:** additional information within an ad, like phone number and links to other pages, are called ad assets. Assets and other components can impact an ad's performance.

Because Ad Rank is an important component in determining where an ad is displayed, it is important to understand how to improve Ad Rank and compete within the auction. There are a few factors that can be improved upon over time to help increase Ad Rank. These are used in a variety of ways and can affect important things like ad auction eligibility, the cost per click, and ad asset eligibility. The factors that can help improve the quality components of Ad Rank are:

- **Expected click-through rate for an ad:** this is partially based on historical click-through performance within a campaign, but adjusting things like ad assets can affect ad visibility and clicks.
- **Ad's relevance to search:** how relevant an ad is to what a user searches for, using keyword research, match type, and other targeting options.
- **Landing page quality:** landing pages must be relevant, transparent, and easy to navigate.

Ad Rank contains certain thresholds which help to decide if and where an ad appears and how ads compete within an auction. These thresholds are determined dynamically, in real time, during the auction process. They are factored into whether an ad is displayed or not, the price of the ad, and the position of the ad. The actual cost per click (CPC) of an ad is calculated based on the Ad Rank, which includes these thresholds and competition from other advertisers. If only one ad is eligible to display for a specific search, that ad will pay the reserve price, meaning that ad costs can vary, depending on ad quality and Ad Rank thresholds.

The various important factors for Ad Rank thresholds are:

- **ad quality:** highly relevant and determined to be high-quality ad text
- **ad position:** ads appearing higher are more likely to be seen
- **signals like location and device type:** different countries and device types carry different thresholds
- **topic and nature of the search:** different industries and levels of competition determine different topical thresholds
- **related auctions:** related queries can determine various thresholds

Ad Quality

Search engines use specific factors to help predict the experience that users will have when they click on a certain ad. This can include relevance, click-through rate and landing page experience. There are also misconceptions about certain things that do not actually impact the assessment of ad quality.

Ad quality affects many specific things within the ad auction, including:

- **If an ad will show:** Ads must meet a certain level of quality to be accepted into the auction.
- **Where an ad will show:** Ad quality determines positioning of ads on the search engine results page with the goal of showing users the best possible ads at the top of the page, above the fold.
- **Ad assets showing:** Some assets only show above search results and must have high ad quality in order to show in that position.
- **Cost per click:** Higher-quality ads typically cost less per click than lower-quality ads.
- **Ad performance:** Higher-quality ads and landing pages typically deliver higher-quality clicks and conversions.

There are many common misconceptions about things that do not impact ad quality, including:

- **Bidding:** The amount being bid may affect Ad Rank, but it does not impact ad quality.
- **Account structure:** Ad groups with the same ads and keywords can be moved to another campaign or account without impacting ad quality.

However, if a keyword is moved to a new ad group with new ad text, it can change ad quality because it affects the user experience.

- **Frequency of ads:** The frequency of ad display is determined by bids, budget, and competition of keywords, but it does not impact ad quality.

- **Conversions:** Reported numbers of conversions do not affect the ad quality.

SEM Strategy

Ads aligned with clear goals will lead to a well-optimized SEM strategy. Understanding how paid ads work, setting campaigns up correctly, and monitoring their progress will impact the performance. Other essential aspects that affect results are keywords, account structure, bidding, targeting, and ad text. Let's take a closer look at how to create a winning SEM strategy. We will examine each of these plus additional elements in closer detail later in this section.

Keywords

As with SEO, keywords are the backbone of a successful SEM strategy. The first step in the keyword process involves research, brainstorming, and analysis. Brand terms, keywords that include brand names and identifiers, are the low-hanging fruit and can be a good place to start. Additionally, tools such as Google Trends, competitive analysis, and SWOT (strengths, weaknesses, opportunities, and threats) analysis can help find new areas of focus for keywords. Seek to fully describe categories, products, services, locations, and other areas of the business. Concentrating on user intent, think about how a potential customer might define or describe products at each stage of the customer decision journey.

Remembering that search volume and competition impact bids and costs, research these as well, looking for the sweet spot of high-volume, low-competition keywords. Keyword research tools can help widen the scope while providing volume, competition, and cost estimates. The initial goal with keyword research is to cast a wide net. From there, capturing data to be used for future campaign optimization becomes the focus. Table 7.2 provides an example, and the Lookout suggests helpful tools for keyword research.

TABLE 7.2 An Example of a Keyword Research Tool

Keywords	Search Volume	CPC	Competition
rescue dogs	100,500	$1.55	High
rescue dogs evanston	65,000	$0.95	High
rescue dogs chicago	120,000	$1.75	High
least expensive dog to rescue rockford, il	5,000	$0.75	Low
labradors for adoption	90,500	$1.05	High
golden retriever for sale	110,500	$1.75	High
affordable low cost dog breed joliet	7,000	$0.75	Low
puppies for sale	120,000	$1.20	High

LOOKOUT

Keyword research tools generate suggestions for search terms. Here are a few free options:

1 Keywordtool.io

2 Wordtracker

3 WordStream

4 Moz Keyword Explorer

5 Ahrefs Keyword Generator

6 Ubersuggest

7 ChatGPT or other AI plugin tool

In addition to those tools listed, both Microsoft Excel and AI are important tools when dealing with extensive keyword lists. Excel offers many critical formulas, including CONCATENATE for creating new combinations and long-tail keyword variations, VLOOKUP and XLOOKUP for data correlation, and COUNTIF or SUMIF for trend analysis. Excel also offers graphing and charting tools to create visuals for metrics like trends and rankings. By processing large amounts of data, AI tools such as ChatGPT can automate tasks such as identifying and removing duplicates, splitting keyword strings, keyword grouping, and offering suggestions and predictions for keyword trends. It can also offer enhanced decision-making by identifying trends and patterns within large datasets. More advanced marketers can use ChatGPT to develop a script that runs functions automatically, such as removing duplicates or cross-checking data. In many cases, using Excel and ChatGPT can save time and increase efficiency with keyword research.

Account Structure

The structure of the account is an essential aspect of an effective SEM campaign. Google Ads account structure comprises five specific elements: ad campaigns, ad groups, keywords, ad text, and landing pages. Campaigns are the highest level for managing ads. Ad groups should be grouped by themes. Keywords are the search queries that are included within the campaign and ads are the text and path that will be displayed for the user's searches that are selected. Finally, landing pages are the pages within the website where users will go once they click on an ad. Budgets are set at the campaign level and bids set at the keyword level. Figure 7.1 shows the structure of a Google Ads campaign.

FIGURE 7.1 Basic Structure of a Google Ads Account

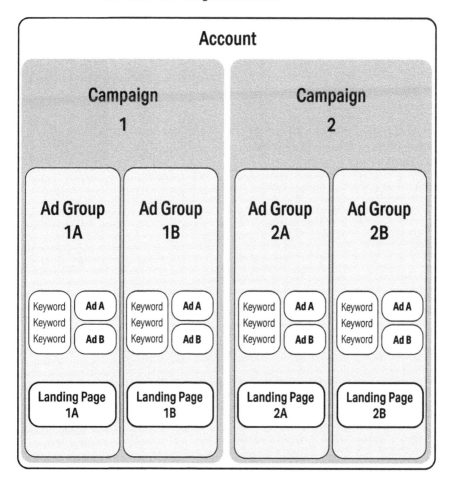

This is an example of account structure. The overall account is for an online shoe retailer. Campaign 1 is for athletic shoes; Ad Group 1 is for tennis shoes and Ad Group 1B is for walking shoes. Many keywords and ad variations can be used with each ad group. For example, in the tennis shoes ad group, keywords might incorporate: tennis shoes, best tennis shoes, shoes for tennis, white tennis shoes, tennis shoes for women, and kids tennis shoes. Ad variations might use different call-to-action words like shop, buy, or free. Landing pages will be specific to the ad group or keywords and can include a vanity URL, rather than a longer string of characters. Table 7.3 depicts the account structure with the ad group, keywords, and ad copy trifecta.

Bidding

Various bid strategies are tailored to different campaigns or goals. For search ads, the goal is typically clicks. Manual bidding and automated bidding are the two main types of bidding strategies for Google Ads. Within those general categories, marketers can target actions or conversions, clicks or impressions. Search ads typically target actions or clicks, meaning that advertisers only pay when a user clicks on the ad or completes a predetermined action. Those actions can include a purchase, an email signup, or a lead generated, for example. With manual bidding, the advertiser retains maximum control by setting the bid amount, which they are willing to pay for each click or action. Automated bidding takes away the heavy lifting but also some of the control.

TABLE 7.3 Account Structure for an Online Shoe Retailer

Ad Group	Keywords	Ad Copy
Tennis Shoes	tennis shoes best tennis shoes shoes for tennis white tennis shoes womens tennis shoes kids tennis shoes	Tennis shoes Buy Now—the largest selection of tennis shoes with free shipping www.samsshoes.com/tennis-shoes
Walking Shoes	walking shoes travel walking shoes , black walking shoes best travel walking shoes mens walking shoes kids walking shoes	Walking Shoes Shop a large selection of walking shoes. Save 10% today. www.samsshoes.com/walking-shoes

Manual Cost Per Click (CPC) Bidding

Advertisers set a maximum price they are willing to pay for a user who clicks on an ad; this is called a max CPC. A default CPC will be set automatically when selecting manual CPC for the bidding strategy. This can be changed to max CPC. Max CPC should be calculated based on the value of a new customer or a sale. For example, a new customer is worth more if you are selling a new expensive watch that costs $5,000 compared with a new pair of walking shoes that cost $100. It is best practice to consistently revisit max CPCs, based on market, competition, and search fluctuation. The max CPC is the maximum amount that you will pay. The actual CPC is the final amount you are charged and can often be less than the max CPC, because of the ad auction and Ad Rank thresholds described earlier in this chapter. Max CPC can be applied at the ad group or the keyword level. This should be determined based on the amount you are willing to pay and at which level within the campaign.

Automated Bidding, Also Called Maximize Clicks, Conversions, or Conversion Value

Here, advertisers set an average daily budget and the system automatically manages bids to bring the most clicks within that average daily budget. This is a simplified bidding strategy because there is little to no work involved. However, many advertisers do not like to use automated bidding because it removes much of the control for running campaigns to drive conversions or specific targeted actions at the ad group or keyword level. Automated bidding can also be used to maximize conversions, which focuses on as many sales, leads, or actions as possible within the constraints of a predetermined budget. Within the maximize conversions bidding strategy, you can set a target cost per action (CPA) value, meaning you are only willing to pay up to that amount for each completed action. Finally, you can target the return on ad spend (ROAS) value with your bidding strategy. This strategy can only be used in conjunction with conversion tracking and at least 15 conversions in the previous 30 days. Targeting ROAS can be an optimal strategy when used effectively, as it basically guarantees a specific return on investment for the ad campaign.

Targeting

There are several ways to incorporate targeting into an SEM strategy. Keywords, audiences, locations, devices, and ad scheduling are the most impactful targeting options. Consider the audience that is being targeted and how they will search for products and services. Consider options like demographics, affinity segments, geographic locations, device types, and timing of ad scheduling. Each of these can be controlled within the campaigns. You can also target users based on whether they are in-market, which is based on recent purchase intent, as well as your own data segments, meaning users who have interacted with your business. This includes website and app visitors, customer matching from your data, or similar segments, which are new users with similar interests to your website visitors or current customers. Audience targeting can be used at the campaign or ad group level.

Ad Text

Text ads include three parts: headline text, display URL, and description text. Headlines are usually the first thing seen by a searcher and should be eye-catching. Each text ad comprises three headlines, each up to 30 characters and separated by a vertical pipe (|). Display URLs are up to 15 characters and are usually displayed in green, showing the website address. The display URL does not have to match the actual URL, as it is meant to provide a path for the user to understand where they will go once they click on the ad. Finally, descriptions highlight the details about the product or service on offer. These should include a call-to-action word, such as "free," "buy," "shop," "try," "ship," etc. Descriptions can be up to 90 characters apiece and there are two descriptions per ad.

Website Success

Driving users and traffic through SEM campaigns is an essential digital marketing technique. However, converting those users into customers is equally important. Websites must be designed to encourage users to take action. This can be accomplished in several ways. Site design should always focus on making the most important information easy to find. Navigation, buttons, and visual hierarchy help users find information quickly and clearly. Users prefer not to have to scroll and click around to discover what they are looking for.

Website copy helps users understand what the site offers. It should be attention-grabbing, simple, and direct. Clearly highlight the customer benefits and provide links to helpful information. Using visuals, bullet points, videos, and clear language are all best practices. Also, transparency and trust are critical components of converting traffic into customers. Sharing specifics about shipping and return policies and including testimonials can build transparency and trust. Also, include third-party verification wherever applicable and include valuable, educational content in the form of articles, blogs, videos, and FAQs.

Optimizing the website for a mobile experience is also key. Many searchers use different digital devices such as tablets and smartphones. Smaller screens provide a much different user experience than a larger desktop viewing experience. Site load speed, videos, and large images can all be impacted by smaller device viewing and are important considerations for the success of the website. When advertisers spend valuable marketing dollars on SEM ad campaigns, it is imperative that the website is ready to take that high-quality traffic and convert it into new customers and new leads. Landing pages provide a distinct opportunity with SEM and will be explored in detail in Chapter 8.

Hiring an SEM Specialist

Running SEM campaigns can be time-consuming, depending on the nature of the business, the competition, and many other factors. There are several options for how to handle the development, management, and optimization of SEM campaigns. Some smaller companies have an internal staff member or external freelancer or consultant doing this work. For larger companies, campaigns might be outsourced to an agency specializing in SEM or they could have an internal team focused on paid digital media. Regardless, when hiring for SEM, it's important to understand what an SEM specialist really does and how to develop the proper communication and accountability.

SEM specialists should have expertise with both strategy and tactics, meaning that they understand the importance of goals and objectives and can align and measure those with campaigns. They should have a full understanding and knowledge of the Google Ad platform as well as Bing if that will be part of the strategy. That means that they understand all the various campaign settings and how to structure and set up campaigns meticulously. They must also know how to select proper targeting and matching options and how to do extensive keyword research. Google Ads is always changing, adding features, and incorporating new technology like AI and machine learning. Strong SEM professionals will stay up to date on the evolving world of SEM.

Budgeting is a critical component of SEM, and the specialist will be an active participant in budgeting, knowing how to oversee and stay within an agreed-upon budget. Finally, measurement and analysis are crucial to overall success with SEM. The experienced specialist knows how to measure campaigns using data, KPIs, and reporting. They must take data and find insights and create meaningful, compelling reports. SEM specialists must be able to take a micro and a macro look at campaigns, identifying issues as well as opportunities by closely evaluating performance and data.

In some cases, a team of specialists with different focus areas will be the right approach for SEM. There are many options for working with outside partners or individuals for SEM. There are agencies that specialize in digital marketing, search engine marketing, or paid digital advertising. There are also many skilled and talented freelancers who specialize in paid search. Freelancing platforms like Upwork, Mayple, Indeed, and MarketerHire often have SEM specialists that are available for hire.

LOOKOUT

Agencies Specializing in SEM

1 HawkSEM

2 LeanSEM

3 Merkle

4 JumpFly

5 KlientBoost

6 Titan PPC

7 Ignite Digital

Professionals in SEM must have precise knowledge and expertise. A good hiring process combined with asking good questions will help hire the best people for developing and running SEM campaigns. Here are focus areas, processes, and questions to aid in hiring.

Research and Analysis

Research and analysis are fluid within SEM. As competitors enter and leave the market, as new products are launched, as technology, AI, and search engines evolve, an SEM specialist must always be researching and analyzing.

To get a sense of experience level with SEM research and analysis, consider asking the following questions:

- Can you describe the detailed process prior to setting up and launching campaigns?
- What tools do you use and what are you looking for?
- How do you stay organized? Can you walk me through what that looks like?

Software

Full knowledge of Google Ads and Google Analytics is a requirement, and certifications may be a prerequisite. Bing's Webmaster Tools and Google's Search Console can also be important, along with SEM-specific software like Semrush, WordStream, and Moz. There are other technical skills that are useful, such as content management systems like WordPress or Drupal, marketing automation such as Pardot or Marketo, analytics systems like Power BI or Adobe Analytics, and reporting software like Data Studio. In some cases, knowledge of HTML, CSS, R, and JavaScript are also beneficial. Specific software expertise will largely depend on the organization's tech stack.

Communication

Skilled professionals must understand communication at a deep level. They must be able to communicate the business and marketing messaging within the confines of a text ad while also being able to summarize their strategy, procedures, and outcomes to the rest of the organization. An accomplished SEM professional will not regurgitate data and facts. Rather, the difficult job is finding issues, insights, and opportunities within the data and sharing that with the key stakeholders, involving customers and internal teams. To better establish the communication experience level, try using this line of questioning:

- Describe your process with creating text ads, and can you share a successful example?
- How do you typically approach reporting for SEM campaigns?
- What is the best method you've found for communicating with particular groups of stakeholders, like customers or management?

Excel

Microsoft Excel is a necessary tool for SEM organization and management. It is used for general purposes like organizing keywords and ad groups, bid management, ad text, and key calculations. However, with advanced knowledge, it can also be used for character counting and to batch tasks like replacing keywords, trimming unnecessary spaces, making comparisons, finding results, joining cells, capitalizing (or lower-casing), appending text, grouping, converting dates, and much more. Also, Google Ads provides the capability to upload Excel files directly into the platform, through a feature called bulk uploads.

Attention to Detail

Keeping track of many moving parts is part of SEM. To do so, organization and attention to detail are at the forefront. This starts with campaign setup and goes all the way through to managing the budget and measuring campaign outcomes. To determine the level of focus on detail, consider asking the following questions:

- How do you organize the different components of paid search?
- Can you describe your budgeting process?
- How would you ensure that overspend is minimized?

Moreover, there are several "nice to have" skills for an SEM specialist, such as copywriting, UI/UX, e-commerce knowledge, landing page optimization, design capabilities, statistics, testing and experimentation, customer service, and understanding of other types of digital marketing like SEO and social media marketing. While no individual can have all the skills as described here, those who demonstrate a confident understanding of the intricacies of SEM as well as a proven track record will stand out. Whether recruiting and hiring internal SEM specialists or agency partners, taking the time to find the right fit is essential.

Wrapping Up

The immediacy of SEM campaigns can be an important way to drive qualified traffic quickly and efficiently. However, SEM has a multitude of factors that impact its effectiveness. To maximize value, marketers must understand and implement a wide variety of best practices.

This includes a very detailed consideration of the keywords and bidding strategy, the structure, ad text and targeting within the account, and the way the website is set up and optimized to receive new visitors. Companies may need several SEM professionals to effectively research, set up, and oversee campaigns, and these SEM specialists should have a deep understanding of the tools, methods, and decisions essential to create successful campaigns. In different cases, SEM specialists will be internal team members, freelancers, agencies, or a combination. Regardless of who is overseeing the efforts, a great level of skill, communication, and attention to detail is required.

CHAPTER SUMMARY

1 SEM necessitates acute attention to detail. While results can be immediate, there are many factors and moving parts.

2 Ad auctions and pricing models must be understood to determine the best strategy for budgeting and bidding.

3 Other key factors of the ad auction that should be monitored include Ad Rank and ad quality.

4 For SEM to be successful, a strategy must be focused on keywords, account structure, bidding, targeting, and ad text.

5 Once traffic is being paid for and driven from search engines, the website must be in good shape to receive that traffic and convert it into customers and leads.

6 Attention to navigation, copy, site speed, and other factors will deliver a strong user experience.

7 When hiring an SEM specialist, consider research and analysis, software, Excel, and communication skills, as well as attention to detail.

Reflection Questions

- Is our organization successfully pursuing SEM and are we aligned on its importance within the marketing and digital marketing ecosystem?

- Are we aware of the ad auction model, pricing models, and the factors that impact how we pay for the traffic generated through SEM?

- Are we budgeting and bidding effectively to ensure the best possible return on our efforts?

- Do our SEM team members fully understand Ad Rank and ad quality factors and how they impact our costs and our campaigns?

- Is our SEM strategy fully embracing and implementing the most critical factors? Are we being intentional and proactive with keywords, account structure, bid strategy, targeting, and ad text?

- Is our website fully optimized for different device types? Is our navigation and visual hierarchy clear and easy to use? Do we have attention-getting copy and content to help users make good decisions?

- Who oversees our SEM efforts?

- When hiring SEM specialists, are we asking the right questions, identifying the proper skill sets, and finding the right fit?

8

Successful SEM Campaigns

WHAT TO EXPECT

- Prior to Liftoff
- Launching Successful Campaigns
- SEM Wins and Fails
- Reflection Questions

OBJECTIVES AND KEY RESULTS

- Understand the fundamentals involved in SEM prior to launching campaigns.
  - Research and planning will save valuable time and drive positive campaign outcomes.
- Tools should be used for analyzing the market, the audience, and the messaging.
  - Create better-performing ads with research, tools, and targeting.
- Thoroughly examining best practices for landing pages drives value for SEM.
  - High-performing landing pages are relevant, trustworthy, easy to navigate, and reliable.
- Examine the nuanced steps involved in properly designing, developing, and launching an SEM campaign.
  - Campaign setup includes several factors and requires sharp attention to detail.
- Knowledge of particulars involved in ad creation will lead to better outcomes.
  - Meticulous focus on keywords, match type, bidding, quality score, and other features is critical for effective ads.

Prior to Liftoff

Before the launch (or relaunch) of an SEM campaign, there are several important steps that will deliver positive results. A deep understanding of the audience, the fundamentals of Google Ads, and other factors will set campaigns up for success. Here we will review all the essential SEM aspects that need attention prior to launch.

Audience

Before creating a new campaign or recreating an old one, it is important to take the time to research and analyze both the current market conditions as well as the audience. Messaging should directly correlate to a defined audience. Tracking search trends and competitors, and creating personas can be worthwhile activities to identify the campaign audience.

- **Market:** Competitive analysis, Google Trends, and other tools can help assess the market conditions at a particular moment in time. Remember to consider factors like seasonality, holidays, and current events when studying the market.

- **Audience:** Personas, customer demographics, and consumer research are useful when reviewing the audience focus for campaigns. Consider the different categories and products and how specific audience targeting parameters, like geography, can bring in the right users.

- **Messaging:** Keywords, calls to action, and tools like gap analysis (see the Lookout for a three-step process) can be beneficial when brainstorming the correct messaging for SEM. Evoking specific actions will drive users toward desired behaviors and increase conversions. Take time to free-associate all the possibilities with calls to action that may resonate with the audience being targeted. See Figure 8.1 for examples of successful words that are used as calls to action in SEM ad text.

LOOKOUT

Three-step Gap Analysis for SEM

1 What keywords are competitors using for their SEM ad strategy?

2 Review competitors' ad text.

3 Use tools like SpyFu for additional intelligence.

FIGURE 8.1 Word Cloud Depicting Call to Action Words

SOURCE WordStream®, 2023, https://www.wordstream.com/

Google Ads Basics

Learning and understanding the fundamentals of Google Ads and making certain decisions ahead of time will benefit campaigns and outcomes in the long run. There are many things to do in the setup phase, but prior to launch, a few quick decisions can save time thereafter.

- **Naming:** Consistent and clear naming conventions for campaigns help provide control, organization, shareability, and filtering of data. Common variables to use when naming campaigns include location, traffic source, brand, category, subcategory, ad type, objective, audience, product, and promotion.
- **Account split:** Different campaign types should be split for easier tracking and data analysis. Campaigns can be segmented or split based on bidding strategy, keywords, languages, or budgets.
- **Integration:** SEM campaigns deliver a wealth of data about traffic patterns, user preferences, search intent, and more. To fully capture, analyze, and derive insights from this data, integration into a web analytics platform like Google Analytics or something similar is key. Taking the

time to integrate Google Ads up front will ensure that the large amount of valuable SEM data lands in the right place once campaigns are running.

- **Smart mode vs. expert mode:** The Google Ads experience is different depending on which mode is selected. Smart mode is a simplified, automated experience using machine learning to determine most factors like keywords and targeting. It also provides simplified reporting. Expert mode offers the full range of features and gives control to the advertiser. The management is more complex and time-consuming but delivers better results due to the enhanced control from the advertiser. In most cases, expert mode is preferable.

Defining Objectives

Every campaign starts with selecting a goal focused on delivering a specific outcome. The objectives for search campaigns can be narrowly focused or broader in reach. When creating a campaign, an objective is selected. Campaign objectives can be added, changed, or removed at any time. The campaign objective must be correlated with the desired outcome. When running campaigns outside of search, such as display, additional objectives can be selected, including reach or predetermined data segments.

The objectives available for search campaigns include:

- Sales
  - used to drive sales and conversions online, in app, by phone, or in store
  - engages customers in the purchase phase of the customer decision journey (CDJ)
- Leads
  - drives relevant prospects to sign up for something, thereby sharing relevant contact information
  - engages users in the consideration phase of the CDJ
- Website traffic
  - delivers a relevant audience to become aware of brands and products of interest
  - engages users in the awareness phase of the CDJ

Campaign Types

Once the objectives have been defined, campaign types are selected. For the purposes of this book, we are focused on search ads. However, there are many campaign types and ad format options in Google Ads. Below is a full list and description of campaign options.

In search marketing, it is a best practice to narrowly focus campaign type on search to avoid overspending budget on inventory with lower conversion rates. When running app campaigns, taking the time to manually select where ads will appear can have a significant impact on results. Avoid using default settings and allowing ads to run across large app site networks, whenever possible. Use a critical eye when determining which apps, if any, your ads will run on. There are massive quantities of apps in the network, and many can be low quality with poor ad performance. Stick with search engines like Google and Bing for the best quality and results.

The list of Google Ads campaign types below starts with the most narrowly focused campaigns (search) and ends with the broadest campaign type (performance max). Carefully consider campaign goals, budgets, and audiences when selecting the campaign type.

- search campaigns: text ads appearing in search results
- display campaigns: image ads showing on websites, search results, Gmail inboxes
- discovery campaigns: multi-image carousel ads displaying on YouTube, Gmail inboxes, and Google Discover, a personalized feed for users logged into their Google account
- shopping campaigns: product listing ads displaying on search results, shopping tab, websites, and Gmail inboxes
- video campaigns: video ads appearing on YouTube
- app campaigns: text, image, video, HTML5 assets combine to display on search results on mobile devices, Google Play, YouTube, AdMob, and 3 million sites and apps
- local campaigns: text and image ads appearing on Google Maps, websites, and YouTube
- performance max campaigns: text, image, and video ads, multi-image carousel, and product listing ads displaying across all sites and platforms within the Google Network

Conversion Tracking

Prior to launching a campaign, goals and objectives will be set. Marketers then align those goals with the proper tracking metrics. Google defines a conversion as an action that is counted when a user interacts with an ad. Actions include things like filling forms, viewing videos, email signups, event registrations, purchases, app installs, and downloads. Implementing conversion tracking helps understand which keywords, ad groups, and campaigns are driving customer actions and return on investment. In order to track conversions, they must first be defined. Then the proper tracking tag or code snippet must be installed. Multiple kinds of conversions can be tracked by setting up different conversion actions for each type of conversion being tracked. The Lookout defines important terminology regarding conversion tracking.

LOOKOUT

Important terms regarding conversion tracking:

Conversions: meaningful actions taken by users who have seen an ad, such as purchase, phone calls, clicks, video views, form fills, chat interactions, and more.

Conversion tracking: the process of tagging ads for the purpose of counting each of the meaningful interactions and which ads led to them.

Conversion value: an option within some conversion actions which allows for the assignment of a specific value given to an action.

Google Tag: code snippet added to a website to enable conversion tracking.

Conversion categories: meaningful actions, such as purchase or submit lead form, selected from a list of possibilities, as outlined in Table 8.1.

TABLE 8.1 Conversion Categories in Google Ads

Business Goal	Sale categories	Leads categories	Further categories
Updated conversion categories	• Purchase • Add to cart • Begin checkout • Subscribe	• Submit lead form • Book appointment sign-up • Request quote • Get directions • Outbound click • Contact	• Page view • Other

The Step by Step offers a checklist for setting up conversion tracking.

STEP BY STEP

Enabling Conversion Tracking in Google Ads

1 Identify the website where the Google Tag will be placed.

2 Create conversion action—choose either URL (which is faster but only tracks page load as a conversion) or manual setup (which takes more time but allows tracking of clicks, buttons, or links and can be customized with conversion value tracking, transaction IDs, and other parameters).

3 Set up Google Tag—once the conversion action is selected there will be instructions for how to set up the tag based on URL or manual setup.

4 Install Google Tag—paste a short snippet of code onto each page on the website that will have conversion tracking enabled.

5 Check Google Tag—sign into Google Ads and check under "Goals" to see that the tag is installed properly and is tracking desired conversions.

6 Analyze conversion data—check the tracking status and analyze data in the conversion actions report in the Google Ads account.

Attribution modeling

Attribution models are used to measure success, based on all ad interactions, not just the click that led to the conversion. If a user interacts with but does not convert on more than one ad before completing an action, the attribution model determines which ad gets credit for the action.

The Lookout describes the three types of attribution models currently used in SEM. Today's customer decision journey encompasses many different channels, platforms, devices, and touchpoints. Attribution modeling helps marketers track each touchpoint and assign credit in the right places.

LOOKOUT

Multi-touch attribution models used in Google Ads are:

1   Last click: All credit for the conversion goes to the last-clicked ad and keyword.

2   First click: All credit for the conversion goes to the first-clicked ad and keyword.

3   Data-driven: Credit is distributed for an action based on the past data for said conversion action.

SIDEBAR

Analyze CPA or ROAS for different attribution models to determine the best approach. Using the "model comparison" report in Google Ads, identify undervalued campaigns or keywords across the conversion path and adjust bidding strategy as a result.

Landing Pages

Optimizing the pages users land on after they have clicked on an SEM ad is critical to the conversion process. Landing pages are the opportunity to convert prospects into customers. Each ad that is running has a specific URL which determines the landing page for that ad. Landing pages and display URLs must share the same domain. However, the display URL does not have to be the true URL with a long string of characters. It can be shortened to indicate a product or category page that matches the search query. Users should not be sent to the home page when they click an ad. Rather, they should be taken to a tailored page that is optimized for user experience and conversion.

Landing page performance can be quickly gauged using metrics like click-throughs and conversions. Consider what users expect to see once they click from an ad to a landing page. If they don't find what they need immediately, they are more likely to leave. Well-constructed landing pages lead to a positive user experience resulting in more conversions. The performance of the landing page is monitored by search engines and has a direct effect on SEM campaign performance, including bounce rate (an indicator of a single page session), ad positioning, and quality score.

- **Decreased bounce rate:** Better landing pages draw in users, making them less likely to click back to the search results page, or bounce, immediately.

- **Improved ad position:** The better experience users have on landing pages, the more likely ads will show up in higher positions.

- **Improved quality score:** Relevance of landing pages is a key indicator to quality score, which impacts ad rank and lowers the cost per click.

Users expect to find landing pages that are relevant, trustworthy, easy to navigate, and reliable. Best practices to ensure that landing pages deliver a positive user experience include the following.

RELEVANT

- Match ads and keywords: Landing page must fulfill the promise of the SEM ad and should incorporate keywords, providing consistency from ad to website.

- Call to action: Customized buttons drive users to act. Incorporate words like "buy," "free," or "save" that indicate the same call to action from ads to landing pages.

- Audience focus: Gear the language and tone of the landing page toward the audience. Clearly demonstrate the value proposition for the user by sharing unique features and benefits.

- Ad groups: Grouping ads for similar products or offers with the same ad group helps keep the campaign organized. Keywords within ad groups should be applicable to what the user will be searching for.

TRUSTWORTHY

- Transparency: Sharing key information regarding purchases, returns, fees, and policies delivers an honest and transparent experience.

- Contact: Make it easy for users to find contact information so that if there is a problem, they know how to get support.

- Verification: Safety and security help put users' minds at ease. Make it easy for customers to find verified factual details and policies, such as policies on data, privacy, returns, shipping, security, and terms and conditions. Also, prominently display certifications, awards, or reputable affiliations to improve credibility.

- Testimonials: Product reviews, case studies, and testimonials build trust. Showcasing unaltered reviews helps users understand the different ways customers interact with the brand.

EASY TO NAVIGATE

- Simplify: Give customers what they are looking for straight away and do not make them try and find it. Navigation should be easy to use, with offers and calls to action front and center. Clear and concise content highlighting customer benefits works best. Avoid long, wordy introductions.
- Visuals: Use lists, bullet points, high-quality images, headlines, and varying font sizes and weights. These all help provide visual hierarchy and draw users to the most important information quickly and easily.
- Shareable: Landing pages should have social media buttons at the top, and all images and videos should be easy to share.

RELIABLE

- Fast: Page load time is an important factor in user experience. Pages that take too long to load will be abandoned. The Lookout offers tools to test page load speed. This should be done frequently to ensure fast load time.
- Consistent across devices: Mobile friendliness is imperative for user experience. Users should have a consistent experience, whether using a desktop computer or a mobile device and across different browsers and operating systems.
- Minimize distractions: Certain features like pop-ups, flashing ads, or JavaScript can negatively impact user experience and can slow down page load time.

LOOKOUT

Tools to Test Page Load Time

1 Pagespeed.web.dev

2 GTmetrix.com

3 WebPageTest.org

4 Pingdom

Helpful Features

There are various useful features within Google Ads for creating a successful search campaign. Using these features can provide predictions as well as checks and balances for campaign structure and settings while also identifying and troubleshooting any issues that arise.

- **Campaign navigation menu:** allows for easy navigation between steps to get a holistic view of progress. Warnings for things like bidding, targeting, and budget selections will be highlighted here.
- **Campaign health check:** indicates any issues which could result in decreased performance or could lead to ads not being approved for serving.
- **Campaign forecast:** provides performance predictions based on selected options for bidding, targeting, and budget as well as other settings.
- **Campaign review:** specifies review of all campaign settings and provides notifications of any issues needing to be addressed to submit the campaigns for approval.
- **Drafts:** progresses campaigns from drafts to ads, providing there are no issues with campaign settings.

Disapproved Ads

Problems can occur as campaigns are being created. Some problems will slow down the progress of ad approval, and some can lead to the ads not being approved at all. Health checks can help find problems and provide guidance on how to correct them. When ads are disapproved, a notification email is sent which usually contains specifics on why the ad was rejected and how to correct it. Understanding the potential issues up front helps develop ads more likely to be approved. Some of these potential problems with ads can include:

- **Ad text length:** Keep in mind the length restrictions for ad text headlines (30 characters), descriptions (90 characters), and display URLs (15 characters). Exceeding the limits will result in ads being disapproved.
- **Spelling or grammar:** Strict spelling and grammar policies are used to ensure a high-quality user experience. Ads with typos or misspellings will be rejected. In the case of grammar, fragmented sentences are allowed, and minor grammar errors will usually not cause ads to be rejected.

- **Capitalization:** Using all capitals is a violation of the policy. First letters of proper nouns must be capitalized, and random capitalizing or non-proper noun capitalizing will cause ads to be rejected.

- **Punctuation and symbols:** Use of exclamation points in the headline or overuse in description will cause rejection of ads. Other repeated punctuation, non-standard symbols, or characters including asterisks, spaces, bullet points, and ellipses are also not allowed. Emojis, or excessive use of superlatives, numbers, or punctuation will lead to rejected ads.

- **Destination mismatch:** Ads must accurately reflect where the user is being directed. The root domain of the actual destination URL must match the display URL within the ad text.

- **Copyright or trademark infringement:** Avoid names or products that might be trademarked by competitors or other companies. Only the copyright owner or authorized representatives have rights to use a trademarked name within an ad.

- **Misleading or alternate call to action:** Ad copy cannot include a phone number, email address, or website address. The cost-per-click model is meant to encourage people to click on the ad. However, ad extensions and call-only ads can be used to direct users to alternate contact methods.

- **Unsuitable content:** Topics deemed inappropriate cannot be included in ads. This includes counterfeit goods, dangerous products or services, dishonest claims, and shocking or derogatory words.

- **Conversion potential limited by budget:** Specific numbers will be provided to help marketers understand the full potential of their campaign. While target cost per click or conversion may remain the same, a larger budget may lead to more conversions. Increasing the budget may lead to wider audience reach and higher conversion rates but also will obviously result in higher spend. The note will specify the recommended budget increase to deliver higher conversions.

- **Audience targeting too narrow in scope:** The targeting settings can sometimes narrow too much in terms of audience scope. This can limit the potential to reach the targets set out in the campaign. Removing or editing some of the audience targeting parameters can fix this issue.

- **Bidding and other settings prevent maximizing the set budget:** At times, the set budget cannot be spent due to bids being too low or targeting parameters being too tight.

Launching Successful Campaigns

To be successful with SEM, there are many important components that go into the launching of campaigns. We will review each of these in detail.

1 keywords

2 campaign setup

3 advertisements

4 match type

5 targeting

6 bidding

7 ad rank

8 quality score

9 advanced techniques

Keywords

Queries are the words a searcher types into a search engine, and keywords are what marketers use to match their marketing strategy with user queries. Keywords are the bullseye at the very center of an SEM (and SEO) strategy. Several components are involved in successfully building out a keyword strategy for SEM.

- research: determine most effective keywords by category
- grouping and organization: best practice is 10–30 keywords per ad group
- negative keywords: exclude specific keyword searches from a campaign
- keyword bid optimization: manually bidding at the keyword level allows maximum flexibility for overseeing ads at the most specific level, rather than a one-size-fits-all approach; this allows marketers to spend more on highest-converting keywords

One of the trickiest parts of keyword usage in SEM campaigns is juggling the head terms as well as the long-tail keywords. Shorter keyword phrases of three words or less are called head terms and are more generic terms that have higher search volume but, because they are broad, will not convert as well. On the other hand, long-tail keyword phrases containing four or more words are narrower in focus and convert better but have lower search volume. For example, if we are advertising our online shoe store, the keyword "running shoes" is very broad and will be more competitive with higher search volume. Even the keyword "women's running shoes" is broad and high level. However, the variation keyword "best running shoes for women" might see lower volume because it is more specific but could perform better and at a lower cost. See Figure 8.2 for an example of how long-tail keywords work.

The best bet when setting up keywords is to stay organized and test different variations. Using variants, variability, and words that may seem redundant can be a good way to test. Keywords and how they are organized should be revisited on a regular basis. Consider reviewing keywords weekly, monthly, and quarterly. Keyword reviews should focus on performance, relevance, and market forces. Identifying the top-performing keywords can help inspire new ideas and variations. Similarly, finding and pausing or removing the low performers can save budget and help reallocate. Relevance, market forces, and competitors change frequently and can drive changes to

FIGURE 8.2 Graphical Depiction of Long-tail Keywords

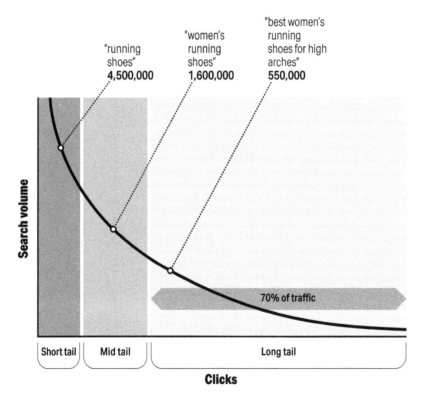

SEM keywords. Taking all of this into account will help determine the right changes to make during keyword research. Also, tools, chatbots, and AI plugins for software such as HubSpot and WordPress can accelerate the process of keyword research.

Campaign Setup

Paid search campaigns require an in-depth setup process. If they are not initially set up correctly, it can create unnecessary work in the future, possibly leading to a rebuild from scratch and loss of valuable data and insights. As we have learned, there are different campaign types within Google Ads, including search, display, shopping, video, and more. For our purposes, we will focus on the setup of search campaigns. Figure 8.3 provides a visual guide for setting up Google Ads Accounts.

- Primary settings: campaign type, daily budget, location targeting, bidding method, and ad rotation and scheduling.
- Goals: conversions, clicks, impressions, interactions, views, etc.

FIGURE 8.3 Google Ads Account Structure

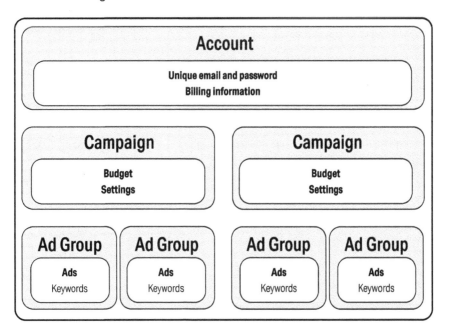

SOURCE WordStream®, 2022, https://www.wordstream.com/blog/ws/2022/05/10/google-ads-account-structure

- Account: determine the goal of the campaign when setting up the account.
- Campaigns: where targeting and budgets are determined. Campaigns should contain approximately 7–10 ad groups.
- Ad groups: campaigns are typically made up of more than one ad group. Ad groups should be organized by groups of related keywords with ads around a common theme.
- Each ad group should have several versions of ad copy and landing pages for optimal testing purposes. Ad groups have an indicator of status levels. When an ad group status is "eligible," that means the ad group is set to run. If an ad group has been labeled "not eligible," there is an issue. Issues could include a campaign suspension due to low funds or a campaign pending because it lacks creative elements or keywords. Ad groups should contain a maximum of around 20 keywords per ad group, with two or three ads per ad group.
- Keywords: use the keyword planner to develop keyword lists by product, category, or service.

Advertisements

Text ads have three parts: headlines, descriptions, and display URLs. The length limits are the same across all languages. Each character in double-width languages like Japanese, Korean, or Chinese counts as two characters.

- Headline: up to 30 characters, which can be up to three headlines separated by a vertical pipe (|). Using keywords in the headline is a best practice.
- Description: up to 90 characters, highlight information or details about a product, service, or brand. Best practice is to include a call to action. For example: "Buy Now," "Learn More," "See Pricing," or "Get a Quote."
- Display URL: this is usually in green and consists of the domain from the website and the text in the optional "path" field, which is up to 15 characters. The display URL is designed to help searchers understand where they will go if they click it; it does not have to match the actual URL path, which may be a much longer string of characters.

Google text ads allow for up to three headlines, two descriptions, and two paths. See the Lookout for a table with Google ad length limits. Text ads can also be created to automatically update with important information for customers. One ad can be created with text that updates dynamically based on keywords, business data, or time of day. New or existing ads can include dynamic text by using a brace ({) and select the type of dynamic text from the drop-down menu. For example, an ad selling walking shoes could use dynamic text to include keywords, highlight a specific product or price, or a countdown to a Black Friday sale.

Dynamic text ads can include:

- Keywords: dynamically inserted based on user search query. This increases relevancy for the searcher by including the keyword used in their search within the headline.

- Countdowns: to a certain event. This triggers a countdown widget and includes start and end timing for the countdown, as well as time zone and language preferences.

- Ad customizers: parameters that change based on a predetermined attribute like products, categories, or prices. This can be used to promote sale items, product details, discounts, or other variables.

- IF function: specific text inserted if a predetermined condition is met for device or audience. The parameter within the braces gets replaced by specified text as triggered by the user's search. This is beneficial when tailoring ads for mobile experiences or cart abandoners, for example.

LOOKOUT

TABLE 8.2 Length Limits

Field	Max length
Headline 1	30 Characters
Headline 2	30 Characters
Headline 3	30 Characters
Description 1	90 Characters
Description 2	90 Characters
Path (2)	15 Characters each

Match Type

Keyword match type helps refine when ads will show up. There are three types of matching in Google Ads: broad, phrase, and exact match. Negative keywords are also a tool to use in conjunction with match type to control when and how ads will display for different searches. Below is a description of the three match types, followed by additional information about negative keywords.

- **Broad match:** ad shows for searches that contain those keywords in any order and for related terms. Selecting broad match means that your ad shows for the broadest variety of searches. Be careful because this is the default setting for all campaigns. However, broad match takes several factors into account, such as user's recent search activity, landing page content, and other keywords within an ad group. This can lead to ads displaying for irrelevant searches and non-converting traffic.
- **Phrase match:** matches keywords to a phrase and close variations. Phrase match will reach fewer searchers than broad match but more searchers than exact match. Use quotation marks around those specific keywords that you want to include, such as "running shoes."
- **Exact match:** excludes searches other than the exact keywords selected. This match type gives advertisers the most control about when the ad will be displayed and who views it. Brackets can be used to indicate keywords for exact matching, such as "[running shoes]."

Negative Keywords

Advertisers can exclude undesirable or unwanted words or phrases from triggering an ad. Negative keywords can be used for broad, phrase, or exact match types. Use a minus sign (-) in front of words to exclude and be sure to also list out misspellings, synonyms, singular, and plural versions as well as close variations. Negative keywords can be broad, phrase, or exact match and can be added to campaigns or to ad groups. They can also be removed or edited at any time.

Many advertisers neglect to use this important feature. Negative keywords provide a critical layer of control for advertisers. For example, if the online shoe store does not sell sandals, the keyword sandals can be used as an exact match negative keyword to ensure that ads don't display for customers looking to purchase a product that is not available. Several free tools exist for discovering negative keywords, including Google's search term report and WordStream's negative keyword tool.

Targeting

Ideal customers may use certain devices or search from specific locations. Ad targeting allows marketers to select parameters for finding the right customers.

- **Device:** Target searchers based on mobile or desktop; take care to avoid unwanted ads on mobile by customizing device.
- **Location:** Target searchers by country, region, areas, or radius.
- **Day and time:** Creating an ad schedule allows ads to display during certain times.
- **Language:** Target ads to potential customers based on the language(s) they understand.
- **Demographics:** Include demographics such as age group, gender, and household income.
- **Exclusions:** Leave out specific audience segments from search campaigns.

Bidding

Bidding determines what you are willing to spend per click. Bid adjustments can increase or decrease bids when ads are competing to appear on specific devices, locations, or days and times.

- **Automated:** Smart bidding automates bids using machine learning to optimize campaigns based on goals such as cost per action (CPA) or return on ad spend (ROAS).
- **Manual:** Manual bidding allows marketers to manage their own bids either by ad group, keywords, or placements.

Ad Rank

Ad Rank thresholds are used to determine the position where an ad will show on a page relative to other ads. It is calculated using factors such as the bid amount, the auction-time ad quality, the context of the search, and others. Figure 8.4 visually demonstrates Ad Rank.

- **Bid amount:** Bid amounts depend on several factors, including campaign type, search volume, competition, and cost of keywords.
- **Ad relevance:** Ads must be relevant to the audience to be successful.

FIGURE 8.4 Ad Rank

Advertiser	Max bid	Quality score	Format impact	Ad rank
Henry	$4	Low	Low	18
Iris	$3	High	Low	10
Priya	$2	High	High	15
Sebastian	$1	Medium	Medium	8

- **Ad quality:** This is an estimate of the user's experience with an ad on Google and is based on several factors, including relevance to initial search, click-throughs, and quality of experience.

- **Format** (see below for more information on format): The ad format must be relevant and high quality.

Quality Score

Quality score is a diagnostic tool, on a scale of 1–10 and available at the keyword level, indicating how well your ad quality compares with other advertisers. Quality score is calculated based on three elements and evaluated as either above average, average, or below average. Quality score is based on historical impressions for exact searches, so keyword match type is not an indicator in quality score. This metric is important because higher quality scores drive better ad positions, lower costs, and increased exposure.

See the Lookout for four ways to use quality score to improve ad performance. Here are the three elements of quality score:

- expected click-through rate: likelihood that an ad will be clicked
- ad relevance: how closely an ad matches the search intent of the user
- landing page experience: relevance between the landing page and the ad itself

Quality score should be leveraged to help identify areas for improvement with ads, or what is commonly called ad quality. Ad quality is important in SEM because it is a metric that estimates the user experience with your ads. Ads must be relevant to searches, which is proven with ad clicks and landing page experience. Higher ad quality is generally an indicator of better performance, better ad positions, and lower costs. Ad quality affects whether an ad can display or not and where it will show up on the results page. It also affects which ad assets display and the cost for each click.

Because quality score is a keyword-level metric, there is no quality score for an entire campaign or account. However, that can be calculated based on taking an average of the metric across all keywords. A good quality score should be in the range of 7–10. Branded keywords should be on the higher end, while more general or ambiguous keywords would likely be on the lower end.

LOOKOUT

Four Ways to Use Quality Score to Improve Ad Performance

1 Review quality score components:

   a. expected click-through rate

   b. ad relevance

   c. landing page experience

2 Make ads more relevant to keywords:

   a. Use keywords within ad text.

   b. Split ad groups based on keyword groupings.

3 Work to improve ad metrics:

   a. Edit ad text or write new ads.

   b. Align details within each ad to the intent of the ad group and keywords.

   c. Experiment with calls to action, test different ideas.

4 Increase landing page effectiveness:

    a. Align landing pages with search intent.

    b. Include the same keywords from ad text within landing page copy.

    c. Improve mobile friendliness and load speed.

SEM Wins and Fails

Wins—robust campaign setup leads to a well-organized and data-driven account; there is no one-size-fits-all solution.

1 Set up campaigns wisely—focus on creating ad groups with themed groups of keywords and specific ad text and extensions.

2 Strong CTA—calls to action encourage people to take action. Try words like: "buy," "sell," "order," "learn," "shop," "browse," "try," or "find."

3 Utilize ad copy wisely—make the most of the available space by writing unique and creative ad copy.

4 Ad extensions—include useful information and help users find exactly what they're looking for, such as phone numbers, locations, price, reviews, and product pages.

5 Experiment—create several versions of the ad and allow Google to automatically rotate them and dynamically optimize the best-performing ad.

6 Landing pages—make sure the landing page matches the ad and track key metrics like conversions from landing pages.

7 Create device-specific ads—mobile searchers often want a phone number or address.

8 Optimize—make regular updates to SEM campaigns. There are many levers to pull. If something isn't working, the tricky part is figuring out the right lever.

Fails—garbage in leads to garbage out; don't set it and forget it.

1 Forgetting the CDJ—utilize SEM across the customer decision journey, not just for purchases; this delivers a competitive advantage.

2   Misuse of keywords—most Google advertisers include too many or too few keywords or underutilize match type by using default settings like broad match.

3   Competition lag—many insights about competitors can be gathered from SEM campaigns or AI, which informs campaign decisions like bid and position.

4   Not dayparting—one of the best features in Google Ads is "dayparting," which is the ability to target ads by day and time. For many businesses, weekend, holiday, or evening traffic can be low-converting. For some businesses, it's the opposite. Utilizing this feature can improve conversions and lower costs over the life of a campaign.

5   Mistakes—Google has an editorial and style guide that all ads must follow. Misuse of style, spelling, grammar, symbols, or characters will lead to ad disapproval.

6   Format—similarly, Google has requirements with formatting ads. For example, dynamic search ads can be removed by Google if duplicate URLs are being used.

7   Set it and forget it—this is the best way to waste marketing budget on Google Ads. Be sure to watch closely or work with people who will align goals with metrics.

8   Ditch SEO—SEO and SEM (and other digital marketing tactics) provide lift and attribution. Just like with traditional media, the more a user is exposed to a brand, the more likely they are to recall it. SEM delivers valuable insights into search behavior, demographics, and performance that is difficult to ascertain with SEO. When SEO and SEM work together, everyone wins.

Wrapping Up

Too many companies use a "set it and forget it" approach to SEM. Skipping steps like research and analysis and setting campaigns up in a rush can result in poor ad performance, reduced user experience, and misspend or over-spend of budget. SEM platforms like Google Ads include many settings and controls. Learning about the way these work will benefit the campaigns in various ways. Setting campaigns up correctly from the start will save time and reduce costs in the long run. Organizations with large budgets or small would benefit from taking a close look at campaign settings, structure, and organization to better understand the intricacies within. Factors like quality score, Ad Rank, bidding, targeting, and landing page have a large impact on costs as well as performance and should not be taken lightly.

CHAPTER SUMMARY

1 Research and analysis are important preliminary steps in effective SEM.

2 For successful outcomes, researching the market and the audience helps to determine the proper messaging.

3 Key pre-launch fundamentals of campaigns include naming, organizing, and integrating.

4 Defining objectives and selecting effective campaign types helps organize campaigns up front.

5 Installing conversion tracking, understanding attribution modeling, and preparing landing pages will all lead to SEM success, while knowing about helpful features and disapproved ads can help troubleshoot when issues arise.

6 When setting up campaigns for launch, there are numerous steps involved with no shortcuts. Attention to detail leads to better ad performance and lower costs.

Reflection Questions

- Have we taken the required steps prior to launching our SEM campaigns by researching and analyzing the market, competitors, audiences, trends, and messaging?

- Are we taking any shortcuts when it comes to SEM or do we have a full understanding of the nuances involved in effective campaigns?

- Are we using the right campaign types? Do we have conversion tracking? What is our attribution model?

- What are our defined objectives and how are we tracking those?

- Are our landing pages relevant, trustworthy, easy to navigate, and reliable?

- When were our campaigns set up and how often are they updated? Are they organized well and are we using long-tail keywords as part of the strategy?

- How well are we using match type, negative keywords, targeting, and ad text to drive performance?

- Do we have a grasp of indicators like ad rank and quality score?

- Are we spending enough time managing and monitoring our SEM campaigns and could they benefit from an overhaul?

9

Refreshing the SEM Approach

OBJECTIVES AND KEY RESULTS

- Review and revise campaigns after they have been set up, using helpful tools.
  - o Google Ads Performance Grader, the Preview and Diagnosis tool, and Ad Strength provide indicators of successful SEM outcomes.
- There are different types of ads within search, including responsive, dynamic, and performance max.
  - o Deliver the best possible ad campaigns by thoroughly understanding and selecting the right options.

- Examine ad enhancements to determine what formats, assets, and extras will improve campaign performance.

    o Stronger ad performance metrics reflect specific selections.

- Knowledge of the automation options within Google Ads opens opportunities.

    o Use machine learning and AI to automate bidding, targeting, and ad text when appropriate to provide efficiency and engagement.

- Comprehension of enhanced tracking options will drive improved outcomes.

    o Deliver increased performance measurement with URL options, URL parameters, and tag management.

Reviewing Campaign Setup

Once the Google Ads account and campaigns have been set up, there are tools to examine things at a closer level. In Chapter 10 we will cover measurement and optimization in more detail. However, using tools, marketers can get a sense of the performance to expect from their SEM campaigns. Tools can be used during ad campaign setup but can also be helpful after a campaign has launched.

Google Ads Performance Grader

Google Ads Performance Grader is a free assessment tool that grades Google Ads accounts and provides insights and action steps. Through a partnership with Google, this tool from WordStream offers helpful tips by comparing industry benchmarks and uncovering issues within the account. Google Ads Performance Grader can be used for many different purposes, but, ideally, it provides insight into any issues or problems within an account prior to or just after launch.

Ad Preview and Diagnosis Tool

Similarly, Google provides a tool within the Ads account to identify why ads or ad assets might not be displaying. If assets are not showing, the tool will provide causes and help troubleshoot issues. Using the tool, marketers can preview a search result page for specific search words to view ads and ad assets as they are appearing.

The Ad Preview and Diagnosis tool is a better way to preview ads than doing a search on Google, for two main reasons:

1 Using the Ad Preview tool will not impact campaign metrics and results, meaning it won't accumulate impressions for the searches performed within the tool.

2 Previewing offers a controlled environment to preview ads, removing some of the targeting and budgeting parameters that may influence how, where, or if an ad displays within a search.

Ad Strength

Another tool provided by Google helps advertisers focus on providing the best messages to their customers. Ad Strength is a metric measuring the relevance, quality, and diversity of ad text. It is measured as either incomplete, poor, average, good, or excellent, and provides action steps for improvement opportunities. Higher Ad Strength leads to better-performing ads and a better user experience. It is recommended that each ad group contains at least one high-performing ad, as determined by either a good or excellent ranking.

Ad Strength does not impact the serving eligibility of an ad, but it does offer improvement opportunities. Ad Strength includes two components: the overall ranking and the specific actions for improvement. Ad Strength can change over time and should be monitored frequently. Missing components, such as final URL, ad group, or keywords, will often trigger lower Ad Strength ratings.

Common recommendations for Ad Strength improvement:

1 Additional headlines or descriptions needed: Up to 15 headlines and four descriptions can be used in responsive ads. Many combinations can be created by maximizing the number of headlines and descriptions. Suggested assets will be provided in the ad creation process and can be accepted, edited, or ignored.

2 Unique headlines and descriptions: Avoiding repetitive words and phrases helps provide unique, different, and interesting combinations. Highlight

unique selling points and use words that spark interest and action whenever possible.

3 Inclusion of keywords: Including keywords within headlines and descriptions can increase relevancy. Suggestions will be provided based on keyword volume and popularity.

Responsive Search Ads

Responsive search ads provide automatic testing of different combinations of headlines and descriptions to find the highest-performing ads. Up to 15 descriptions and four headlines can be included, which leads to thousands of different combinations and versions of the ad, based on what the user searched for and search history. Responsive search ads can provide a more personalized and optimized experience for users, taking device type and preferences into account.

Advertisers still have control with responsive ads, meaning ads can be edited and closely managed. Pinning is a way to control outcomes. The default setting for responsive search ads will be that any headline and description combination can appear in any order. However, use of pinning allows control over where individual headlines and descriptions appear. For example, if there is a disclaimer that must appear in every ad, it can be pinned to description position 1 and thus will be included in all ads. Be aware that pinning a description to position 1 means that it will prevent other descriptions from showing, so the overall number of combinations is reduced. It is a best practice to consider pinning a couple of headlines or descriptions to each position to increase the number of combinations, when possible. Many advertisers avoid pinning altogether to increase the number of combinations and allow for greater testing and optimizing of ad text.

Benefits

Responsive search ads are not applicable for all campaigns; however, they can create efficiency and flexibility. The Lookout offers best practices for use of responsive search ads. Here are the main benefits of responsive search ads:

- **Flexibility:** Ads adapt to device size and location.
- **Efficiency:** Time is saved by providing opportunities for combinations of ad options.

- **Customization:** Headlines and descriptions are tailored to users based on preferences like search history, previous behavior, and keywords.

- **Increased reach:** Combinations provide opportunities to reach more queries and compete in more auctions.

- **Improved performance:** More auctions and search queries result in more visibility, clicks, and conversions.

LOOKOUT

Best Practices for Responsive Search Ads

1 Include unique and varied headlines and descriptions.

2 Test different offers within descriptions.

3 Utilize concise call to action (CTA) words.

4 Include keywords, products, and features whenever possible.

5 Experiment with different lengths for descriptions for device types.

Location Insertion

Another feature that creates efficiency for responsive search ads is location insertion. Using this tool, advertisers can tailor responsive search ad text to specific locations. The benefits of location insertion are creating efficiency and tailored messages that are localized based on physical locations or locations of interests. For example, a company that offers products that are delivered to all cities in the Bay Area would not need to write individual headlines containing each specific city. Instead, using the headline code "{LOCATION{City}}," the location within the ad group will be inserted automatically. Locations can be set up for city, state, and country, and there must be default headlines without the location insertion included in the ad group.

Dynamic Search Ads

Advertisers with a large inventory of products or a well-developed website can consider dynamic search ads (DSA), which use website content to target ads and to develop dynamic headlines and landing pages. Advertisers must create the descriptions for the ad text for DSAs. For campaigns where advertisers prefer a high level of control over their targeting, keywords, and ad text, this approach may not be the best option.

The main benefits here are increased reach and time-saving. Because DSAs use the website content to create headlines, it is essential that website content is relevant, clear, and up to date. An important difference between Bing and Google is that Bing's DSAs will allow advertisers to control their ad text, while Google Ads only allows customized descriptions. DSAs broaden reach by identifying keywords based on website content and search queries. This can be beneficial for larger organizations.

Targeting Options

DSAs offer different ways to target based on web pages or categories. DSAs can be set up with one of these options:

- **Specific web pages:** Select the exact URLs included in the campaign, ensuring that users land on well optimized pages.
- **All web pages:** Target the whole site with the option to exclude irrelevant pages to the campaign.
- **Categories:** Select from a list of categories and examples with keywords and landing pages.
- **Page feed:** Upload spreadsheet of URLs for focused, controlled targeting.

Exclusions

Because DSAs create scale and increase in audience size, understanding how to tighten targeting and increase advertiser control is beneficial. Negative keywords can be a favorable tool when creating DSAs. Just like with any ad group, to avoid ads displaying for irrelevant searches, create negative keyword lists for DSAs, or bring them over from other campaigns or ad groups. Negative keywords can be used at the campaign or keyword level and should not overlap with regular keywords.

There is also control over the dynamic ad targets, the bidding, and the budgets for DSAs. Additionally, advertisers have the option of layering further targeting over DSAs. It is recommended to test DSAs and, based on performance, consider changing the default setting from "observation" to "targeting," which provides ways to narrow the reach of the campaign to specific segments. For example, ads can be shown only to audiences who have previously visited the website. Overseeing these options helps maintain control even when using dynamic functions for ads.

Performance Max Ads

For advertisers looking to maximize the reach and scale of their ad campaigns, performance max ads (Pmax), which use artificial intelligence, can be an option. This goal-based campaign type provides access to all Google Ads inventory from one campaign, meaning that it works across all of Google's channels, including YouTube, Search, Discover, Gmail, and Maps. These campaigns are based on conversion goals and combine automation across bidding, budget, audiences, creative, and more. Figure 9.1 demonstrates the reach of performance max campaigns, which is not limited to search.

Pmax Ad Assets

Because Pmax will include ads outside of search, there will be additional ad assets needed, such as images, videos, and others. Unlike search campaigns— which rely on text ads consisting of headlines, descriptions, and destination

FIGURE 9.1 Performance Max Ads

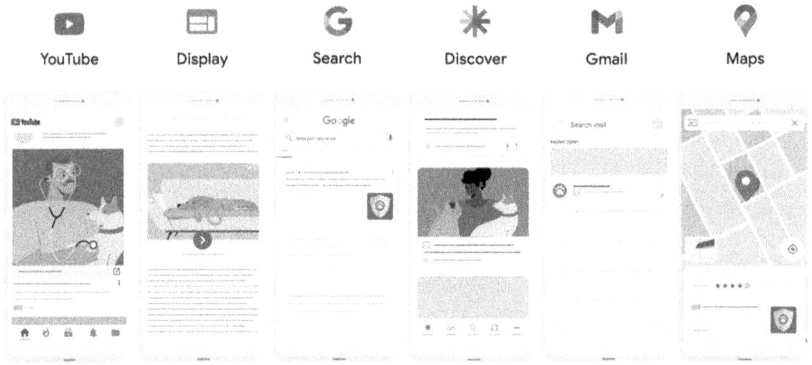

SOURCE Eduardo Indacochea (2021) Google Ads and Commerce Blog, Performance Max campaigns launch to all advertisers https://blog.google/products/ads-commerce/performance-max/

URLs—Pmax campaigns rely on additional resources. These campaigns are based around resource groups that contain specific asset groups with unique names.

Each asset group must contain the following elements:

- images: up to 20 images
- logos: up to five logos
- videos: up to five videos (if you do not add videos, they will be automatically generated)
- titles: up to five titles, 30 characters maximum
- long titles: up to five long titles, 90 characters maximum
- descriptions: one short description, 60 characters maximum, and up to four long descriptions, up to 90 characters maximum
- call to action: choose from different layouts and enter company or brand name
- ad URL: path to visible URL and final URL for mobile devices

Key Considerations

Here are a few things to keep in mind when considering if Pmax ads are the right choice for specific campaigns:

- Keywords from search campaigns are prioritized over Pmax campaigns: Pmax campaigns are prioritized over shopping campaigns but not search. Rather, the intention is that a Pmax campaign will allow display and video ads to run alongside a search ad campaign.
- Pmax is a performance-driven campaign type: Conversion tracking is key to informing the machine learning aspect of these campaigns.
- Budget allocation is not channel-specific: Machine learning will optimize budgets dynamically over time, but there is no ability to manually allocate budgets at this time.
- Exclusions are available at the account level: Excluding things like locations, products, or keywords can be a helpful way to provide exclusions from the automation. Brand terms and other brands can also be excluded.
- Video creation is available: Google provides integrated video creation tools to make it easier to create high-quality video assets.

Benefits and Challenges

Pmax ads can be powerful for organizations that are looking to scale campaigns and increase performance. However, like anything, these automation capabilities also have drawbacks.

Automation can be a helpful tool with time-consuming aspects of SEM. Here are valuable benefits to Pmax ads:

- **Efficiency:** Automation provides efficiency by using machine learning for specific time-consuming campaign components. Setting up Pmax ads is quick and easy in most cases.

- **Optimization:** Automated adjustments to bids and targeting can provide increased efficiency with ad optimization. Because these campaigns are goal-based, achieving conversions can happen faster and more efficiently with automation.

- **Increased reach:** Ads shown across a massive network like Google's have the potential to reach larger audiences through a single campaign through YouTube, Gmail, and more. These campaigns will have much higher levels of ad impressions.

- **Identify new audiences:** Utilizing search engines' real-time data around user preferences and search intent, Pmax campaigns provide opportunities to target similar audiences across multiple channels.

- **Creative:** Google's automation makes it easier and more cost-effective to create multiple versions of ads with creative assets including video, images, and logos.

Automation has its limitations. As such, several weaknesses exist for Pmax ads, including:

- **Visibility into campaign specifics:** A lower level of detail is provided about campaign specifics, leading advertisers to trust the automation engine rather than maintain comprehensive control over campaign aspects like locations and keywords.

- **Campaign control:** Bidding and targeting are automated through machine learning, meaning that advertisers cannot control these campaign components at the keyword level. Rather, advertisers must trust that the automation process will deliver the best results of the campaigns.

- **Limited insights:** Advertisers cannot see keyword-level reporting on impressions, clicks, and overall insights. The AI function of Pmax campaigns is meant to automatically optimize without providing the same level of detailed reporting as a manually run search campaign.

- **Ad cannibalizing:** It is possible that ads can be cannibalizing because Pmax covers such a broad range of ads, meaning that an AI-generated, broad Pmax ad could supersede a manually created, specific search ad.

Advanced Features

There are many other advanced features within Pmax ads, such as ad extensions, audience signals, and asset optimization. As with search ads, ad extensions for Pmax ads can be used for sitelinks, location, and call extensions. We will examine ad extensions closely later in this chapter. Audience signals help by using audience insights to determine where ads will display. This provides the ability to enhance ad targeting by segmenting audiences based on demographics, interests, browsing history, and search history. It is important to note that although audience signals can be used, they will not be the only targeting criterion for Pmax ads, which will go beyond those targeting parameters based on AI-generated data and information. Finally, asset optimization offers performance data on how ad assets, including text, images, and videos, are performing. This provides optimization opportunities for removing low-performing ad assets and focusing on delivering the top-performing ads within the campaign.

Pmax ads are relatively new to the world of SEM and should be monitored closely. As with anything—even automation—understanding and scrutiny are key components. Using this approach may be better suited for experienced SEM professionals with a thorough understanding of the tools, reporting, and optimizations available with Pmax ads. Testing is also recommended to see if automation works in specific aspects of the SEM strategy. Knowing that Google offers automation tools to save time for advertisers also comes with the understanding that automation delivers increased revenue to Google and decreased control for advertisers.

Enhanced Ads

Apart from using automated ad types like responsive, dynamic, and performance max, there are other ways to enhance campaign performance at the ad level. Comprehensive understanding and use of ad formats, ad assets, sitelinks, and ad extensions can provide closer control and increased performance of SEM campaigns in the long run.

Ad Formats

Visual enhancements can be included with ads to assist with displaying information or content about a business such as phone numbers, website domain, reviews, or third-party content. Within ad formats are ad assets that can include various types of information that help users obtain additional information directly within the ad. Enhancements to ads can be added manually or automatically, or in combination, based on selected settings within the Google Ads system.

Ad Assets

Ad assets, formerly called ad extensions, are the different pieces of content that make up an ad. For search ads, these are headlines, descriptions, links, call buttons, and location information. Depending on individual search queries, assets will come together to create the right ad for each search. It is generally understood that including more assets leads to better performance because, over time, the best assets and combinations will be automatically generated through machine learning. Some assets are manually created, and some are automatic, depending on the campaign type and other factors. Assets can be added, removed, pinned, and edited within the account.

The most common assets are sitelinks and account-level automated assets. There are also callout assets, image assets, app assets, lead form assets, and more. Using sitelinks and automated assets, advertisers can include helpful links and information within ads that deliver a better user experience and higher performance metrics. Ads containing links to specific pages, information about hours and locations, and seller ratings are more comprehensive and get higher click-through rates, in general. To get a deeper understanding, let's explore sitelinks and account-level automated assets at a closer level. Also, ad assets are covered in greater detail in Chapter 10.

SITELINKS

Including supplementary links to interior site pages delivers a better ad experience with more opportunities for users to find what they need. Users can select specific pages based on important information, such as a specific product, phone numbers, or locations. Sitelinks provide an easy-to-use and easy-to-manage feature for advertisers. They are typically created at the account level and can be used across campaigns and ad groups. Link text should be short and concise, making it easy for users to understand the destination of the link. Sitelinks are limited to 25 characters in most languages and can be added, edited, paused, removed, and scheduled within ad assets. Sitelinks can also be optimized to show specifically on mobile devices.

Sitelinks appear in different ways, based on campaign aspects like device, position, and other factors. Link text repetition, punctuation, symbols, and duplicate URLs are not allowed. Similarly, third-party URLs will lead to disapproved ads. Figure 9.2 illustrates the use of sitelinks within a Google Ad.

In search campaigns:

- Sitelinks appear in text ads at the top and bottom of search results pages.
- Desktop-displaying ads:
  o must have at least two sitelinks
  o can show up to six sitelinks
  o can appear on the same line or fill up to two lines
- Mobile-displaying ads:
  o must have at least one sitelink
  o can show up to eight sitelinks
  o can appear side by side or single in carousel format, or can swipe left to right for viewing multiple sitelinks

FIGURE 9.2 Ad on Google with Sitelinks

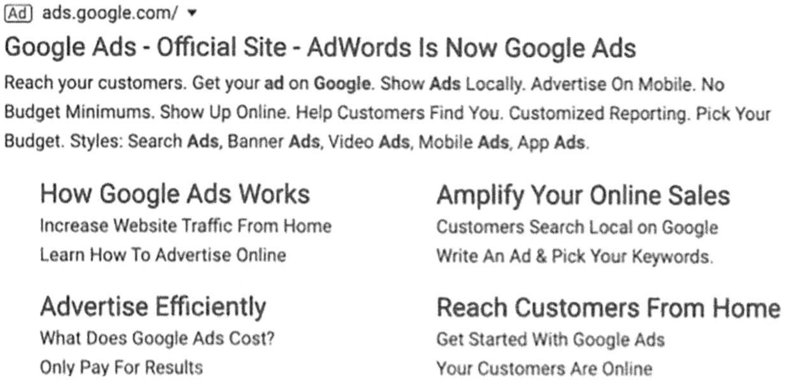

[Ad] ads.google.com/ ▾

Google Ads - Official Site - AdWords Is Now Google Ads

Reach your customers. Get your **ad** on **Google**. Show **Ads** Locally. Advertise On Mobile. No Budget Minimums. Show Up Online. Help Customers Find You. Customized Reporting. Pick Your Budget. Styles: Search **Ads**, Banner **Ads**, Video **Ads**, Mobile **Ads**, App **Ads**.

How Google Ads Works
Increase Website Traffic From Home
Learn How To Advertise Online

Amplify Your Online Sales
Customers Search Local on Google
Write An Ad & Pick Your Keywords.

Advertise Efficiently
What Does Google Ads Cost?
Only Pay For Results

Reach Customers From Home
Get Started With Google Ads
Your Customers Are Online

NOTE Screenshot of Google search, 2023, keyphrase: Google Ads. Google and the Google logo are trademarks of Google LLC.

AUTOMATED ASSETS

Account-level automated assets are created automatically and can be used in conjunction with manually created assets. These are often a good idea to test alongside manual assets to optimize performance and combinations. There are different types of account-level automated assets:

- **Dynamic sitelinks:** drive people to the right place on the website. For example, a restaurant may include links to a menu or map page.

- **Dynamic structured snippets:** provide additional descriptions about a business or its products and services. Advertisers can control dynamic structured snippets by pausing or removing them from the ad assets.

- **Automated location assets:** help people quickly find business location information, such as address, directions, or distance to location. This may also include a phone number or call button.

- **Seller ratings:** show reviews and additional seller rating information, such as stars, number rating, or a qualifier like delivery time.

- **Dynamic callouts:** display relevant information about products and services, like "10 years of experience" or "Book online."

Automation

Over the past several years automation has played an increasingly large role in SEM. Google has and will continue to focus on automation and AI-based tools for the Google Ads platform. Many of these tools are useful for increasing efficiency and reducing the manual burden and heavy lifting of campaign creation and management. However, advertisers must fully understand automation and test it prior to becoming reliant on it for all of their campaign needs. Bidding, targeting, and ad creation are three of the top areas where automation can be employed to increase exposure while reducing workloads and manual operations. Keep in mind that there is a learning period with any automation and patience may be required to get to the point of advanced automation strategies.

Automated Bidding

While manual bidding is still an option in Google Ads, for most advertisers the automated option can be useful by creating efficiency. The bidding strategy should be tailored based on the goal of the campaign. For lead generation or sales goals, the bidding strategy should be tied directly to conversions. For brand awareness or recognition campaigns and for website traffic campaigns, bidding can be aligned with target clicks or maximum cost-per-click strategies. As stated, there is a learning period with automation and specific to automated bidding. See the Sidebar for more information on Google's learning period. To minimize or avoid the learning period, consider the best bid strategy and test it prior to using automated bidding. Also, only change budgets by 20 percent or less to minimize impact during testing. Google's learning period applies to smart bidding and should be understood prior to testing.

SIDEBAR

Question: What does Google mean when they say "learning"?

Answer: Bid strategies take time for performance data collection and analysis. This learning period only applies to smart bidding and typically lasts seven days.

More information: The learning period can be triggered by a new bidding strategy, changes in settings or with conversion tracking, changes to budget or bid, or significant campaign changes.

Automated Targeting

Missed opportunities can be avoided using automated targeting options in Google Ads. Using a combination of performance data and machine learning provides two ways to automate targeting within a search campaign.

1 dynamic ad groups: leverages the website instead of keywords to automatically target the right queries to the ads within a campaign

2 broad match keywords: uses broadly defined keywords to automatically find large quantities of other queries that are seemingly relevant to the campaign

Ad Text

Dynamic text ads, as described earlier in this chapter, offer dynamically generated ads using different combinations of ad assets. This can create efficiency across campaigns. Dynamic keyword insertion is another way to create automatic, customized ads that include the keyword or keywords that were used in the search query. This easy-to-use tool delivers higher engagement and a better experience for the user. This is simply formatted using the following code: "{Keyword: Your Phrase}" for sentence case. If the search term is too long to fit within the set character limits, Google will insert the text included within the keyword insertion code.

Although this can be a useful tool, it is important to remember not to use dynamic keyword insertion for competitors' names or anything else that could be a trademark violation. This tool works best in ad groups with tight themes, like products or services. Dynamic keyword insertion should be monitored to ensure strong performance within ad groups and for specific keywords.

Similar to dynamic keyword insertion, other automation is available at the ad text level, including countdown customizers, IF functions, and more. Experimenting with automation is the best way to determine what works best for particular campaigns, ad groups, and keywords.

Automated Rules

To set up automatic changes based on preconfigured settings and conditions within a campaign, automated rules can be used. Automated rules can be applied to ad scheduling, status, bids, budgets, positions, and more. Automated rules can take specific actions or can simply trigger an email alert, which saves time monitoring campaigns. Additionally, using JavaScript code, automated scripts can be used to create automated changes and rules within accounts and campaigns. Scripts are recommended for large campaigns or multiple accounts within a managed account. Below are examples of common uses of automated rules.

- **Promotional events:** Turn specific ads on or off for a promotional event.
- **Repeating ads:** Turn ads on or off based on a schedule, such as weekends or holidays.
- **Pause keywords:** Low-performing keywords can be paused based on performance metrics, such as high cost per conversion or low click-through rate.
- **Apply labels:** Create groups of labels within campaigns, ad groups, keywords, and ads.

- **Target position:** Change bids based on desired average position for an ad.

- **Bid scheduling:** Raise bids higher during certain hours within the day.

- **Budget cap:** Pause campaigns that have reached a specified budget.

- **Increase budget:** Raise budgets based on performance metrics, such as cost per conversion.

Enhanced Tracking

Running SEM ads will automatically deliver certain tracking information, such as how many times an ad was displayed and the number of clicks. There are ways to enhance the tracking of SEM campaigns using tags and URL parameters. This can provide additional information about the device type, source, and keyword for particular users. There are several ways to enhance tracking with SEM campaigns, including URL options, URL parameters, and tag management. These can be used in combination or separately and should be used with an enhanced analytics solution. Enhanced tracking provides deeper understanding of campaign performance and improved optimization.

URL Options

URL options provide additional tracking and are created at the account, campaign, keyword, or sitelink level. URL options should be used at the campaign, account, or ad group level. That way these can be changed without the need to resubmit ads for approval. If URL options are included at the keyword, ad, or sitelink level, they will need to go through the review process whenever the URL options are updated. There is a "test" button that will check that the URL tracking is set up properly.

There are three main sections within URL options:

1 Tracking template: the field containing tracking information that will be added to a final URL to create a landing page. This is an advanced and sophisticated feature that may not be needed in most cases.

2 Custom parameter: a URL parameter that is created and customized by the advertiser and added to tracking templates. This allows for maximum advertiser customization to tracking.

3 Final URL suffix: parameters that will be attached to the end of the landing page to track specific information.

URL Parameters

Tracking specific information, such as the source or keyword for specific traffic, is passed along through destination URLs using URL parameters. These parameters consist of a key and a value, which is separated by an equals sign (=). Parameters always come after a question mark (?) within a URL and each parameter can be separated by an ampersand (&). An example of a URL using parameters is: www.sample.com?product=12345&utm_source=google. In this example, we are able to track this specific destination URL and its source (Google). In other words, this click will be attributed to Google as the source.

In Google Ads, two types of parameters can be used for enhanced tracking:

1 Content modifying parameters: passing information to the landing page and exclusively within the final URL. For example: www.sample.com?product=12345 will send a user directly to the product 12345 page.

2 Tracking parameters: passing information from the campaign, account, ad group. These can be either custom or ValueTrack:

   a. Custom: advertiser-defined value such as a campaign like Black Friday.

   b. ValueTrack: URLs within the parameter tracking predefined values like "device," which provides tracking of the user device type.

Tag Management

A system for managing digital marketing deployments and data sources is commonly referred to in digital marketing as tag management. Tags, or short code snippets, are added to URLs to enable data collection and analysis. Typically, tags are executed by browsers and instruct browsers to send data to a collection server, which stores and analyzes the data. Web analytics, digital marketing, and data science are common uses for tag management.

Different third-party software options can be used to manage tracking tags. Some companies that offer tag management systems include Google Tag Manager, Adobe Launch, Tealium, and Signal. Tag management systems (TMSs) offer tag management capabilities to marketing teams without heavy lifting from IT or technical teams. A TMS is a container for all marketing tags that can be used across web pages, videos, and apps. Tags are sometimes referred to as beacons or pixels and collect various types of information, including user context, user profile, and user behavior data. Cookies, as opposed to tags, are textual strings of code that are stored, usually within a browser, to remember user preferences like username, password, or shopping cart contents. Tags and cookies are not the same thing, and with the ongoing deprecation of third-party cookies, tags are becoming the most important method of tracking for digital marketing.

One of the benefits of using a TMS is the enhanced data provided for marketers. Tags are easy to use and reduce dependence on technical teams for setup and management. Tagging systems like Google Tag Manager also offer useful templates and supported tags, making it easier for marketers to tag and track the most important campaign elements. Another key benefit is that well-configured tag managers provide enhanced performance, including load speed optimization. Because many tag managers are free, including Google Tag Manager, they are frequently used by businesses for enhanced tracking in an organized, easily updated solution. Figure 9.3 shows how a tag management system works between the website and the third-party systems like Google Ads, Bing, Facebook, and more.

FIGURE 9.3 Tag Management Systems

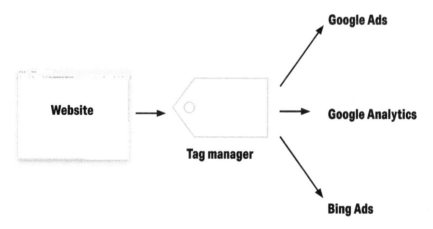

Google Ads

Website → **Tag manager** → **Google Analytics**

Bing Ads

Tags are generally used for:

- **user context:** information such as IP address, browser type, referral type
- **user profile:** anonymous data stored within a browser cookie, such as profile ID or specific targeting parameters
- **user behavior:** product, category, or content within ads viewed, links clicked, time on site

Although tagging has become an important and widely used tracking mechanism, there are challenges associated with tagging in digital marketing, particularly about third-party solutions. Several considerations exist when analyzing tag management systems and whether to use them. Answering specific questions will help determine the right course of action with tagging.

- **Ownership:** Who owns the data and its collection process? The more tags, the more potential third parties accessing the data.
- **Implementation:** Processing and managing is a well-known and well-documented challenge requiring custom coding and management. Who is responsible? Tagging can fall to busy IT teams, marketing teams, or third-party agency partners.
- **Privacy:** Various tags can cause privacy concerns due to third-party access. Privacy regulations across different industries and geographies are continuously being updated and can cause challenges for operational oversight. What are the privacy issues at hand?
- **Performance:** Multiple tags can produce latency and delay page load speed, thus degrading the user experience over time. Manually configured tags can have a particularly negative impact on load speed. How can tagging increase performance?

Google Tag

The Google tag (gtag.js) is a single tag ID that is added to a website to measure performance in Google Ads and in Google Analytics. A tag ID is a unique identifier that is managed and configured within Google and used across Google destinations. It is important to provide users with privacy and consent options that clearly represent the data collection, sharing, or use. Setting up the Google tag can be done manually or using a website builder like Wix or Squarespace or a content management system like WordPress, Drupal, or HubSpot. Google Analytics can also be used to set up a Google tag. Once the Google tag is set up, it can be configured and managed to provide specific tracking information. With the Google tag, the following configuration settings are available:

- **Manage automatic event detection:** Configure specific events to automatically detect.

- **Configure domains:** Specify a list of domains to be included in cross-domain tracking.

- **User-provided data capabilities:** Include or leave out any specific user-provided data.

- **Define internal traffic:** Define specific IP address to define traffic as internal.

- **List unwanted referrals:** Specify domains whose traffic should not be counted as referral traffic.

- **Adjust timeout sessions:** Define how long sessions last before being considered a timeout.

- **Override cookie settings:** Change settings for cookie tracking, such as how long cookies last.

Google tags can be accessed through both Google Ads and Google Analytics. Managing the tag allows editing the tag name, combining multiple tags, and adding or removing destinations for tagging. The Tag Assistant can be used to check the implementation of a tag or troubleshoot and debug tags. Often connection issues are the root cause of tag issues and can be corrected easily by updating the URL or testing the debug parameter, which can cause pages to break or behave differently. Tag Assistant also has a Chrome extension that can be installed in the browser to provide detection and debugging sessions for Google tags. Tagging is an increasingly important part of successful tracking and measurement of SEM campaigns and should be thoroughly understood and implemented strategically to enhance performance.

CASE STUDY
BFO and Arizona Tile Use SEM to Drive Awareness and Conversions

Introduction

Arizona Tile, a family-owned business founded in 1977, imports more than 230 varieties of granite, marble, limestone, travertine, quartz, and quartzite slabs and tile, and is one of the leading tile and slab distributors in the United States. Carrying over 40 series of porcelain and glass tile, their relationships with manufacturers allow them to develop new product lines, many of which are only available at their locations throughout the western United States. Arizona Tile partnered with BFO to drive their digital marketing strategy, specifically with paid search (SEM) initiatives.

Goals

Arizona Tile and BFO worked together to establish their goals for SEM. Utilizing key features of Microsoft and Google Ads, they could maximize qualified traffic to drive conversions and sales. Monitoring traffic quality metrics combined with conversion metrics would deliver the best approach and provide optimization insights for the future.

Strategy

In a crowded marketplace, Arizona Tile found it hard to stand out. Not having the brand reach like "big box" home improvement stores and balancing the multi-channel approach of selling to the trade as well as directly to the consumer, Arizona Tile needed to be able to control their messaging while reaching a targeted audience. Utilizing Google and Microsoft Ads, with multiple ad formats, and leveraging SEM insights, first-party data, and machine learning, Arizona Tile was able to reach new users to drive efficient site traffic, driving conversions.

Actions

Leveraging SEM insights, first-party data, and machine learning, Arizona Tile selected Google and Microsoft Ads, given the ability to target users actively searching for the products they offer. The capabilities of paid search, including ad formats, audience targeting, and customization, were primary drivers. Keyword targeting included Arizona Tile brand terms, specific geographies, and surface types: quartzite, granite, porcelain.

Beyond keyword targeting, in-market and affinity audiences were also used to reach prospective customers based on their browsing interests and behaviors. In addition, retargeting ads allowed for re-engaging previous site visitors to bring them back to the Arizona Tile site to complete on-site conversions.

Google Search ads, Google discovery ads, performance max ads, and YouTube ads were used given their ability to reach users throughout the research and buying process. To showcase additional features and their unique value proposition, Arizona Tile utilized advanced features including sitelinks, callout extensions, structured snippets, image extensions, and location extensions across search campaigns.

Through ongoing bid and budget management, the BFO team developed and optimized campaigns as granularly as possible, going so far as to adjust bids at the audience, demographic, and device level, to maximize efficiency and drive successful results. Initially, maximize conversion goals were set at the campaign level, but it was soon realized that this bidding strategy limited site traffic and ad spend. As a result, the bidding strategy was changed to maximize clicks, resulting in an increase in site traffic, alongside increased conversions at a lower CPA.

Results

Through this combination of targeted paid search advertising combined with an omnichannel strategy, Arizona Tile was able to increase the number of qualified users visiting their site, leading to an overall increase in site visitors, visitors' time on site, and on-site conversions year over year. Figure 9.4 illustrates the top-performing ad in Google Search from May 2023. Results from the campaign include:

- New users increased 40 percent.
- Click-through rate improved 29 percent.
- Conversion rate improved 38 percent.
- Cost per conversion decreased 9 percent.

Insights

- Leveraging SEM advertising to target specific products and geographies can drive traffic and increase sales.
- Advanced SEM techniques like automation and machine learning can drive the performance of ad campaigns and provide optimization opportunities for future planning.

FIGURE 9.4 Google Text Ad for Arizona Tile

Ad · www.arizonatile.com/tiles/kitchen ▼
Arizona Tile Near You Stone, Granite, Marble & More | Unique, Hand-Selected Surfaces
No matter the project, Arizona Tile helps visualize your design before committing. Stop in to see and touch extraordinary surfaces we've hand selected from around the world.
Porcelain & Ceramic · Della Terra® Quartz · Marble · Limestone
Types: Porcelain, Quartzite, Granite

| Product Finder | Tile Visualizer |
| Find a Location | New Products |

NOTE Screenshot of Google search, 2023, Google Ads top-performing search ad. Google and the Google logo are trademarks of Google LLC.

Wrapping Up

SEM campaigns offer various and advanced tools that must be fully identified and understood. Organizations must leverage the right tools, options, automation, machine learning, and AI to be fully successful with advertising. To do so, businesses can leverage different ad types and automated processes that deliver efficient management of campaigns. However, we can never forget the importance of close monitoring of campaign budgets, bidding, targeting, and ads—even when automation is present. Similarly, proper tagging and management of tracking delivers the best performance and outcomes for SEM campaigns in the long run.

CHAPTER SUMMARY

1   Reviewing and revising campaign setup can be made easier with useful tools like Google Ads Performance Grader, the Preview and Diagnosis tool, and Ad Strength.

2   There are different types of ads within Search, including responsive, dynamic, and performance max. Understanding the features, benefits, and drawbacks of each will help determine the right fit for SEM campaigns.

3   Ad enhancements including formats, assets, and sitelinks can increase engagement and performance of ads.

4   Automation options using machine learning and AI, like automated bidding, automated targeting, and automated ad text options, can produce efficiency in the creation and management of SEM campaigns.

5   Enhanced tracking options, like URL options, URL parameters, and tag management, will drive improved ad performance measurement over time.

6   Tag management systems and the Google tag offer solutions for deeper tracking and measurement of SEM campaigns.

Reflection Questions

•   Do we have a strong process in place to review and revise our SEM ad campaigns?

•   Are we using the right tools to help identify issues or troubleshoot when needed with SEM campaign setup?

- Do we have a thorough understanding of the different types of ads within Search and are we using them effectively?

- Do we know how to leverage responsive, dynamic, and performance max ads as needed within our search marketing strategy?

- Is our organization leveraging ad enhancements like sitelinks to display the best possible advertisements for our customers?

- Are we fully utilizing ad formats and ad assets to create the most effective combinations of headlines, descriptions, and destination URLs for our ads?

- Do we have the full picture of how machine learning, artificial intelligence, and automation can enhance our strategy with bidding, targeting, and ad text?

- How can tag management systems like Google TMS, Signal, or others help us store, manage, and update our digital marketing tags?

- What are the challenges, such as privacy and ownership, associated with tag management and how will they impact our organization?

10

Advanced Techniques to Measure and Optimize a Campaign

OBJECTIVES AND KEY RESULTS

- Measuring outcomes starts with metrics and key performance indicators (KPIs).
  - Tracking metrics such as CTR, CPC, CPA, and ROAS will lead to better SEM outcomes.
- Google Analytics and Google Ads data can be combined to deliver meaningful data and insights.
  - Custom and advanced reporting can provide meaningful insights and future optimization opportunities.

- Keyword research is an ongoing part of SEM.
    - Progressive techniques such as match types, monitoring, and long-tail strategies pay long-term dividends.
- SEM campaigns benefit from testing, optimization, and advanced methodologies.
    - Utilize experiments with ad copy, targeting, and CTAs along with advanced methods like ad extensions, match type mirroring, and dynamic keyword insertion to take SEM campaigns to the next level.
- Fraud is a reality in digital marketing and in SEM.
    - Knowing how to identify, detect, and defend against ad fraud, or invalid activity, is an important component in SEM success.

Key SEM Metrics

When measuring the success of a paid search campaign on Google Ads, there are several important KPIs. These can help businesses understand how their campaigns are performing and drive data-driven decisions to optimize future advertising efforts.

1 Impressions: An impression refers to the number of times an ad is displayed on a user's screen. Each time an ad is displayed on a search results page, a website, or a mobile app, it is counted as one impression. For some marketers, impressions are an important metric in online advertising because they represent the potential reach of an ad. However, impressions do not equate to clicks or conversions, and therefore are considered less important than metrics like CTR, CPC, and quality score.

2 Click-through rate (CTR): This metric measures the percentage of users who clicked on your ad after seeing it. A higher CTR indicates that your ad is relevant and engaging to your target audience.

3 Cost per click (CPC): This is the amount paid for each click of an ad. A lower CPC indicates more value for advertising dollars.

4 Conversion rate: This metric measures the percentage of people who took a desired action, such as making a purchase or filling out a form. A higher conversion rate indicates that the ad is effectively driving the right type of traffic.

5 Cost per acquisition (CPA): This metric measures the cost of acquiring a new customer or lead. It considers both the cost of advertising and the conversion rate of a campaign.

6 Return on ad spend (ROAS): This metric measures the revenue generated from your advertising campaign compared with the cost of the campaign. A higher ROAS indicates that a campaign is generating a positive return on investment (ROI).

7 Quality score: This metric measures the relevance and quality of your ads and landing pages. A higher quality score can lead to a lower CPC and better ad placement.

By tracking these KPIs, marketers can glean valuable insights into the effectiveness of paid search campaigns. This data can be used to measure and optimize campaigns, improve ROI, and make informed decisions about future advertising budgets and efforts. These are the key calculations for SEM campaign measurement:

$$ROAS = \frac{Campaign\ Revenue}{Cost\ of\ Campaign}$$

$$Cost\ per\ Acquisition = \frac{Total\ Amount\ Spent}{Total\ Conversions}$$

Google Analytics and SEM

Google Analytics (GA) is a powerful tool that can be used to track and analyze the performance of Google Ads campaigns. By linking Google Ads with Google Analytics, marketers gain a deeper understanding of ad performance, leading to data-driven decisions to optimize campaigns.

Here are several ways that GA can be used in conjunction with Google Ads to deliver deeper measurement and analysis:

1 **Track conversions:** Google Analytics can track website conversions that result from clicks on specific ads. This helps in understanding which ads are driving the most conversions and therefore adjusting campaigns accordingly.

2 **Analyze user behavior:** Using GA, marketers can identify insights into how users interact with website pages after clicking on ads. Tracking time on site, pages per visit, and exit pages can help optimize landing pages and improve user experience.

3 **Evaluate demographics:** GA can provide demographic data about the users who click on your ads, such as age, gender, and location. This information can be used to create more targeted and effective campaigns.

4 **Monitor bounce rates:** Tracking the bounce rate of landing pages within GA helps monitor performance and user experience. A high bounce rate indicates that users are leaving without taking any action, which can be a sign that ads or landing pages need to be improved.

5 **Monitor ad performance:** Deeper performance data from Google Ads campaigns can be integrated into GA, including click-through rates, cost per click, and conversion rates. This information can be used to optimize campaigns and to identify trends and patterns compared with other digital marketing channels.

Reporting

Creating reports that summarize and analyze campaign data from Google Ads and Google Analytics can be an important step in optimizing campaigns. Combining data from these two sources delivers a deeper understanding of how ads are performing across campaigns, landing pages, and the customer journey. Also, tracking trends and metrics over time allows for the identification of patterns within the data. For example, seasonality can be recognized with campaigns over time, and future recommended adjustments to budgets or bids can be made to accommodate spikes or drop-offs in traffic or conversions.

Here are the necessary steps to take for creating reports that summarize and analyze campaign data from Google Ads and Google Analytics:

1 **Identify KPIs:** Before creating reports, it is important to determine which KPIs are most important to the business and the campaign goals. These may include metrics such as click-through rate, conversion rate, and cost per acquisition. Focusing on KPIs can help gain a clearer understanding of how campaigns are performing.

2   **Use Google Ads and Google Analytics:** Google Ads provides extensive SEM data and Google continues tracking after a user clicks an ad. Using these tools together gathers data on selected KPIs, as well as other relevant metrics, and connects the customer journey back to ad performance. Consider behavioral data, landing page metrics, and content and engagement performance when determining what to include within reporting.

3   **Organize data:** Once the data has been gathered, organize it in a way that creates a flow and makes it easy to understand. This may involve creating tables or charts to visualize data or grouping data by specific metrics or time periods.

4   **Analyze data:** Once the data is organized, analyze it to identify patterns or trends. Look for areas where your campaigns are performing well, as well as areas where improvements can be made. This analysis can help optimize campaigns for enhanced future performance. Analysis is a key ingredient for strong reporting and cannot be skipped.

5   **Create your report:** Finally, use the organized and analyzed data to create a report that summarizes campaign performance. This report should include KPIs, as well as relevant metrics or insights that can help business marketing executives and stakeholders make informed decisions.

By following these steps, reports can summarize and analyze campaign data from Google Ads and Google Analytics. These reports can provide valuable insights to drive optimization campaigns for better performance and greater ROI. Review the Lookout for SEM reporting best practices.

LOOKOUT

SEM Reporting Best Practices

1   Use visuals to convey information: Visuals such as charts and graphs help make data more understandable and digestible. Use them to highlight trends and patterns with data.

2   Customize reports: Every business has unique needs, goals, and stakeholders, so tailor reports accordingly. Use customizable reporting options to create reports that provide the information needed to make informed decisions. Also, consider developing customized reports for unique audiences. For example, technical teams use different data than marketers or executives.

3   Keep it simple: Avoid overwhelming reports with too much information or data. Focus on the most important metrics and keep reports concise and easy to read.

4   Include actionable insights: Use reporting to provide actionable insights that drive improved campaigns. This could include recommendations for optimization or areas for further testing.

5   Tell a story: The best reports help people understand the most important aspects of SEM campaigns and provide insights that are not readily available in the data.

6   Update reports regularly: SEM data can change quickly, so it's important to update reports regularly to ensure they reflect the most current data. Consider setting up automated reporting to make this process easier and more efficient. Determine the proper cadence for reporting—weekly, monthly, quarterly, annually—and what will be included within each report.

Reporting on SEM often falls on the shoulders of third-party partners such as agencies, consultants, or freelancers. Clear communication about goals, needs, and expectations for reporting can save time and frustration in the long run. See the Lookout for essential tips on working with third-party partners for reports.

LOOKOUT

Working with Third-party Partners for Reports

- Data sources: Does the partner have access to all data sources that will be included in reports?

- Goals and objectives: What do you hope to accomplish with the reporting?

- Delivery and communication: Will reports be emailed, and what is the frequency? Will there be a meeting, call, or presentation to accompany reports?

- Metrics: Which metrics will be included in reports and how will these be obtained or calculated?

- Tools: Which tools will be used to develop the reports?

Advanced Reports

Along with the above recommendations, there are additional advanced reporting techniques for Google Ads which can provide marketers with a more detailed and comprehensive understanding of campaigns. Here are some techniques that can be used to create advanced reports for Google Ads:

1 **Custom reports:** Google Ads provides a range of predefined reports, but custom reports can be created to suit specific business needs or for particular stakeholder groups. Custom reports can include data on a range of metrics, such as geographic performance, ad position, device performance, and audience demographics. These reports can be set up to run regularly and provide up-to-date performance data.

2 **Multi-channel reporting:** Linking Google Ads to other marketing channels such as social media, email marketing, and display advertising provides additional insights. Creating multi-channel reports tracks performance across all channels and gains a more comprehensive view of the digital marketing efforts and how SEM fits.

3 **Attribution modeling:** Attribution modeling can help marketers understand how different touchpoints in the customer journey contribute to conversions. Google Ads provides attribution models, including last click and data-driven. These models can be used to determine which touchpoints are most effective and optimize advertising campaigns accordingly.

4 **Data visualization:** Advanced data visualization techniques can help business marketing executives understand complex datasets. Dashboards, heat maps, and charts can be used to present data in an easily digestible format that highlights key performance indicators and trends. Tools like Google Looker Studio (formerly called Data Studio) or Tableau can provide meaningful and compelling data visualizations to enhance reporting. See the Lookout for best practices for using Google Looker Studio for data visualizations.

5 **Cohort analysis:** Cohort analysis can help with understanding how different groups of customers behave over time. By grouping customers based on shared characteristics such as acquisition date or demographic information, cohort analysis can provide insights into customer behavior that can be used to optimize campaigns.

By implementing advanced reporting techniques, marketers and key stakeholders can gain a more comprehensive understanding of campaigns.

Campaigns can be examined at a more precise and advanced level, driving decisions regarding optimization, budgeting, and more.

LOOKOUT

Best Practices for Looker Studio (formerly Data Studio)

1   Connect marketing platforms like Google Ads, Google Analytics, Search Console, MySQL, Facebook Insights, Microsoft Ads, Salesforce, HubSpot, and many more.

2   Use templates to cut down on time spent creating manual reporting dashboards. Keep in mind that templates can still be customized.

3   Customize with fonts, colors, and text while adding and removing widgets, dashboards, labels, filters, and more.

4   Create engaging data visualizations such as bar charts, pie charts, tables, scorecards, bubble maps, bullet charts, scatter charts, pivot tables, heatmaps, and more.

5   Share reports by scheduling email delivery, inviting others, getting a shareable link, embedding, or downloading reports.

6   Manage report sharing access by creating reports as either restricted, unlisted, or public.

Progressive Keyword Research

Consistent keyword research and maintenance techniques are essential for ensuring the success of Google Ads campaigns. Refer to Chapter 9 for additional information on keyword research, tools, and use of AI. By continuously analyzing keywords and applying advanced keyword research, marketers can improve campaign performance, increase conversions, and maximize ROI. Here are some advanced techniques and tools for keyword research and maintenance in Google Ads campaigns:

1   **Keyword research tools:** There are several keyword research tools that can help marketers find new keyword opportunities for their campaigns. Google Keyword Planner is a widely used keyword research tool. It provides insights into keyword search volume, competition, and cost-per-click (CPC) data. Other tools include Semrush, Ahrefs, and ChatGPT.

2 **Negative keywords:** Negative keywords are search terms that are irrelevant to your business or not likely to result in conversions. By including negative keywords in campaigns, you can prevent ads from showing up for irrelevant search queries. Google Ads provides tools to help identify negative keywords, such as the search terms report.

3 **Keyword match types:** Keyword match types can help ensure that ads are displayed to the right audience. Match types include broad match, phrase match, and exact match. Over time, match types may evolve, and marketers may want to move from broad or phrase match to exact match. Match types are reviewed in detail in Chapter 8.

4 **Keyword bidding:** Keyword bidding is the process of setting bids for specific keywords. Advanced bidding strategies, such as automated bidding based on performance, can help optimize bidding and improve campaign performance.

5 **Keyword monitoring:** It is important to regularly monitor the performance of keywords and adjust as needed. Setting up alerts for underperforming keywords and looking for trends can be important strategies for keyword monitoring.

Another crucial methodology for progressive keyword research is a long-tail keyword strategy. This involves targeting highly specific, low-volume keywords that are longer and more specific than broad, high-volume keywords. There are several ways to think about long-tail keywords as a strategy.

- Focus on specific products or services.
- Target precise or particular geographic locations or areas.
- Use long-tail keywords to target niche markets or specific audiences.
- Incorporate long-tail keywords to increase relevance and target more specific search queries.
- Experiment with long-tail keyword variations to find top performers.

Testing and Experimentation

Testing and experimentation provide the opportunity for marketers to test different elements within an ad and optimize based on results. One of the main benefits of search ads is the ability to perform testing and experimentation quickly and easily across different ad elements.

Google Ads provides tools such as campaign experiments and ad variations that allow advertisers to set up controlled experiments to test different campaign elements. By using these tools, advertisers can make data-driven decisions to optimize their campaigns and improve performance.

Here are some specific examples of experiments that an advertiser can run with Google Ads:

1 **Ad copy experiments:** An experiment can be set up to test different versions of ad copy to see which version performs better. For example, the advertiser could test different headlines, descriptions, or calls to action to see which version results in higher click-through rates (CTRs) or conversion rates. See the next Lookout for specific ideas for ad copy testing options.

2 **Landing page experiments:** Testing different landing pages or landing page elements can help identify which version results in higher conversion rates. For example, testing different headlines, images, colors, or form fields on the landing page and monitoring conversions can help find the version that performs best.

3 **Keyword experiments:** An advertiser can run an experiment to test different keywords or keyword match types to see which version results in higher conversion rates or lower cost per acquisition (CPA). For example, testing phrase match versus exact match for a specific keyword can determine which match type performs better.

4 **Bid adjustments testing:** Test different bid adjustments to see how they impact your ad performance. Try increasing or decreasing your bids based on factors like time of day, device type, or location to see how it impacts costs and conversions.

5 **Ad extension testing:** Experiment with different ad extension variations to see which drives the highest click-through rates (CTR) and conversions. Try testing different ad extensions like callout extensions, sitelink extensions, and structured snippets to see which combination drives the best performance.

6 **Targeting testing:** Try different targeting options to see which drives the highest conversion rates. Create tests by targeting different audiences, locations, and device types to see how it impacts the campaign.

LOOKOUT

Ad Copy Testing Ideas for Search Ads

1   Numbers vs. abbreviations: Use of numbers can increase activity by grabbing attention.

2   Including pricing: Using pricing within ad copy can often either help or harm the ad engagement.

3   Promotional language: Test elements like percentage discount, currency amount, or written-out description of promotion.

4   Punctuation: Use of exclamation points, commas, question marks, and dollar signs can impact ad performance.

5   Emotional appeal: Consider increasing engagement with ads by tying in emotions such as surprise, guidance, curiosity, joy, or fun.

6   Call to action: Test words that are seemingly similar, such as: get, shop, discover, call, try, join, learn, subscribe, and more.

Additionally, marketers can use automated functions to test and experiment with search ads. Two ideas for this are dynamic keyword insertion (DKI), which allows advertisers to automatically insert the user's search query into the ad copy, and descriptions using the IF function, which allows advertisers to customize their ads based on predetermined conditions. These methodologies are also explored in Chapter 9.

Dynamic Keyword Insertion

DKI can make ads more relevant to the user and increase the likelihood of a click by including their specific search words right in the ad. Here's how it works.

When an advertiser uses dynamic keyword insertion in their ad copy, they can specify a parameter in the ad text, such as "{KeyWord:default text}." When someone searches for a term that matches a keyword in the campaign, Google will replace the parameter with the actual keyword that was searched. For example, if the keyword is "red shoes," and someone searches for "red shoes," the ad copy could read "Buy Red Shoes Online" instead of "Buy Default Text Online." If someone searches for a keyword that doesn't match any of the keywords in the campaign, the default text specified by the advertiser will be used instead.

Dynamic keyword insertion can be a valuable tool for advertisers who want to create more relevant ad copy and increase click-through rates. However, it should be used carefully and strategically. Advertisers should make sure that the ad copy still makes sense with the dynamically inserted keyword, and that it doesn't violate any ad policies. Advertisers should also monitor their campaigns closely to make sure that they're not spending money on irrelevant clicks.

Descriptions Using the IF Function

Descriptions using the IF function in Google Ads is a feature that allows advertisers to customize their ad copy based on certain conditions. With this feature, you can create different versions of ad descriptions based on the user's search query or device.

The IF function in Google Ads works by setting a condition and creating two different versions of the ad description: one for when the condition is true, and one for when the condition is false. For example, an advertiser could set a condition based on the user's device, creating one ad description for desktop users and a different ad description for mobile users. The IF function would then automatically show the appropriate ad description to each user based on their device.

Here's an example of how the IF function in Google Ads can be used in ad descriptions:

- Ad description 1: Get 10% off your first order! Use code NEWCUSTOMER at checkout.
- Ad description 2: Welcome to our store! Browse our selection of products and save on your first purchase.

Using the IF function, the advertiser could create the following ad description:

- Ad description: {=IF(device="Mobile","Welcome to our store! Browse our selection of products and save on your first purchase.","Get 10% off your first order! Use code NEWCUSTOMER at checkout.")}

In this example, if the user is on a mobile device, they will see the second ad description. If they are on a desktop device, they will see the first ad description.

The IF function in Google Ads can be a useful tool for advertisers who want to create more personalized and relevant ad copy for their target audience. However, this should also be used carefully. Always test different variations and monitor results to ensure that the function is effective in driving clicks and conversions.

Further Advanced Methods

Metrics, reporting, testing, and experimentation are critical components of successful SEM campaigns. In addition, there are several further advanced methods and account strategies to consider for better optimizing campaigns. Search ads can benefit from some of these techniques, tips, and strategies to increase performance over time. Below is a list of several advanced methods and strategies for SEM campaigns. Additional information is provided for each, keeping in mind that with the proliferation of generative AI, some of these may change or become obsolete in the future:

- **SMART ad automation:** Use machine learning to automate ad campaigns based on goals.
- **Ad extensions:** Include details like locations, links, pricing, and more within ad text.
- **Call recording:** Record calls made through ads.
- **Match type mirroring:** Structure duplicate ad groups according to keyword match type, thereby breaking up high-volume campaigns into smaller, easier-to-manage sections.
- **Single keyword ad groups (SKAG):** Ad groups focus on one keyword for close analysis and monitoring.
- **Single theme ad group (STAG):** All keywords match one particular theme, such as a company, service, or category.
- **Single product ad group (SPAG):** All keywords focus on one product or brand.

SMART ad automation is a feature in Google Ads that uses machine learning to automate the creation and optimization of ad campaigns. It provides an opportunity to create and manage ads more efficiently and effectively by using data-driven insights. As we learned previously, the term SMART stands for "specific, measurable, achievable, relevant, and timebound," which are the criteria used to set goals for campaigns. SMART ad automation uses these criteria to automate the creation and optimization of ads, often making them more targeted and effective. As always, ad performance with SMART ad automation should be monitored for successful metrics and measurement.

Here are some ways SMART ad automation can help:

1 Ad creation: SMART ad automation can create and test different ad variations to see which perform best based on the goals set by the advertiser. It can automatically generate headlines, descriptions, and other ad elements.

2 Bid optimization: SMART ad automation can adjust bids in real time based on data such as location, device, and time of day to optimize ad performance.

3 Targeting: SMART ad automation can analyze user data to identify patterns and target ads to specific audiences. It can also adjust targeting parameters to improve performance.

4 Performance monitoring: SMART ad automation can monitor ad performance in real time and make adjustments based on data to improve performance.

Ad assets, formerly called ad extensions, are supplementary pieces of information that can be added to your Google Ads to provide further context or details about your business or product. Assets are visual cues with links that help users gain specific information right from the ad. They are enhancements, making ads more prominent, relevant, and informative, thus improving the user experience and driving higher conversion rates.

Here are some common ad assets that can be used in Google Ads campaigns:

1 Sitelink: Add additional links to specific pages within the website, giving users more options to find what they are looking for. Commonly used sitelinks are: contact us pages, promotions, pricing, products, or FAQ pages. Because sitelinks help ads stand out, they are considered the most important ad assets. Up to six sitelinks can appear on desktop ads and up to eight can appear on mobile. Sitelinks should be under 25 characters, and desktop ads need at least two while mobile needs one. Figure 10.1 offers an example of sitelinks in a Google ad. Also, consider using dynamic sitelinks, which allows Google to automatically add links and descriptions for ads that best match a user's search behavior.

FIGURE 10.1 Example of the Use of Sitelinks

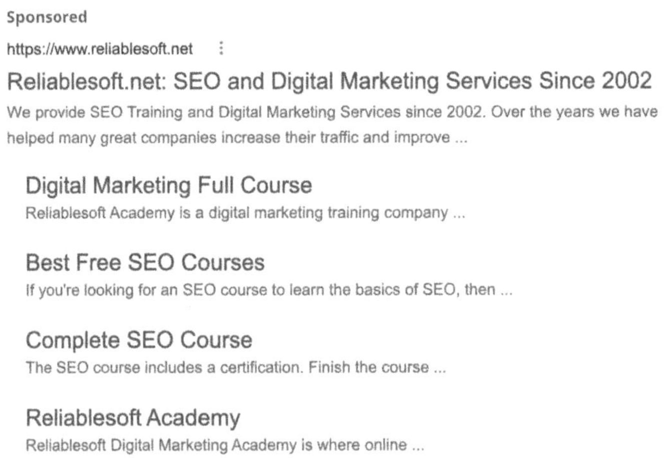

Sponsored

https://www.reliablesoft.net   ⋮

Reliablesoft.net: SEO and Digital Marketing Services Since 2002

We provide SEO Training and Digital Marketing Services since 2002. Over the years we have
helped many great companies increase their traffic and improve ...

Digital Marketing Full Course
Reliablesoft Academy is a digital marketing training company ...

Best Free SEO Courses
If you're looking for an SEO course to learn the basics of SEO, then ...

Complete SEO Course
The SEO course includes a certification. Finish the course ...

Reliablesoft Academy
Reliablesoft Digital Marketing Academy is where online ...

NOTE Screenshot of Google search, 2023, keyphrase: digital marketing course. Google
and the Google logo are trademarks of Google LLC.

2 **Product:** Link a Google Merchant account to Google Ads to show
product listings.

3 **Seller rating:** Including business reviews can build trust and reputation.

4 **Call:** Allow users to call your business directly from your ad, making it
easier for them to get in touch using click-to-call technology.

5 **Location:** Show your business's physical location on a map, making it
easier for users to find your business and visit your physical location.

6 **Structured snippet:** Provide more detailed information about products or
services, such as product categories or specific features.

7 **Callout:** Add supplementary descriptive text, 25 characters, to your ad,
highlighting key selling points or promotions.

8 **Price:** These allow you to showcase your products or services with their
respective prices, making it easier for users to compare and choose from
your offerings.

9 **App:** Provide a download link in ad text for app downloads.

10 **Lead form:** Eliminate the need for users to fill out a form by pre-populating
the relevant information for users logged into their Google accounts.

11 **Image:** Complement text ads with a relevant visual or image.

Ad assets can improve the visibility, relevance, and effectiveness of search ads, by providing extra information, links, and calls to action from within the ad. By using appropriate ad assets and regularly reviewing their performance, you can improve campaign effectiveness.

Call recording is a feature available in some Google Ads that allows you to record and track phone calls made through your ads. It can help you better understand your customers' needs and preferences, improve customer service, and optimize your advertising campaigns.

Here are some benefits of call recording in Google Ads:

1 **Call tracking:** Call recording allows you to track and measure the number and duration of phone calls made through your ads, helping you evaluate the performance of your campaigns.

2 **Customer insights:** Call recording can provide valuable insights into your customers' needs, preferences, and pain points. By analyzing recorded calls, you can identify common issues and adjust your products or services to better meet their needs.

3 **Quality control:** Call recording can help you monitor the quality of your customer service and identify areas for improvement. You can review recorded calls to ensure that your agents are handling calls properly and providing excellent customer service.

4 **Legal compliance:** Call recording can help you comply with legal requirements related to call monitoring and data protection. It can also help you resolve any disputes or misunderstandings that may arise from phone conversations.

It is important to note that call recording is subject to various legal and ethical considerations, such as obtaining the consent of the parties involved and protecting personal data. It's important to familiarize yourself with the applicable laws and regulations before using call recording in your Google Ads campaigns.

Match type mirroring is a technique in Google Ads that involves creating ad groups with identical keywords but different match types, usually focusing on broad and exact match campaigns. This strategy allows you to tailor your ad copy and bids to each match type, monitor performance, and drive more visibility over time. This can be an especially beneficial technique for business-to-business (B2B) campaigns, where cost per click is high and keywords may be limited or campaigns limited by daily budget.

Here's how to implement match type mirrored campaigns:

1 **Create ad groups:** Create ad groups for each set of keywords you want to target with different match types. Consider using labels such as "Mirrored—Broad" and "Mirrored—Exact" for campaign naming.

2 **Add keywords:** Add the same keywords to each ad group, but with different match types (e.g., broad, and exact match). Also, add the exact keywords as negative keywords in the broad campaign to ensure that those keywords are only active in the exact campaign.

3 **Write ad copy:** Write ad copy for each ad group that reflects the corresponding match type. For example, you might write more specific ad copy for exact match keywords, and more general ad copy for broad match keywords.

4 **Set bids:** Set bids for each ad group based on the performance of each match type. For example, you might set higher bids for exact match keywords that have a higher conversion rate.

5 **Measure and optimize:** Check the search queries for the broad campaigns to see which keywords convert. Then add the converting keywords to the exact campaigns. Also, exclude underperforming keywords in broad campaigns.

By using match type mirroring, you can create more relevant and effective ads for each match type, improving the performance of your Google Ads campaigns. It allows you to target users at different stages of the buying funnel, from those who are actively searching for your products or services (exact match) to those who are researching potential solutions (broad match). It also allows you to better control your ad spend by setting bids based on the performance of each match type.

Another way to increase ad effectiveness is to consider an ad group strategy such as SKAGs, STAGs, or SPAGs. These strategies involve setting up ad groups specifically around either single keywords, themes, or products. Using these strategies can provide greater control over messaging and landing pages. The benefits and challenges of each strategy overlap and may not be right for every organization.

Single keyword ad groups (SKAGs) are a strategic way of organizing your Google Ads campaigns by creating a separate ad group for each individual keyword you are targeting. This allows you to create highly targeted ads that are tailored specifically to each keyword, which can result in higher click-through rates (CTRs) and better conversion rates. Typically, SKAGs are more time-consuming to manage because it is a manual process but delivers higher ROI and relevance and also improves quality score over time.

Here are some benefits of using SKAGs:

1 **Improved relevance:** SKAGs ensure that your ads are highly relevant to the specific keyword you are targeting, which can improve your quality score and ad relevance.

2 **Better control:** SKAGs give you more control over your ad groups, allowing you to make specific optimizations for each keyword.

3 **Higher CTR:** SKAGs can result in higher click-through rates as your ads are targeted directly to the user's search query.

4 **Improved conversion rates:** By tailoring your ads to each specific keyword, you can improve your conversion rates and get a better return on investment.

However, there are also challenges to using SKAGs, such as the time and effort required to create and manage multiple ad groups, as well as the potential for overlap and redundancy in keyword targeting. Overall, SKAGs can be an effective strategy for improving the performance of certain Google Ads campaigns, but it is important to weigh the benefits and challenges to determine if this is a viable option.

Single theme ad groups (STAGs) are a Google Ads strategy that involves creating tightly focused ad groups that contain keywords that match a particular theme. This strategy can help improve the ad relevance, increase CTRs, and drive more conversions. STAGs focus on creating hyper-focused ad groups with a specific theme, which could be a product or service category or a location. By implementing this technique, highly relevant ads can be created to the user's search query, which can increase the likelihood of clicking through. In addition, because the ad is so closely related to the user's search query, they are more likely to find what they are looking for on the landing page, which can drive conversions.

STAGs can also help create more targeted ad copy and landing pages. When you have a single theme in an ad group, you can create ad copy and landing pages that focus directly on that particular theme. Unlike with SKAGs, using STAGs allows for multiple keywords in an ad group with the same theme, making it easier to perform experiments with ad copy and utilize automated bidding strategies. This can help to improve the user experience and increase the likelihood of conversions.

The use of STAGs can have several benefits, potentially improving the performance of your campaigns. Here are some of the key benefits:

1 **Improved ad relevance:** STAGs allow you to create highly relevant ads that are tailored to a specific theme. This can help to increase ad relevance, resulting in higher CTRs and better overall performance.

2 **Better quality score:** By improving ad relevance, STAGs can also help to improve quality score. Quality score is a metric used by Google to measure the quality and relevance of your ads and landing pages. A higher quality score can result in lower CPCs and higher ad positions.

3 **More targeted ad copy:** With STAGs, you can create and test ad copy variations tailored to a specific theme. This can help to improve the CTR and increase the likelihood of conversions.

4 **More targeted landing pages:** STAGs allow you to create landing pages that are tailored to a common theme. This can improve the user experience and increase the likelihood of conversions. It is also less manual work because a themed landing page can be used across the STAG ad group.

Overall, STAGs can help improve campaign performance by increasing ad relevance, improving quality score, and creating more targeted ad copy and landing pages.

Single product ad groups (SPAGs) are a Google Ads strategy for creating specific ad groups for individual products. This strategy can help increase the relevance of ads, improve your quality score, and increase conversions. The idea with SPAGs is to create ad groups that are hyper-focused on a single product or SKU, thus creating ads that are highly relevant to the user's product search query, which can improve clicks and conversions.

SPAGs can also help you create more targeted ad copy and landing pages. When you have a single product in an ad group, you can create and test ad copy that speaks directly to that product, and you can create landing pages that are tailored to that specific product. This can help to improve the user experience.

Overall, SPAGs can be an important strategy that can help improve the performance of your campaigns, particularly if you have a large product catalog. However, it does require more time and effort to set up and manage than traditional ad groups. If you have a small product catalog, it may not be necessary to use SPAGs for every product. Instead, you may want to use it for your top-performing products or those with the highest potential for conversions.

Single product ad groups (SPAGs) have several benefits that can improve the performance of campaigns. Here are some of the key benefits:

1 **Increased ad relevance:** SPAGs allow you to create highly relevant ads that are tailored to a specific product. This can help to increase your ad relevance, which can result in higher CTRs and better ad performance.

2 **Improved quality score:** By improving ad relevance, SPAGs can help improve quality score and drive down costs.

3 **More targeted ad copy:** With SPAGs, ad copy can be tailored to a specific product. This can help improve ad performance and user experience.

4 **Campaign management:** By focusing on specific products, campaign management can become simpler by easily identifying what is working and areas for improvement.

Overall, SPAGs can help expand the performance of Google Ads campaigns by increasing ad relevance, improving quality score, and creating more targeted ad copy and landing pages. By focusing on individual products, a more personalized experience is created for potential customers, which can lead to higher conversion rates and, ultimately, more sales.

Use of ad group strategies can be an interesting opportunity to find what works best. Each business is unique. SKAGs, STAGs, and SPAGs offer different approaches for managing ad groups while offering similar benefits. The best practice is to try different strategies and gather the data to determine which results in the best alignment with the goals of the campaigns.

A Note on Invalid Activity

Unfortunately, invalid activity, or fraud, in digital marketing has become a reality. Invalid activity refers to an interaction that does not come from real people with a real interest in an ad on Google. This can be accidental, or it can be deliberate and can take several forms. Google uses both automated and manual methods to identify invalid activity and protect advertisers from fraud.

Google has several systems and policies in place to detect and prevent fraud in their advertising platform, including automated algorithms and human reviewers. The IAB Tech Lab and the Trustworthy Accountability Group also oversee these processes. If you suspect fraud in your Google Ads campaign, you should report it to Google immediately and take steps to protect your account, such as by using fraud detection tools or setting up IP exclusions.

Some common types of fraud in Google Ads include:

1 Invalid user activity: A mobile user may reach for a link but accidentally click an ad instead.

2 Click fraud: When someone clicks an ad repeatedly without any intention of making a purchase or engaging with your business, this is called click fraud. This can artificially inflate your ad spend and reduce the effectiveness of your ad campaign.

3 Impression fraud: When a user artificially inflates the number of impressions your ad receives, typically by using bots or other automated software. This can result in wasted ad spend and reduced campaign performance.

4 Ad injection: An unauthorized website or app displays your ad without your permission, typically by overlaying your ad on top of their own content. This can lead to a decrease in ad visibility and click-through rates.

5 Fake engagement: Fake accounts or bots are used to engage with your ad, such as by liking, sharing, or commenting on it. This can make it appear as though your ad is performing better than it actually is and can reduce the effectiveness of an ad campaign.

Wrapping Up

Metrics, measurement, testing, and reporting are critical components of the SEM puzzle. Without the proper tracking, analysis, experiments, and optimization, campaigns will become stagnant over time. Focusing on continued advancement of campaign performance through testing different ad components and strategic account methodology ensures that campaigns never become dormant. The "set it and forget it" approach simply will not work in the dynamic world of SEM.

CHAPTER SUMMARY

1 Key performance indicators and metrics such as CTR, CPC, CPA, and ROAS help marketers measure the effectiveness of SEM campaigns.

2 Integrating Google Ads and Google Analytics combines campaign data with web analytics to create meaningful and insightful reporting.

3 Advanced reporting provides a window into next-level digital measurement, such as attribution modeling and cohort analysis.

4 Progressive keyword research, monitoring, and analysis is critical to develop focus on advanced tactics like long-tail keyword strategy.

5 Testing and experimenting with key ad elements such as copy, landing pages, and targeting, alongside implementation of automated functions like dynamic keyword insertion, can deliver a data-driven boost to ad performance.

6 Further advanced techniques including ad assets for things like locations, sitelinks, callouts, and more, provide an enhanced user experience and ultimately higher conversion rates.

7 Invalid activity, or ad fraud, is a fact of life in digital marketing and SEM but can be monitored and reported when marketers know what to look for.

Reflection Questions

- Is our team of internal and external stakeholders aligned on the proper metrics and KPIs to track for a thorough understanding of our SEM campaign effectiveness?

- Are we aligned on our reporting goals, and do we have the right combination of data and actionable insights? Are the reports customized for the proper audiences and do they incorporate visuals to tell the story of our campaigns?

- Is our reporting providing advanced insights about our customer demographics, their user journey, and the attribution of our campaigns?

- Are we dedicating the proper time and resources to continuous keyword research to ensure that we have the right strategies in place now and into the future?

- Does our SEM campaign reflect an environment of testing and experimentation to demonstrate data-driven optimization?

- Are we up to date on all the available advanced techniques, including ad assets like dynamic sitelinks, images, locations, prices, reviews, and more?

- Do we have full understanding of ad fraud and invalid activity and what that could look like within our SEM accounts? Do we have a process for identifying, reporting, and solving ad fraud issues?

PART FOUR

Conclusion

11

Working Together with SEO and SEM

> - Maintain SEM and SEO—don't set it and forget it.
>   - Follow specific innovative strategies and techniques to continue progress with search visibility, clicks, and conversions.
> - Know the specific steps for both SEO and SEM for maximum value.
>   - The best results are achieved with full attention to detail.

SEO and SEM: Better Together

SEO and SEM are two different but complementary digital marketing strategies, two sides of the same coin. However, many marketing organizations keep them separate. In some cases, two different agencies will oversee them, working with different internal teams. SEO can fall into a more technical department and SEM often lives with other paid media efforts. While this makes sense because SEO is more technical and SEM is paid advertising, there are also many advantages to SEO and SEM working in tandem, with teams aligning to share data, results, and brainstorm new ideas.

SEO and SEM are both important components of marketing that complement each other in driving both organic and paid search website traffic to increase online visibility.

Here are some advantages of doing SEO and SEM together:

1 **Increased visibility:** By combining SEO and SEM, businesses can improve their visibility in search results. SEO can help a website rank higher in organic search results, while SEM can ensure that a website appears at the top of the page as a sponsored result. When a business appears on SERPs as both an organic and a paid listing, it drives increased activity, clicks, and conversions.

2 **More qualified traffic:** SEO and SEM can both drive more qualified traffic by targeting users who are actively searching for products or services. Because SEO takes more time, SEM provides faster results.

3 **Improved brand recognition:** Consistent exposure in both organic and paid search results expands brand recognition while providing a level playing field for businesses across size and industry.

4 **Diversified traffic sources:** Relying on one search marketing strategy can be risky. By combining SEO and SEM, businesses can diversify their traffic sources and reduce their reliance on a single channel. This can help

businesses weather changes to search algorithms and competitors as well as fluctuations in ad costs.

5 **Increased control:** With SEM, businesses have greater control over their messaging, targeting, and landing pages. However, they have less control over costs. On the other hand, with SEO, marketers can closely oversee their budgets but have less control over their rankings, listings, and positioning.

6 **Improved analytics:** By combining SEO and SEM, businesses can gain more insights into their website traffic and conversions. They can use tools like Google Analytics to track both organic and paid traffic and gain a better understanding of how different channels are contributing to their marketing efforts. Data from paid campaigns can help drive strategy for SEO and lead to improvements in efficiency.

7 **Better ROI:** By using both SEO and SEM together, businesses can optimize digital marketing spend and improve ROI. Budgets can be allocated to the channels that are driving the most traffic and conversions, and strategies can be adjusted to maximize ROI.

Overall, SEO and SEM are both essential components of a comprehensive digital marketing strategy. While SEO takes time to produce results, SEM can provide immediate traffic and leads. By using both together, businesses can achieve maximum search engine visibility and attract high-quality traffic, conversions, and sales.

Leverage SEM for SEO

Because SEO takes longer to see results, a best practice is to use SEM to drive the optimization strategy. In other words, paid search can provide a testing ground for many aspects of SEO, thus making the strategy more focused, deliberate, and results-driven. Here are a few tips for how SEM can drive the SEO strategy.

- **Keyword testing:** Testing new categories and keywords is easier with SEM. By monitoring the data and results, the best-performing keywords with the highest optimization appeal can be found and incorporated into the SEO strategy.

- **Data and analytics:** Using Google Analytics and Google Ads, marketers can obtain significant keyword-level reporting, including metrics like CTR, CPC, and CPA. However, for SEO, we do not have those metrics at the keyword level. By leveraging SEM data and analytics like behavioral and demographics, we can get a fuller picture.

- **Enhance SEO content:** Testing ad copy with SEM provides an important opportunity for marketers to maximize their efforts with SEO. Through SEM testing and refining, you can identify the messaging that resonates best with a target audience and use that to push the SEO strategy forward.

- **Analyze competitors:** Using SEM, marketers can identify the audiences and the keywords that competitors are using in their strategy. Thus, it becomes easier to identify gaps and opportunities, which can become a valuable part of the SEO plan.

Working with Agencies

SEO and SEM include detailed and specialized skills and knowledge. As such, many companies will work with agencies to develop, deploy, and manage SEO and SEM. Agencies come in many types and sizes. Knowing roles and responsibilities is critical. It may also be important to understand where team members are located, how often collaboration occurs, and what the timelines are for different components.

Agency Types

Some of the most common agency types for managing SEO and SEM are:

1 **Full-service digital marketing agency:** Full-service agencies offer a wide range of digital marketing services, including SEO and SEM. They may have in-house specialists who can handle all aspects of SEO and SEM campaigns. They may only have somewhat broad knowledge and understanding of SEO and SEM, so it is important to thoroughly vet the SEO and SEM professionals who will be working on your account.

2 **SEO agency:** SEO agencies specialize in SEO and focus solely on improving your website's organic search rankings. They may offer services like keyword research, on-page optimization, and link building. It is important to thoroughly understand the services offered, who will oversee implementation, and how. Some SEO companies outsource aspects like backlinks or use automated processes. It is important to have a full understanding of what is included when working with an SEO agency.

3 **SEM agency:** SEM agencies specialize in paid advertising, often including Google Ads and other PPC platforms. They can help set up and manage paid search campaigns to drive traffic and conversions. Again, certain aspects can be outsourced or automated, which should be clarified up front.

4 **Content marketing agency:** These agencies focus on creating and promoting high-quality content to improve user experience and the website's search rankings. They may offer services like content creation, SEO, social media marketing, and email marketing. It is important to understand the process and resources focused on SEO if considering a content agency for SEO work.

5 **Inbound marketing agency:** Inbound agencies typically use a combination of SEO, content marketing, and other inbound strategies to attract and convert leads for business-to-business companies. They may focus on creating a comprehensive inbound marketing strategy that includes SEO and SEM. They may be more focused on B2B marketing and, thus, lead or demand generation. Clarity around which services are on offer and the resources for implementation is key with an inbound marketing agency.

6 **Boutique agency:** Small boutique agencies are very specialized, offering a niche set of services like local SEO or e-commerce optimization. Some boutique agencies offer both SEO and SEM, which can be an interesting option for marketers looking to home in on these strategies while sharing data, analysis, best practices, and optimization opportunities.

7 **Large ad agency:** Big agencies often have an in-house digital marketing department with specialization in SEO and SEM. However, big agencies also may outsource specialized aspects that require very particular skillsets around areas like link building, content creation, and paid search campaign setup and maintenance. Be sure to fully understand how a large agency approaches SEO and SEM and what the realistic expectations are for how it will manage these aspects of marketing.

8 **Web design agencies:** Companies that specialize in website design and development often offer SEO and sometimes offer SEM. This can be beneficial because they oversee the website and can easily deploy SEO-related changes as well as landing pages. However, it is essential that a web design company has specific individuals and tools that will deliver high value for search marketing. This cannot be done by designers, developers, or engineers.

Agency Factors

When choosing an agency of any type or size, there are many factors to consider, such as experience, expertise, and track record of success. Additionally, take factors like pricing, communication, and transparency into account, to ensure that the agency is a good fit for your business needs. Encouraging as many people as possible from the agency and the company to meet and collaborate is an important step. Working with an agency can be tricky, and the more collaboration the better.

When hiring an agency partner for SEO and SEM, marketers should consider the following factors:

1 **Expertise:** The agency should have a deep understanding of SEO and SEM best practices, including keyword research, on-page optimization, link building, and paid advertising. They should also have experience in the client's industry and be able to provide case studies and references to demonstrate their expertise. Their expertise should be cutting-edge with knowledge about the very latest developments in both SEO and SEM, including algorithm updates, software, AI, and machine learning.

2 **Transparency:** The agency should be transparent about their process, providing regular updates and reports on progress and results. They should also be up front about their pricing and any potential additional costs. This is important to thoroughly vet as, unfortunately, many search marketing agencies are not forthcoming about all aspects of their process, including what they are doing, what is automated versus manual, how pricing works, contact people, and roles and responsibilities. If team members are located overseas or in different geographical locations, transparency and openness is key.

3 **Communication:** Effective communication is crucial for a successful agency–client relationship. The agency should be responsive to emails and phone calls and should provide clear and concise communication throughout the engagement. Understanding exactly what the communication loop is, knowing how often to expect reports, and regular meetings are vital. Some agencies prefer email to phone calls or meetings, but some clients expect consistent face-to-face or online, teleconference, or phone interactions. Aligning expectations about communication up front is critical to a long-term relationship.

4 **Collaboration:** The agency should be willing to work collaboratively with the client, taking the time to understand their business goals and objectives

and tailoring their approach to meet those needs. Again, a deep dive into who does what, including team members from both the agency and the client, is a valuable exercise in collaboration.

5 **Results-driven:** The agency should be focused on driving results and should have a track record of achieving measurable outcomes for their clients. Understanding specifics around metrics, reporting, tools, and resources will help set the tone for a results-driven partnership. Agencies should also be willing to set realistic expectations and provide guidance on how to achieve those goals.

6 **Flexibility:** The agency should be flexible and adaptable, able to pivot their strategy as needed based on changes in the industry or client needs. It is very common to try different tactics with both SEO and SEM, determining what is successful, what is not, and how best to move ahead.

7 **Ethical practices:** The agency should adhere to ethical SEO and SEM practices, avoiding any techniques that may be deemed spammy or manipulative.

By considering these important factors, marketers can often find a reputable and effective agency partner for their SEO and SEM needs. Having the right agency partner can make all the difference for successful outcomes and business growth while also saving time and creating efficiency.

Questions to Ask

Here is a list of questions to ask during the agency selection or review process.

1 What is your approach to SEO/SEM? This will give you a sense of the agency's philosophy and methods.

2 What is your experience with my industry or niche? This will help you gauge the agency's familiarity with your business and target audience. Look for an agency that has worked with businesses similar to yours and can provide relevant case studies and success stories.

3 What metrics do you use to measure success? The agency should be able to provide clear metrics for measuring the success of your SEO/SEM campaigns, such as increased traffic, higher rankings, and improved conversion rates.

4 How do you stay up to date with changes in search engine algorithms? SEO/SEM is an ever-evolving field, and you want an agency that stays on top of the latest trends and updates. Look for an agency that participates

in industry conferences, follows thought leaders in the field, and has a process for staying up to date with changes in search engine algorithms.

5 What is your reporting process? The agency should be able to provide regular reports on the progress of SEO/SEM campaigns, including insights into performance and areas for improvement.

6 What is your team's level of expertise? Ask about the agency's team members and their areas of expertise. You want an agency with a team that includes SEO/SEM specialists, content creators, and data analysts. You also want to understand who you will be working with, the chain of command, and escalation points.

7 What is your process for creating and implementing SEO/SEM strategies? Look for an agency that has a clear process for researching, creating, and implementing SEO/SEM strategies tailored to your business and target audience.

Benefits and Challenges of SEM and SEO

An advertiser can create and launch an SEM campaign quickly. Tools like Google Ads provide maximum control over every element of a text ad. With the right attention to detail, successful campaigns with specific landing pages and calls to action can drive tremendous growth for businesses. However, depending on how competitive the landscape, costs per click can be high. SEM can often represent the largest line item on a digital marketing budget.

SEO, on the other hand, takes time, resources, and patience to implement and drive results. Once first page visibility and rankings are achieved, organic traffic can significantly increase, and website conversions can soar. That said, the waiting, trial and error, and overall difficulty of SEO can be trying for even the most patient marketers.

SEM Benefits and Challenges

SEM has numerous benefits, but it also presents challenges that advertisers should be aware of. Here are some of the key benefits and challenges of SEM.

BENEFITS

1 Immediate results: With SEM, you can start driving traffic to your website and generating leads immediately. This is because your ads appear at the top of search results pages as soon as you launch a campaign.

2 Targeted advertising: SEM allows you to target specific audiences based on their search queries, location, device, and other factors. This means you can reach people who are actively searching for your products or services, making your advertising more effective.

3 Cost-effective: SEM is generally cost-effective, compared with other channels, because you only pay when someone clicks on your ad. This means you can control your ad spend and optimize your campaigns for maximum return on investment (ROI).

4 Measurable results: SEM provides detailed analytics that allow you to track your ad performance and make data-driven decisions to optimize your campaigns.

CHALLENGES

1 Cost: While SEM can be cost-effective, it can also be expensive if you don't manage your bids and budgets carefully. This can be particularly challenging for small businesses with limited finances.

2 Competition: Depending on your industry and target keywords, you may face stiff competition from other advertisers. This can drive up the cost of clicks and make it harder to achieve a good ROI.

3 Constant optimization: To get the most out of your SEM campaigns, you need to constantly monitor and optimize your ads, keywords, bids, and targeting. This requires time and expertise, which may be a challenge for some advertisers.

4 Ad fatigue: SEM campaigns can become less effective over time if users see the same ads repeatedly. This can lead to ad fatigue and lower click-through rates and conversions.

In summary, SEM can be a highly effective way to drive traffic and generate leads, but it requires ongoing management and optimization to achieve optimal results. Advertisers should be prepared to invest time and resources in their SEM campaigns to get the most out of them.

SEO Benefits and Challenges

Similarly, SEO has many benefits for businesses, but it also presents some challenges that need to be addressed. Here are some of the key benefits and challenges of SEO.

BENEFITS

1 Cost-effective: SEO is generally cost-effective because it involves optimizing your website and content to rank higher in organic search results. This means you don't have to pay for clicks or impressions like you would with SEM.

2 Long-term results: SEO is a long-term strategy that can generate sustainable traffic and leads over time. Unlike SEM, which provides immediate results but stops as soon as you stop paying, SEO continues to work for you as long as your website remains optimized.

3 Improved user experience: SEO involves improving the user experience on your website by optimizing content, navigation, and design. This not only helps you rank higher in search results, but also makes your website more user-friendly and engaging.

4 Credibility and trust: Ranking high in organic search results can boost your credibility and trust with potential customers. People are more likely to trust businesses that appear at the top of search results, which can lead to higher click-through rates and conversions.

CHALLENGES

1 Time-consuming: SEO is a time-consuming process that requires ongoing optimization and monitoring. It can take months or even years to see significant results, depending on industry and competition.

2 Constantly changing algorithms: Search engines like Google constantly update their algorithms, which can affect your website's rankings. This means you need to stay up to date with the latest SEO best practices and algorithm updates to maintain your rankings.

3 Competition: Depending on your industry and target keywords, there may be competition from other businesses. This can make it harder to rank higher in search results and generate organic traffic.

4 Limited control over search results: While you can optimize your website and content for SEO, you have limited control over how search engines display your content in search results. This can make it challenging to ensure that your content appears as you intended.

In summary, SEO can be a highly effective way to generate sustainable traffic and leads, but it requires ongoing optimization and monitoring to achieve optimal results. Advertisers should be prepared to invest time and resources in their SEO efforts to see the long-term benefits.

Helpful Checklists

SEM Checklist

1 Research keywords and develop groups for campaigns.

2 Set up and organize campaigns using Google Ads.

3 Write compelling text ads (many versions per ad group) which include calls to action and ad assets.

4 Develop a budget and bidding strategy.

5 Set keyword match types and targeting.

6 Design and set up landing pages.

7 Connect Google Ads to Google Analytics.

8 Develop a set of metrics and identify key performance indicators to measure the success of the SEM campaigns.

9 Incorporate testing and experimentation with ads and assets.

10 Analyze search ad performance and user behavior by developing intuitive reports combined with an ongoing optimization strategy for SEM. Optimization includes keyword and ad group review, experiments, and refreshed landing pages.

SEO Checklist

1 Conduct in-depth keyword research: Research relevant keywords and phrases that your target audience is searching for and use them to optimize your website content. Incorporate high-level keywords as well as a long-tail strategy.

2 Optimize website structure: Ensure that your website has a clear and organized structure, including a logical hierarchy of pages and easy-to-use navigation.

3 Optimize tags: Optimize your title tags, meta descriptions, and header tags to include target keywords and accurately describe content.

4 Improve page load speed: Ensure that your website loads quickly, as slow load times can negatively impact search engine rankings.

5 Create quality content: Create high-quality, relevant, and engaging content that incorporates target keywords and provides value to your audience.

6 Optimize images and videos: Optimize images and videos with descriptive file names, alt tags, and captions that include target keywords.

7 Build quality backlinks: Build high-quality backlinks to your website from reputable and relevant sources, as this can improve search engine rankings.

8 Utilize social media: Utilize social media to promote your website and content, as social signals can impact your search engine rankings.

9 Monitor and analyze results: Use tools like Google Analytics to track and analyze website performance and adjust your SEO strategy accordingly.

10 Continuously improve: Continuously monitor and improve your website's SEO by testing new keywords, creating fresh and relevant content, and optimizing your website based on performance data.

By following these checklists, you can ensure that your website is optimized for search engines and improve your search engine rankings, which can lead to increased visibility, traffic, and conversions.

Maintenance

Regular reviews of both SEM and SEO are critical steps within the processes. Maintaining search marketing provides a deeper level of understanding of metrics to drive potential optimization and adjustments. Moreover, the digital marketing and search engine landscape is always changing. Google Ads is consistently adding and changing features within the system while increasing opportunities for automation and machine learning. Google and Bing are dependably updating search algorithms, impacting SEO efforts. Marketers who want to stay competitive while achieving business objectives must have a robust system in place for maintaining both SEM and SEO efforts on a routine and reliable basis. Here is a compiled list of how to maintain SEM and SEO on an ongoing basis.

SEM Maintenance Tips

REGULAR PERFORMANCE REVIEW

With SEM, be on the lookout for keywords with low clicks and conversions, but also look for keywords with high clicks and low conversions or low clicks and high costs. Try pausing those keywords or adjusting them by match type. Allow keywords to run for a while and review the last month, three months, and year of data when making decisions to pause, remove, or revise keywords.

LOW-VOLUME SEARCH TERMS

Google will assign the "low search volume" status to keywords with little to no search traffic volume. In many scenarios, keyword lists are bloated with too many terms that don't drive volume or value. It is important for marketers to pay attention to keyword status and make adjustments as needed. Also important, look for keywords with impressions but no clicks, as ads might be less relevant or require improvement to ad text or landing pages.

MONITOR SEARCH TERM REPORT

Find this report in Google Ads under the insights and reporting tab. This report helps advertisers see the actual search terms used to trigger their ads and can be a great way to identify new opportunities for future keywords and negative keywords. Careful analysis of this report can also provide insights for messaging, targeting, and budget optimization.

USE AUCTION INSIGHTS FOR SEARCH CAMPAIGNS REPORT

This report in Google Ads provides six statistics that can help marketers improve campaigns. This report can be generated for an ad group or specific campaigns or keywords. This report delivers nearly real-time (within one day) data representing exactly where and how ads were displayed, providing specific and competitive data for future optimization of campaigns. The auction insights report can be used to compare how your ad campaigns are performing realistically compared with other advertisers and competitors within the SEM auctions.

Here are the metrics from auction insights and what they mean:

- **Impression share:** how often your ad showed up compared with how often it could show up. This metric is displayed as a percentage, which tells you what percentage of the time your ad shows up when it is eligible to. Impression shares under 10 percent will not be displayed. Impression shares correlate directly to ad spend, so a lower share could indicate a budgeting issue.

- **Position above rate:** shows which competitors' ads are earning top-ranking slots. This is also a percentage and it indicates that a competitor's ad was displayed above yours for a certain percentage of the times it was searched. This metric can help keep tabs on what specific competitors are doing and how they may be ranking above you using bidding or targeting or, perhaps, because of more relevant ad text or better quality score.

- **Overlap rate:** the percentage of times a competitor's ad also achieved an impression at the same time as your ad. Although it is common for competitive ads to overlap, this can help determine if the strategy for those keywords needs to be reviewed.

- **Outranking share:** shows the percentage of the time that your ad ranked higher in the auction than another advertiser's or competitor's ad. It will also specify when their ad did not show up at all. This is particularly useful because it helps to understand how your campaign is doing compared with others. Using this metric to determine relevance and performance against competition can help optimize campaigns with bidding or ad copy adjustments.

- **Top of the page rate:** tells how often your ad appeared above the first set of organic results, at the top of the page. This helps identify how well ads are ranking compared with other advertisers.

- **Absolute top of the page rate:** The percentage of times your ad appeared as the first result at the very top of the SERP. In this metric, your ad is not only above organic listings but also above any other ads. This is a good metric to keep an eye on over time in hopes of seeing it increase along with quality score and other metrics.

There are a few key takeaways from use of the auction insights reports. First off, knowing who your competitors really are and understanding more about their Google Ads strategy, positioning, and performance is key. You can also find out if competitors are bidding on your brand keywords. Next, getting a realistic view of impression share gives you a chance to tweak bidding or ad copy to drive the share higher or identify why an ad is not showing up. You can also see what positioning you hold compared with other advertisers and if or how that might be impacting ad performance. Finally, this report is useful in identifying opportunities which may be lower competition, resulting in better shares of impressions and better positioning, and thus better ad performance over time. Also, review the Lookout at the end of this section for two convenient tools to use for information about competitors and how they are contending for search engine positioning.

SEO Maintenance Tips

CONDUCT ONGOING WEBSITE AUDITS

Regular website audits are an important way to identify any technical issues that may be impacting SEO results. For example, when new pages are added to the website, broken links are common. Additional issues can include missing metadata or alt text for images, slow page load times, or mobile optimization problems. Pages, titles, URLs, and headings may be labeled incorrectly or not labeled at all. Issues with content can include low keyword volume, duplicating content, outdated content, or low-quality content.

INTERNAL LINKING

The process of hyperlinking to other pages within the website is a basic tenant of SEO. However, it is often overlooked, particularly as new pages, images, and assets are added to a website. For SEO maintenance, doing a review of opportunities—such as in-text links, new content pages, anchor text, and footer links—can provide an innovative way to drive more internal links, which encourages site and bot crawlers and, thus, search engine indexing. Internal links also help distribute PageRank, a Google metric for web page authority, delivering better authority and link equity across the website.

BACKLINKS

Continuously monitoring use of backlinks is an essential component of SEO maintenance. Since many backlinks are low quality or even toxic, regularly reviewing the backlinks to ensure that they are reputable and high quality is key. Spammy, low-quality backlinks should be recognized and removed using tools like Semrush or Ahrefs. Leveraging social media, guest blogging, creating valuable content, and participating in online communities and conversations are important ways to monitor and improve backlinks for SEO.

ONGOING ANALYSIS

Web analytics tools and Google Search Console greatly help to monitor KPIs and metrics for SEO maintenance. Consider not only SEO metrics like organic traffic and rankings on SERPs, but also behavioral and engagement metrics to understand not just the quantity but also the quality of organic search traffic. Understanding how long searchers stay on the site, what content they engage with, where they come from, and where they go when they leave can provide valuable insights. Also look for any technical issues that can negatively impact SEO, like crawl errors, bounce rate, page speed, structured data errors, and usability concerns. Finally, explore security issues that may arise, including malware, hacked content, spam, phishing, or unauthorized access. These types of issues inhibit SEO success and can arise at any time, warranting consistent monitoring, analysis, and troubleshooting.

ALGORITHM CHANGES

Google releases algorithm changes on a continual and frequent basis, with two core updates typically taking place in the spring and the fall and frequent smaller updates throughout the year. Follow Google and Bing's official blogs to keep track of major algorithm updates and use industry news sites like Search Engine Land and Search Engine Journal for coverage and analysis of these updates. Notable major updates of the past include Panda, Penguin, Florida, Big Daddy, and Hummingbird. A recent core update from Google was aimed at promoting or rewarding quality content web pages.

Here is a short list of how to monitor algorithm updates to ensure ongoing SEO success.

1 Stay in front of updates by following along and staying informed with Google and Bing's official blogs, Search Engine Land or Search Engine Journal.

2 Review analytics, looking for any sharp drops or changes in organic traffic aligning to timing of algorithm updates.

3 Check organic search rankings and keep track of any significant changes to important keyword rankings. This can be done manually or better yet, automatically using tools like Semrush, Moz, or Ahrefs.

4 Review content quality, relevance, and engagement on an ongoing basis. Be sure to identify and revise low-performing content pages or assets.

5 Diversify traffic sources by including and incorporating SEM into the search marketing strategy and thus protecting against any unforeseen loss of search traffic due to algorithm changes.

LOOKOUT

Two Tools for Monitoring Search Marketing Competitors

1 **SpyFu:** Find out more about how competitors are ranking, what keywords they are using, and which backlinks they have in place. Energize the SEO and SEM strategy by uncovering competitive data and identifying opportunities for entering new markets.

2 **Google Trends:** Find new search terms by tracking what is currently trending. Use Google Trends to see how frequently a given search term is entered into Google relative to the overall total search volume, and discover spikes and dips in keyword volume over time. Use Google Trends to breathe new life into SEO and SEM strategies and find new keyword and category prospects.

SEM Step-by-step Guide

Here are the important steps for SEM:

1 Set up a Google Ads account: The first step is to create a Google Ads account, which you can do by going to ads.google.com and following the prompts to create an account.

2 Choose campaign type: Next, choose search as the type of campaign you want to run; other options include display, shopping, or video. Each campaign type has different settings and options.

3 Define target audience: Define the audience based on factors such as age, gender, location, interests, and search intent. This will help you reach the right people with your ads.

4 Choose keywords: Choose the keywords that you want to target with your ads. Use keyword research tools such as Google Keyword Planner to find relevant keywords and expand the list.

5 Create ad groups: Organize keywords into ad groups based on their relevance to each other. This will help create targeted ads that are more likely to resonate with your audience.

6 Write ad copy: Write compelling ad copy that includes target keywords and a clear call to action. Use ad assets such as sitelink extensions and call extensions to provide more information and encourage conversions. Also try using AI tools like ChatGPT.

7 Set bids and budget: Set your maximum bid for each keyword and your daily budget for the campaign. Use bidding strategies such as manual bidding or automated bidding to optimize ad performance.

8 Launch campaign: Review your campaign settings and make any final adjustments before launching your campaign. Once your campaign is live, monitor its performance and make any necessary changes to improve its effectiveness.

9 Track and analyze results: Use Google Ads reporting and analytics tools to track campaign performance and analyze results. Use this data to optimize campaigns and improve ROI.

SEO Step-by-step Guide

Here are the important steps for SEO:

1 Identify target audience and relevant keywords: The first step is to identify your target audience and the relevant keywords they use to search for your products or services. Use data gathered from SEM campaigns as well as keyword research tools such as Google Keyword Planner, Ahrefs, or Semrush to find relevant keywords.

2 Website analysis: Analyze your website to identify any technical SEO issues such as broken links, slow loading speed, or missing meta descriptions. Use tools such as Screaming Frog, Google Analytics, and Google Search Console to identify and fix these issues.

3 Create high-quality content: Create high-quality content that is relevant to your target audience and includes your target keywords. Use internal linking to guide users to relevant pages on your website.

4 Build backlinks: Build high-quality backlinks to your website to improve your website's authority and search engine rankings. Use outreach strategies such as guest posting, broken link building, and social media promotion to build backlinks.

5 Optimize on-page elements: Optimize on-page elements such as titles, meta descriptions, header tags, and alt tags to improve your website's relevance and visibility to search engines.

6 Monitor and track progress: Monitor your website's progress using tools such as Google Analytics and Google Search Console. Use this data to refine your SEO strategy and improve your website's search engine rankings.

7 Stay up to date with SEO best practices: Stay up to date with SEO best practices and algorithm updates to ensure that your website remains optimized for search engines.

By following these steps, you can create an effective SEO strategy that will help your business improve its online visibility and attract more organic traffic to your website.

Wrapping Up

Because SEO and SEM are like two sides of the same coin, they work well together. While not all organizations combine and collaborate on the two types of search marketing, it can be an effective way to drive visibility, cut costs, and increase efficiency. Identifying the right agency partner can create efficiency with costs and resources while driving successful outcomes. However, selecting the best agency can be tricky, with many factors and considerations. Maintaining and following best practices and taking the proper steps will lead to better outcomes. SEO and SEM take time, energy, and resources without cutting corners. For the most successful results, don't set it and forget it. Rather, hire the best people, invest in the right tools, and follow the necessary steps.

CHAPTER SUMMARY

1 SEM and SEO work best together with many benefits to marketers like shared data, leveraging keyword research, and increased visibility.

2 Consider the size and style of agency that best suits your business and ask the right questions up front to ensure a strong and successful partnership.

3 SEO and SEM, like any marketing tactic, present both benefits and challenges, which is another reason that they work well together.

4 Maintenance is an ongoing component of SEO and SEM and can be an essential success driver when viewed as equally important to the overall strategy.

5 Appreciating the importance of advanced maintenance techniques like the Google search report, auction insights, ongoing website audits, and algorithm changes will enhance the performance of SEO and SEM.

6 Monitoring competitors, as part of ongoing maintenance, can be done using online tools like SpyFu and Google Trends.

7 Following the proper steps and not cutting corners with both SEO and SEM will lead to better online visibility, clicks, and conversions.

Reflection Questions

• How are SEO and SEM currently managed by our organization? Do the teams working on SEO and SEM collaborate, share data, and brainstorm new ideas?

• Are we effectively leveraging SEM for SEO to drive down costs and increase effectiveness?

- Do we currently work with an agency? If so, are we satisfied with the relationship? If not, should we consider it for the future?

- When hiring an agency, are we properly identifying the right size and type to fit our business needs? Are we considering all the factors, including expertise, track record, transparency, communication, and pricing?

- Are we asking the right questions and taking our time to fully examine our options and make the best possible decision?

- Do we have enough focus on the maintenance of our SEM and SEO?

- How, specifically, do we handle maintenance, which advanced tools and reports do we use, and how do we continuously progress the strategy, tactics, and results?

- Do we use tools like SpyFu and Google Trends to monitor our competitors and drive our strategies for SEO and SEM?

- Are we following all the steps for both SEO and SEM, without cutting corners or skipping anything along the way?

12

The Future of Search Marketing

WHAT TO EXPECT

- The Future of Search Marketing
- Mobile Optimization
- Multi-modal Listings
- Voice Search
- Chatbots
- Large Language Models (LLMs)
- Generative AI
- Data Privacy and Regulation
- Brand Safety
- Reflection Questions

OBJECTIVES AND KEY RESULTS

- The future of search marketing includes many changes.
  - Understand and implement best practices with mobile optimization and for multi-modal listings and voice search.
- New technological developments like chatbots, LLMs, and generative AI will impact search marketing.
  - Consider how these technologies can provide opportunities to enhance the user experience and the strategies for SEO and SEM.

- Evolving data privacy and regulation landscapes affect search marketing.
  - o Staying in front of regulatory and legal changes by following a gold standard like GDPR is a best practice.
- Brand safety is a cornerstone of digital marketing and search marketing strategies.
  - o Invest in processes and resources to protect the brand and its reputation into the future.

The Future of Search Marketing

Since the beginning of search engine marketing, in the late 1990s, it has been an evolution. Through many different names, phases, iterations, algorithms, features, updates, and processes, search marketing has become a richer and more engaging way for consumers to find what they need online and for businesses to answer those needs. Although SEO goes back to the previous century, the last several years have proven to be particularly important for the technological development of how listings appear on results pages and how users search. This includes the appearance of results, which now often include rich results, images, videos, news, and more, as well as users searching in new ways and with new and different types of mobile devices. Perhaps the most significant impact on search marketing is and will be that of machine learning and AI.

Modern developments in the search marketing universe include multimodal result listings, voice search, and mobile optimization. Similarly, in very recent times, we have witnessed a movement toward the use of large language models, generative AI, and chatbots, which will only continue. It is essential that business leaders follow along and build their search marketing strategies as technologies and marketing opportunities evolve. Finally, to plan ahead, marketers must understand the always changing dynamics around data privacy and regulations, as these will continue to impact marketing and business for years to come.

Mobile Optimization

Increasingly, people spend their internet time on mobile devices including phones, tablets, and wearable devices like watches and glasses. Similarly, users are more likely to trust a brand that delivers a positive mobile experience. Taking it a step further, search engines prioritize mobile when crawling and indexing websites. In fact, as of 2019, Google has shifted to what's known as a mobile first index, meaning that crawlers and bots will read mobile sites first, thus rewarding mobile-friendly sites with better search positions.

The first step for marketers to fully adopt a mobile-friendly SEO strategy is to check their site's mobile-friendly status. Further, there are no longer separate indexes for desktop and mobile sites; there is just one. Marketers need to focus on fast page load times while avoiding common mistakes such as small font sizes, use of Flash or other incompatible plugins, issues with device width, unloadable resources, popups and interstitials, and many more. The Lookout offers tips for testing mobile friendliness using Google or other online tools.

LOOKOUT

Is My Site Mobile Optimized?

1   Google Search Console: mobile usability

2   Mobile-Friendly test tool from Google

3   PageSpeed Insights from Google: Core Web Vitals

4   MobiReady: device ratings

Sites can be configured for mobile using either responsive design, dynamic serving, or separate URLs. Responsive design allows the same pages to be served to both desktop and mobile users by rendering the page based on the device type. This is considered the best way to provide a mobile-friendly experience for both users and search engines. Dynamic serving will show different versions of pages based on a user's device but is not always accurate, which can create frustration for users and issues for SEO. Separate URLs are a way to essentially create a mobile version of the website where the URL is slightly different and includes an "m" for mobile. This is an outdated tactic that is not recommended as a best practice for SEO.

Mobile SEO is an essential consideration for marketers. Here are tips and best practices for a solid mobile strategy for SEO.

1 Responsive design: A crucial component of mobile SEO, responsive design ensures a good experience across different device types and sizes.

2 Mobile-friendly content: Include short paragraphs that can be easily skimmed or reviewed quickly from smaller screens. Space things out and incorporate white space as a design element. Cramming too much text into a tight space will frustrate users. Also, make calls to action easy to identify and click on. This can include phone numbers, phrases, forms, buttons, or other actions.

3 Focus on site speed: Confirming that pages load quickly is a best practice for mobile SEO and an important way to deliver a solid mobile experience for customers.

4 Clean navigation: Most users will find information directly on a landing page or by accessing the navigation bar on a site. Hamburger menus make it quick and easy for users to find what they need without creating an unnecessary distraction.

5 Avoid pop-ups: Google will penalize sites for intrusive interstitial pop-ups that cover the main content and lead to a poor user experience. Some pop-ups, like cookie policies, may be needed. However, these necessary pop-ups should be reasonably sized without covering up the main content within a page.

6 Voice search keywords: Voice search is increasingly relevant for on-the-go searchers. Be sure to incorporate conversational keywords and phrases, while incorporating voice-search-friendly content to accommodate those users.

7 Structured data: Schema markup and structured data provide organization of content to help search engines quickly understand it. This is especially important for mobile pages with less real estate for content and keywords.

Multi-modal Listings

Multi-modal search listings refer to search engine results pages (SERPs) that display a combination of different varieties of content, such as text, images, videos, news, and featured snippets. This is an advancement in search marketing because it provides marketers with new opportunities to optimize their content for search engines and engage with their target audience in different ways. It also improves the experience for users because they have a wider and more interesting selection of results to choose from when doing their search.

An example worth exploring is image search. Recently Google has added an image icon to their search bar, indicating that image search is more important than ever. In fact, the concept of multi-search was introduced as the next evolution of a more sophisticated search. Google allows users to include text qualifiers to image searches, meaning a user can take a photo of a pair of blue jeans and ask for a particular size. What does this mean for marketers? Simply put, image optimization is critical. Google's image recognition technology automates the analysis of the content of pictures. This is transforming the role of search results to a more immersive, image-focused matching experience for users based on their search intent.

Here are some ways in which multi-modal search listings are advancing search marketing:

1 Improved user experience: Users will have a more engaging and informative experience with multi-modal search. They can quickly find the information they need through a combination of text, images, and videos, without having to navigate through different pages.

2 Enhanced visibility: With multi-modal search listings, businesses can increase their visibility by appearing in different types of content formats. For example, they can appear in featured snippets, image carousels, and video thumbnails, which can drive higher-volume and higher-quality traffic to their website.

3 Higher engagement: Better listings will increase user engagement with the different forms of content. For example, videos can provide more detailed information than text, while images can convey emotion and grab the user's attention.

4 More opportunities for optimization: Multi-modal search listings provide marketers with more opportunities to optimize their content for search engines. They can use different formats, such as images and videos, to target different types of search queries and improve their rankings. Image and video optimization are more important than ever before.

5 Deeper insights: How-to guides, related topics, things to know, refine search, and broaden search are all examples of ways that search engines can provide deeper insights for users by delivering a more structured experience.

Multi-modal search listings are a significant advancement in search marketing. They provide businesses with more opportunities to engage with their target audience, improve visibility, and optimize content for search engines. By improving the user experience, driving higher engagement and deeper insights, multi-modal listings represent many opportunities for SEO and search marketing.

Voice Search

Voice search is becoming increasingly popular, with more people using voice assistants like Amazon's Alexa, Google Assistant, and Apple's Siri, and smart devices like Google Home, Amazon Echo, and Homey, to search for information, products, and services. As consumers continue to embrace mobile devices, smart speakers, and voice assistants, search marketing must continue to evolve. Typically, consumers using voice search are less formal and more conversational, as if they are chatting with a friend. This is a different approach than how consumers usually interact with a search engine, by typing words or phrases into the search bar. As a result, businesses will need to adapt their search marketing strategies to optimize for voice search.

Here are some strategies to consider for voice assistant search marketing:

1   Use long-tail keywords: Voice searches tend to be longer and more colloquial than typed searches. Thus, businesses need to focus on long-tail keywords that match the natural language that people use when speaking. Consider using keyword research tools to identify relevant long-tail keywords while also testing different versions of longer keywords and phrases.

2   Optimize for local search: Many voice searches are local in nature, such as "what are the best Italian restaurants near me?" To optimize for local voice search, businesses should ensure their website and Google My Business listings are up to date with accurate contact information, address, website, and hours of operation.

3   Prioritize mobile optimization: Voice searches are often done on mobile devices, so businesses should prioritize mobile optimization. Ensure your website is mobile-friendly, loads quickly, and has a responsive design that adapts to different device and screen sizes.

4   Invest in schema markup: Schema markup, a scalable SEO component, is a structured data markup that helps search engines better understand the

content on a website. This can help voice assistants provide more relevant and accurate responses to user queries. Use Schema.org or other online tools to manage the schema markup strategy.

5 Focus on featured snippets: Voice assistants often read out featured snippets in response to user queries. Therefore, businesses should optimize their content to appear as a featured snippet. Consider formatting content in a way that makes it easy for voice assistants to extract and read out the most relevant information. Use Google Search Central to maximize the value of featured snippets.

6 Audio-friendly content: Businesses are investing in audio content as an additional way to provide value to customers. Examples of useful audio content can be podcasts, audio guides, and audio versions of written or video content.

In summary, businesses should adjust their search marketing strategies to consider optimizing for voice search. By using long-tail keywords, optimizing for local search, focusing on featured snippets, investing in schema markup, prioritizing mobile optimization, and using audio-friendly content, businesses can improve their visibility and engagement in voice search results.

Chatbots

Chatbots have become increasingly popular in recent years as a way to improve customer service and automate routine tasks. Companies like Spotify, Bank of America, Starbucks, and others have made significant investment in chatbots for their organizations. Chatbots come in many shapes and sizes; they can be built from scratch using a coding language like Python or purchased off the shelf and configured for a specific use case. Either way, chatbots can be a useful way to provide advanced customer service and personalization for website users across geographies and industries.

Typically, chatbots provide users with customer service, troubleshooting, and answers to common questions. When it comes to SEO, chatbots can have both positive and negative impact on rankings. Here are some ways chatbots can impact SEO, positively and negatively:

1 Improved user experience: Chatbots can provide a more personalized and efficient user experience, which can lead to increased engagement

and higher search rankings. For example, chatbots can quickly answer user queries, provide relevant information, and guide users to relevant content on the website.

2 Increased engagement: Increased engagement on a website can be a positive outcome of chatbots, by providing a more interactive experience. This can lead to longer visits, more page views, and lower bounce rates, all of which can positively impact search rankings.

3 Faster response time: Chatbots can potentially deliver a faster response time to user queries than humans, which can improve user satisfaction, increase positive reviews, and reduce bounce rates. This can positively impact search rankings, as search engines place a high value on user experience qualifiers.

4 Keyword optimization: Marketers can use chatbots for keyword research and to optimize for long-tail keywords and conversational language. By analyzing the queries users ask the chatbot, businesses can identify new keywords and opportunities to target and optimize their content accordingly.

5 Duplicate content: Duplicate content is an SEO problem and can become exacerbated by chatbots. To avoid this, businesses should ensure their chatbot's content is unique and not duplicating content from elsewhere on the website.

6 Indexing issues: Search engines may have difficulty indexing chatbot-generated content, particularly if it is dynamic and constantly changing. Businesses should ensure that all of their chatbot-generated content is crawlable and indexable by search engines.

7 Technical problems: Technical issues such as connectivity or software bugs can negatively impact SEO. Businesses should continuously test and check chatbots for quality or technical issues that could lead to a poor user experience or SEO concerns.

There are many factors to consider regarding chatbots and SEO. In fact, chatbots can have both positive and negative impacts on both users and search engines. By carefully considering the value that chatbots can have for SEO, they can be used strategically for marketing purposes. However, businesses should also be aware of the potential issues that can come along with or be caused by chatbots, particularly as those pertain to search rankings.

Large Language Models

Large language models (LLMs) are a type of artificial intelligence (AI) technology that uses deep learning algorithms and vast amounts of data to analyze and generate human-like language. These models are capable of recognizing, summarizing, translating, predicting, and understanding natural language to then generate coherent, contextually appropriate responses to queries. LLMs try and predict sequences of words, after being trained on large quantities of data. This makes LLMs an ideal technology for a variety of technological applications, including chatbots, content creation, and customer service. LLM examples include GPT-3 and GPT-4, which perform tasks like text generation and translation. Additionally, BERT is an example of an LLM that works to understand the context of a sentence or query to then generate a compelling and accurate response. See the Lookout for further examples of large language models. LLMs are being used in many applications, including Gmail and Microsoft Word, for things like auto suggest or smart composing emails.

LOOKOUT

Examples and Descriptions

1 OpenAI's GPT-4.5: One of the most advanced models currently available, GPT-4.5 is a large multi-modal model and can accept image and text inputs while producing text outputs. GPT-4 exhibits human-level performance on various professional benchmarks and can be used for content creation, coding, and more.

2 BERT: Developed by Google, BERT (Bidirectional Encoder Representations from Transformers) is a pre-trained natural language processing (NLP) model that can be fine-tuned for a variety of tasks, including search. BERT helps Google understand the context and meaning of search queries to provide more relevant and accurate results.

3 XLNet: Developed by researchers at Carnegie Mellon University and Google, XLNet is a pre-trained NLP model that has achieved state-of-the-art results on a variety of natural language processing tasks, including search.

4 RoBERTa: Developed by Meta AI, RoBERTa is a pre-trained NLP system that has achieved state-of-the-art results on several NLP benchmarks, including search-related tasks.

In the context of marketing, large language models are often used to improve customer engagement and interactions. For example, chatbots powered by large language models can provide 24/7 customer support, helping businesses improve customer satisfaction and loyalty. Moreover, large language models can be used to create high-quality content, such as blog posts, social media posts, and email marketing campaigns, which can help businesses improve their online presence and reputation.

Search engines like Google and Bing are not considered LLMs, although they do use machine learning and natural language processing techniques to improve their search results with question answering, sentiment analysis, text classification, personalization, and other elements. Because LLMs are capable of processing natural language and generating human-like responses to queries, they become useful for a variety of search-related applications, including chatbots, content creation, and improving search results.

Large language models can also be used to conduct more sophisticated market research, by analyzing customer feedback and sentiment in content such as social media posts and customer reviews, allowing businesses to better understand their customers' needs and preferences. This can help businesses optimize their marketing efforts and improve their overall strategy, which ultimately impacts SEO. Generally, large language models have the potential to transform the way businesses interact with customers and conduct marketing research, providing a more personalized and effective experience for both customers and businesses. Eventually these models, along with machine learning and generative AI, could significantly impact search marketing as well. For now, these models can be used to the advantage of marketers in several important ways.

Currently, LLMs can have an impact on SEO in the following ways:

1 Improved content creation: High-quality content that is optimized for search engines is a critical and time-consuming factor for SEO. LLMs can cut down on the time and resources needed to create voluminous content for businesses. This can help improve SEO by creating relevant, informative, and engaging content that ranks well in SERPs.

2 Enhanced natural language processing: Large language models can process natural language more accurately than ever before. This means that over time, search engines can better understand user queries and user sentiment, thus providing more accurate and relevant search results. Improved accuracy can help businesses and their SEO by optimizing their website content for the types of keywords and queries their target audience is using.

3 More sophisticated chatbots: Businesses using LLMs can create more sophisticated chatbots that understand and respond to user queries in a more conversational and human-like manner. This can improve the user experience and lead to higher engagement.

4 Improved language translation: Language translation can be accomplished quickly and accurately with LLMs, allowing businesses to more easily create multilingual content that can be optimized for SEO. This can help businesses expand their reach and improve their visibility in international markets.

5 Better keyword research: Sophisticated keyword research drives SEO. By providing insights into the types of queries their target audience is using, LLMs can simplify this process for marketers. This can help build the SEO strategy and create content that is optimized for the specific keywords and phrases for a target audience.

Overall, large language models have the potential to significantly impact SEO by improving content creation, enhancing natural language processing, creating more sophisticated chatbots, improving language translation, and facilitating better keyword research. As businesses continue to adopt and leverage these models, we can expect to see continued advancements in SEO.

Generative AI

Generative AI refers to a class of artificial intelligence (AI) models and algorithms that are capable of generating new, original data based on patterns learned from a training set. Unlike discriminative models, which focus on classifying data into predefined categories, generative models focus on creating new data that is similar to the data that they were trained on.

Generative AI models use techniques such as deep learning, neural networks, and natural language processing to learn patterns and generate new data. See the Lookout for examples of generative AI models currently in use.

LOOKOUT

Examples of Generative AI Models

1 Generative adversarial networks (GANs): a type of deep learning model that consists of two neural networks: a generator and a discriminator. The generator creates new data, while the discriminator evaluates the

authenticity of the generated data. These models are used for tasks such as image and video generation.

2 Variational autoencoders (VAEs): a type of neural network that learns to represent the latent features of input data and then generates new data based on those features. These models are used for tasks such as image and music generation.

3 Recurrent neural networks (RNNs): a type of neural network that is particularly well suited for processing sequential data, such as natural language text. RNNs can be used to generate new text, speech, and music.

Generative AI has numerous applications, including creating new art and music, generating realistic images and video, and creating natural language text. In the context of digital marketing and SEO, generative AI can be used to create high-quality content, analyze data, and provide personalized customer experiences. This can be done based on patterns learned from a training set. Generative AI can be used for a wide range of digital marketing tasks, such as creating product descriptions, ad copy, and social media posts.

For example, a generative AI model could be trained on a large set of product descriptions, and then used to create new, unique product descriptions based on the patterns it learned during training. Generative AI can also be used to create personalized marketing content for individual customers. For example, a generative AI model could analyze a customer's browsing history, purchase history, and demographic data, and then generate personalized ad copy or product recommendations based on that data—thus giving it the potential to significantly improve the efficiency and effectiveness of marketing campaigns, by automating the process of creating high-quality, personalized marketing content. However, it is important to note that generative AI is in the early stages of development, and its effectiveness for marketing purposes is still being explored.

Generative AI can be used for SEO purposes in several ways for digital marketing, including:

1 Content creation: Similar to LLMs, generative AI can assist marketers in the creation of high-quality content optimized for search engines, including blog posts, social media posts, and product descriptions. This content can be used to drive traffic to a website and improve its search engine ranking.

2 Keyword research: By analyzing search queries, generative AI can be used to identify new keywords that can be used for SEO purposes. This can help businesses optimize their website content for the keywords and phrases that their target audience is using.

3 Chatbots: Generative AI can be used to create chatbots that provide personalized support and assistance to website visitors. This can improve the user experience and drive higher engagement.

4 Natural language processing: Through analysis of natural language queries, generative AI can be used to help businesses have a more thorough understanding of users' intent and sentiment.

5 Multilingual content creation: Generative AI can help businesses create multilingual content that is optimized for SEO, allowing them to expand their reach and improve their visibility in international markets.

Overall, generative AI can help businesses improve their SEO by creating high-quality content, conducting sophisticated keyword research, creating personalized chatbots, analyzing natural language queries, and creating multilingual content. As businesses continue to adopt and leverage generative AI, we can expect to see significant improvements in how SEO is conducted and optimized for digital marketing purposes. Similarly, companies like Google and Microsoft will continue to build on their use of generative AI for search marketing and innovation. This is expected to continue to include many enhancements in the future.

Data Privacy and Regulation

Technological innovations like voice search, multi-modal listings, and LLMs will continue to drive advancement for search engines and how marketers use them. Additionally, administrations and governing bodies are progressively developing how they oversee consumer privacy. Combined with changes to the way publishers and tech companies collect, store, and manage consumers' data, this has led to big changes in the past several years. Popular browsers like Safari and Firefox have moved away from storing cookies—strings of code that collect and store user data—and Google will be doing the same. Similarly, Apple has moved toward a more closed and secure way of handling its app store.

The current state of data privacy and regulation for digital marketers is rapidly evolving, with new laws and regulations being introduced globally to protect consumer data and privacy. With regard to data privacy and regulation, the European Union has led the charge with the introduction of GDPR. Many other countries and states are following suit. Globally, there is a growing movement toward data privacy regulations and new laws, many of which are modeled on GDPR. Recent examples include: LFPDPPP in Mexico, the updated Privacy Act in Australia, LGPD in Brazil, and PIPEDA in Canada.

There is currently no federal regulation of data privacy in the United States, although it is a hot topic at the state level. Many states and corporations are using GDPR as the gold standard in regulation, as they move toward putting new laws and protections in place.

Some of the most significant developments with data privacy and regulation in recent years include:

1 General Data Protection Regulation (GDPR): The GDPR is a regulation introduced by the European Union that governs how companies collect, use, and store personal data. It applies to any company that processes the personal data of EU citizens, regardless of where the company is located.

2 California Consumer Privacy Act (CCPA): The CCPA is a law introduced by the state of California that gives California residents the right to know what personal information is being collected about them, and to opt out of the sale of that information.

3 Digital Advertising Alliance (DAA): The DAA is a self-regulatory program that provides guidelines for digital advertising companies to protect consumer privacy. It includes a set of principles for online behavioral advertising, as well as an opt-out tool that allows consumers to opt out of behavioral advertising.

4 Apple's App Tracking Transparency (ATT) feature: Apple's ATT feature requires app developers to obtain user consent before tracking their data across third-party websites and apps.

In addition to these developments, there are ongoing discussions about new laws and regulations around the world to further protect consumer privacy and data. Digital marketers need to be aware of these developments and ensure that their practices are compliant with all relevant laws and regulations. This includes obtaining explicit consent from consumers for the collection and use of their data, being transparent about data practices, and implementing strong data security measures to protect consumer data.

Data privacy laws and regulations also have an impact on search marketing. GDPR was designed to help protect the privacy and personal data of citizens in the European Union, which includes their use of online tools like search engines. For example, websites must obtain explicit consent to collect and process personal data from users. This means there must be a clear privacy policy posted for users to easily access. Similarly, GDPR provides users with the right to be forgotten, meaning that users can request that their data be erased from a website database. Finally, data protection is at the center of GDPR, and websites must take steps to ensure that their website is secure, and that user data will be safely protected from breaches. Each of these components is relevant to both SEO and SEM, as websites and advertisers must acknowledge, understand, and implement best practices around data privacy while staying aware and informed as legislation and technologies continue to evolve.

Brand Safety

Brand safety should be a cornerstone of any digital marketing strategy, and that includes search marketing. Although we often hear about brand safety in the context of social media marketing, it is still a concern with search marketing. Brand safety refers to protecting the reputation of a brand when advertising and appearing online. Unfortunately, there are many nefarious factors out to tarnish a brand's reputation, such as: disinformation, malware, fraud, click fraud, fake news, and more. Examples specific to search marketing can include paid search ads appearing alongside harmful, inappropriate, or misleading content. Similarly, fraudulent activity from bots, trolls, or other immoral sources can impact both paid and organic search listings.

Generally, search marketing is considered a safer approach to digital marketing in that it aligns relevant content with user search queries, which is true for both SEO and SEM. However, business leaders and marketers can still take steps to increase transparency and decrease risk when it comes to protecting their brand. A strong first step is to create brand safety guidelines and identify how to handle breaches with clear roles and responsibilities. Brands with a plan in place and resources available to address issues will be prepared in the event that reputation management is needed. To be prepared, it is crucial for marketers to understand how brand safety can impact both SEO and SEM.

Here are a few ways brand safety can impact search marketing:

1 Negative content: Negative content such as reviews, comments, and articles can damage a brand's reputation and affect its SEO. Negative content can rank highly in search results and drive traffic away from a brand's website. For SEO, it is important to monitor and manage negative content by responding to reviews, addressing complaints, and promoting positive content.

2 Ad placement: SEM ad placement is an important factor in brand safety because ads can appear next to content that is inappropriate, misleading, or harmful to a brand's image. This can damage a brand's reputation and lead to a loss of trust from users. Monitoring actual SEM ad placement carefully can help to avoid appearing next to inappropriate or harmful content.

3 Brand reputation management: Reputation management is central for maintaining brand safety in SEO. This involves monitoring and managing a brand's online reputation through strategies such as social media management, review management, and content creation. Reputation management can help businesses to maintain a positive online presence and avoid negative impact on their SEO strategy. Solid reputation management strategies also provide useful tools like sentiment analysis and word clouds, which can provide further SEO value.

4 Legal compliance: Compliance with laws and regulations is important for brand safety in SEO and SEM. Violations of laws or regulations can lead to legal issues and damage a brand's reputation. All content and advertising must be compliant with relevant laws and regulations, such as GDPR and consumer protection laws. Similarly, a clear and concise privacy policy should be used to provide customers with easily accessible information about their privacy and other important matters.

Overall, brand safety is a central concern for businesses engaging in SEO and SEM because search listings can impact a brand's reputation and online visibility. By monitoring and managing negative content, carefully managing ad placement, conducting reputation management, and ensuring legal compliance, businesses can maintain a positive online presence and protect their brand safety in the cases of both SEO and SEM.

Wrapping Up

Like other types of digital marketing, the future of search holds many unknowns. However, understanding the past and the present helps as we plan for the future. Marketers must be aware of the latest developments in SEO and SEM, including factors like the importance of mobile optimization, multi-modal listings, and voice search, as well as the enormous impact of chatbots, LLMs, and generative AI. Considering a cookieless future, data privacy, and regulation, direct marketers need to consider brand safety as a cornerstone of all digital marketing, including both SEO and SEM. Staying current with the changing digital ecosystem and putting processes for reputation management in place are some of the ways to drive search marketing into the future and beyond, as new and exciting innovations emerge.

CHAPTER SUMMARY

1 Search engine marketing has been a consistent evolution since the very beginning.

2 Marketers must be aware of the ever-changing landscape, such as new ways of displaying results on SERPs, new methods for user searches, technological innovations, and fluctuating laws and regulations.

3 With the influx of mobile devices and changing consumer habits, mobile optimization is a critical component of SEO and must be a consistent part of the strategy.

4 Users expect a dynamic experience when they are searching. This includes multi-modal search results, including image and videos, as well as the ability to search using voice assistants like Siri and home devices like Alexa.

5 Innovations to search marketing from new and developing technologies like chatbots, large language models, and generative AI will continue to drive improvements to search engines in new and interesting ways. Marketers must optimize their SEO and SEM strategies according to the latest advances.

6 Data privacy, regulations, and changes to how tech companies collect, store, and oversee data will continue to impact marketers.

7 Brand safety, a cornerstone of a digital marketing strategy, is important for search marketing and impacts both SEO and SEM in many ways.

Reflection Questions

• Does our organization have an understanding of the new and evolving technologies, innovations, regulations, and changes impacting our search marketing efforts?

- Does our strategy include a strong focus on mobile optimization and are we following best practices to ensure a positive user experience from different mobile devices?
- Are we aware of new and different ways that search listings appear, how users search, and how our listings can be displayed? Are we embracing optimization of images, videos, and other multi-modal listing opportunities?
- How are chatbots, LLMs, and generative AI going to impact our search marketing efforts in the future?
- How will the changing data privacy and regulatory environment impact our search marketing strategy?
- Are we aware of and planning for the future impacts of the evolving digital landscape?
- Is brand safety a cornerstone of our digital marketing and search marketing strategy?
- What steps are we taking and what processes do we have in place to protect our brand?

Conclusion

In conclusion, search marketing is a constantly developing and complex field that requires businesses to stay up to date with the latest trends and best practices. Through a combination of SEO and SEM, businesses can increase their online visibility, attract more targeted traffic, and ultimately drive more sales and revenue. These techniques are fundamental and foundational to a digital marketing strategy and should also be considered vital to any comprehensive marketing strategy. By understanding the importance of user intent, leveraging data and analytics, and adopting a comprehensive approach to digital marketing, businesses can succeed in the competitive world of search marketing. As the world continues to shift toward digital, search marketing will only become more important, and those who are able to stay ahead of the curve will reap the rewards of increased traffic, engagement, and revenue. So, whether you are a business owner, marketer, or just curious about the world of search marketing, I hope this book has provided you with valuable insights and strategies for success in this exciting and ever-changing field.

GLOSSARY

Understanding the complex jargon and acronyms that dominate the digital marketing industry can be complicated. Here are key definitions of phrases commonly used by professionals within the search marketing business.

Ad extension   additional information that can be added to an ad, such as a phone number or location.

Ad group   a collection of ads that target a specific set of keywords.

Ad Rank   a formula used by Google Ads to determine the position of an ad on search engine results pages (SERPs).

Ad rotation   the practice of evenly distributing ad impressions between multiple ads in an ad group to test which performs best.

Alt text   descriptive text used to describe images on a web page to search engines.

AMP   accelerated mobile pages—which are stripped-down versions of web pages designed to load quickly on mobile devices.

Anchor text   the visible and clickable text of a hyperlink.

Backlink   a link from an external website to a page on your website. Backlinks are a tool used to increase a website's authority for SEO purposes.

Black hat   slang for unethical SEO that breaks search engine guidelines, in order to artificially rank websites using tactics like keyword stuffing, duplicate content, spammy link building, and negative SEO.

Campaign   a set of ad groups that share a budget and targeting criteria.

Canonicalization   the process of selecting the preferred URL for a page with multiple URLs.

Canonical URL   a tag that tells search engines which version of a web page to index, in cases where there are multiple versions of the same page.

Click-through rate (CTR)   the percentage of users who click on an ad after viewing it.

Conversion rate   the percentage of users who take a desired action, such as making a purchase or filling out a form, after clicking on an ad.

Cost per click (CPC)   the amount that an advertiser pays each time a user clicks on their ad.

Cost per thousand impressions (CPM)   the amount that an advertiser pays for every 1,000 impressions of their ad.

Domain authority (DA)   a metric focused on the weight of a specific domain name that predicts a website's ability to rank on SERPs.

Dynamic keyword insertion (DKI)   a feature in Google Ads that allows advertisers to dynamically insert a user's search term into the ad copy.

Dynamic search ads (DSA)   a type of ad that is automatically generated based on a website's content and targeting.

Enhanced cost per click (ECPC)   a bidding strategy that automatically adjusts the advertiser's bids based on the likelihood of a conversion.

Header tags   HTML tags used to structure the content of a web page, and to indicate the hierarchy of headings.

Hreflang   an HTML attribute that signals to search engines the language and geographical targeting of a web page.

Impression   the number of times an ad is displayed on a SERP.

Impression share   the percentage of impressions that an ad receives out of the total available impressions in its target market.

Internal linking   the practice of linking to other pages on your website to improve its structure and navigation.

Keyword   a word or phrase that users enter into search engines to find relevant content. Keywords are also used for search marketing purposes.

Keyword match types   broad match, phrase match, exact match, and negative match.

Landing page   the web page that a user is directed to after clicking on an ad.

Log file analysis   the process of analyzing server log files to understand how search engines crawl and interact with a website.

Long-tail keyword   a highly specific keyword phrase that typically has lower search volume but higher conversion rates than broader keywords.

Meta description   an HTML tag that provides a brief summary of a web page's content and appears in search engine results.

Meta tags   HTML tags that provide information about a web page to search engines.

Off-page optimization   the practice of building links to a website from external sources to improve its ranking on SERPs.

On-page optimization   the practice of optimizing the content and structure of a website's pages to improve its ranking on SERPs.

Page authority (PA)   a metric focused on the weight of a specific page within a website that predicts a page's ability to rank on SERPs.

Pagination   the process of dividing a large piece of content into multiple pages for ease of navigation.

Pay-per-click (PPC) advertising   a type of online advertising where advertisers pay each time a user clicks on their ad.

Performance max   a type of Google Ads campaign that allows advertisers to create campaigns across multiple Google ad networks and formats, including Google Search, Display, YouTube, and Discover. With performance max, Google's machine learning algorithms are used to optimize ad delivery for audience, placement, and format, based on the advertiser's goals and creative assets.

Quality score   a metric used by Google Ads to measure the quality and relevance of an ad and its corresponding landing page.

Remarketing   the practice of targeting users who have previously interacted with a website or ad.

Robots.txt   a file that instructs search engine bots which pages on a website they can or cannot crawl.

Sitemap index   a file that contains a list of multiple sitemap files for large websites with many pages.

Smart bidding   a set of automated bidding strategies that use machine learning to optimize bids for conversions.

Structured data   data that is organized in a specific format, such as a table, and can be easily read and understood by search engines.

Target CPA (cost per action)   a bidding strategy that sets bids to achieve a target cost per action.

Target ROAS (return on ad spend)   a bidding strategy that sets bids to achieve a target return on ad spend.

INDEX

Printed in the USA
CPSIA information can be obtained
at www.ICGtesting.com
JSHW041636060224
56768JS00019B/235

9 781398 612808